Adobe® Photoshop® 5.5 and Adobe® Illustrator® 8.0

Advanced Classroom in a Book

www.adobe.com/adobepress

Contents

Advanced Compositing

Color Management and Distribution

Introduction

Adobe® Photoshop® 5.5, Adobe Illustrator® 8.0, and ImageReady™ 2.0 are powerful, industry-standard image-editing tools for professional designers who want to produce sophisticated graphics for the Web and for print. Because most design and graphics professionals often use all three applications, Adobe has added many features to these products—such as the Jump To submenu, a common user interface, and shared file formats—that make it easy for the user to move seamlessly between them. This book was written for the advanced user or graphics professional who wants to develop high-level skills using these products both together and separately.

About Advanced Classroom in a Book

Adobe Photoshop 5.5 and Adobe Illustrator 8.0 Advanced Classroom in a Book® is part of the official training series for Adobe graphics and publishing software. These lessons are advanced and were written under the assumption that the student has completed the lessons in both the *Adobe Photoshop 5.5 Classroom in a Book®* and the *Adobe Illustrator 8.0 Classroom in a Book®*. Designed by a variety of professionals who are making their livings using Photoshop and Illustrator, the projects range from painting an illustration, to animating a banner for a Web page, to setting up your system to ensure consistent color as you move between applications.

The lessons are designed to let you learn at your own pace. Although each lesson provides step-by-step instructions for creating a specific project, there's room for exploration and experimentation. You can follow the book from start to finish or do only the lessons that correspond to your interests and needs. Many of the lessons are split into two sections, one for Illustrator and one for Photoshop. For example, Lesson 1, "Preparing Images for Print or Web," teaches you how to take a photograph and prepare it for both a printed exhibition and an online gallery Web site. These split lessons also discuss the advantages and disadvantages to using one application versus the other.

Prerequisites

The lessons in the *Adobe Photoshop 5.5 and Adobe Illustrator 8.0 Advanced Classroom in a Book* require the following knowledge or skills:

- A working knowledge of your computer and its operating system.

• Familiarity with the tools, features, and menus in Photoshop 5.5, Illustrator 8.0, and ImageReady 2.0.

• Successful completion of the lessons in both the *Adobe Photoshop 5.5 Classroom in a Book*® and the *Adobe Illustrator 8.0 Classroom in a Book.*

• Basic knowledge of monitor calibration, setting color management options for print and Web images, and proofing and printing CMYK images.

Memory requirements

Graphics software requires substantial amounts of memory by its very nature; if you don't have enough, you may encounter errors in the lessons. Before beginning the lessons, check your computer's memory:

• Windows computers do not have memory allocation settings, but should ideally have at least 64 megabytes (MB) of RAM to complete the lessons.

• If you have a Macintosh, check the memory allocation on both Adobe Photoshop and Adobe Illustrator (select the application's icon in the Finder and choose File > Get Info. If you have Mac OS 8.5 or later, choose Memory from the window that appears). The Preferred Size setting for Photoshop and Illustrator should ideally be set to 40 MB or more.

Copying the Advanced Classroom in a Book files

The Advanced Classroom in a Book CD includes all the files needed to complete the lessons in this book. These files are stored in individual lesson folders (named Lesson01, Lesson02, and so on), which are, in turn, stored in a single folder called Lessons. To use these files, you must copy the Lessons folder to your hard drive prior to beginning the lessons. To save room, you can copy individual lesson folders to your hard drive as you need them.

To install the Advanced Classroom in a Book files:

1 Insert the Advanced Classroom in a Book CD into your computer's CD-ROM drive.

2 Open the CD-ROM drive icon:

• In Windows, double-click My Computer; then double-click the PS55AI8_ACIB icon.

• In Mac OS, double-click the PS55AI8_ACIB icon on the desktop.

3 Drag the Lessons folder from the PS55AI8_ACIB window to the desktop.

To copy individual lesson folders, open the Lessons folder and drag the desired lesson folder from the Lessons window to the desktop.

4 Close the PS55AI8_ACIB window and remove the Advanced Classroom in a Book CD.

Note: As you work through each lesson, you will overwrite the Start files. To restore the original files, recopy the corresponding Lesson folder from the Advanced Classroom in a Book CD to the Lessons folder on your hard drive.

Restoring default preferences

The preferences files store palette and command settings and color calibration information. Each time you quit Photoshop, Illustrator, or ImageReady, the position of the palettes and certain command settings are recorded in the respective preferences file. When you use the Photoshop color management assistant, monitor calibration and color space information is stored in the Photoshop preferences files as well.

To ensure that the tools and palettes function as described in this book, restore the default preferences for Adobe Photoshop, Adobe Illustrator, or Adobe ImageReady before you begin each lesson. These preferences can be restored by deleting the preferences file or simply moving it from its default location.

Important: If you have adjusted your color display and color space settings, be sure to move the preferences file, rather than deleting it, so that you can restore your settings when you have finished the lessons in this book.

To restore default Photoshop preferences:

1 Exit Adobe Photoshop.

2 Locate and open the Adobe Photoshop Settings folder (which is in the Photoshop application folder).

3 Choose an option:

• If you are removing the preferences file for the first time or have adjusted your color display and color space settings, move the preferences file to the desktop or to another location by dragging the file. Moving rather than deleting the file lets you restore your settings when you have finished the lessons in this book.

- If you have already moved your preferences file, delete the Adobe Photoshop 5.5 Prefs file from the Adobe Photoshop Settings folder by dragging it to the Recycle Bin (Windows) or the Trash (Mac OS).

4 When you are ready to restore your settings, exit Photoshop and drag the preferences file from the desktop back into the Adobe Photoshop Settings folder (which is in the Photoshop application folder). In the warning dialog box that appears, confirm that you want to replace the existing version of the file.

To restore default Illustrator preferences:

1 Exit Adobe Illustrator.

2 Locate the AIPrefs file in the Illustrator 8.0 folder (Windows) or the Adobe Illustrator 8.0 Prefs file in the Preferences folder in the System folder (Mac OS).

3 If you can't find the file, choose Find from the Start menu and then choose Files or Folders (Windows), or choose Find from the desktop File menu (Mac OS). Type **AIPrefs** or **Adobe Illustrator 8.0 Prefs** in the text box, and click Find Now (Windows) or Find (Mac OS).

Note: If you still can't find the file, you probably haven't started Adobe Illustrator for the first time. The preferences file is created after you quit the program the first time, and it's updated thereafter.

4 Choose an option:

- To save the current settings, rename the AIPrefs file (Windows) or the Adobe Illustrator 8.0 Prefs file (Mac OS) rather than throwing it away. When you are ready to restore the settings, change the name back and make sure that the file is located in the Illustrator 8.0 folder (Windows) or the Preferences folder (Mac OS).

- To delete the preferences file, drag the AIPrefs file to the Recycle Bin (Windows) or the Adobe Illustrator 8.0 Prefs file to the Trash (Mac OS).

5 Start Adobe Illustrator.

To locate and delete the Adobe Illustrator preferences file quickly each time you begin a new project, create a shortcut (Windows) or an alias (Mac OS) for the Illustrator 8.0 or Preferences folder.

To restore default ImageReady preferences:

Do one of the following:

• In Windows, hold down Ctrl+Alt+Shift *immediately* after launching the application. (If you get to the application splash screen, you were not quick enough.) Click Yes in the warning dialog box that appears.

• In Mac OS, delete the Adobe ImageReady 2.0 Prefs file from the System Folder/Preferences folder, or (if you want to be able to restore your settings later) move the file to the desktop.

Note: Because of the way that ImageReady restores default preferences in Windows, you cannot restore your own settings later.

Additional resources

Adobe Photoshop 5.5 and Adobe Illustrator 8.0 Advanced Classroom in a Book is not meant to replace documentation that comes with the program. Only the commands and options used in the lessons are explained in this book. For comprehensive information about program features, refer to these resources:

User Guides   For both the Windows and Mac OS, platforms are included with each Adobe software application. These guides provide instructions for using Photoshop, Illustrator, and ImageReady. The text notes any differences in procedures and commands between platforms.

Complete documentation of all Photoshop, Illustrator, and ImageReady features is also available in the online Help systems of the respective applications.

These user guides assume you have a working knowledge of your computer and its operating conventions, including how to use a mouse and standard menus and commands. They also assume you know how to open, save, and close files. For help with any of these techniques, please see your Windows or Mac OS documentation.

Quick Reference Cards   Contain basic information about the Adobe Photoshop, Adobe Illustrator, or ImageReady tools and palettes, and shortcuts for using them.

Tours, tutorials, and movies Are included with the software for advanced users that need to refresh their skills in any of the three applications covered in this book. Chapter 1 of the *Adobe Photoshop 5.5 User Guide Supplement* and Chapter 1 of the *Adobe Illustrator 8.0 User Guide* contain a Quick Tour. The application CDs also contain Tour movies that give you a basic overview and Tutorial movies that demonstrate specific features and commands.

Other learning resources

Other learning resources are available but are not included with your application.

Official Adobe Print Publishing Guide Provides in-depth information on successful print production, including topics such as color management, commercial printing, constructing a publication, imaging and proofing, and project management guidelines. For information on purchasing the *Official Adobe Print Publishing Guide*, visit the Adobe Web site at www.adobe.com.

Official Adobe Electronic Publishing Guide Tackles the fundamental issues essential to ensuring quality online publications in HTML and PDF. Using simple, expertly illustrated explanations, design and publishing professionals tell you how to design electronic publications for maximum speed, legibility, and effectiveness. For information on purchasing the *Official Adobe Electronic Publishing Guide*, visit the Adobe Web site at www.adobe.com.

The Adobe Training and Certification program Are designed to help Adobe customers improve and promote their product proficiency skills. The Adobe Certified Expert (ACE) program is designed to recognize the high-level skills of expert users. Adobe Certified Training Providers (ACTP) use only Adobe Certified Experts to teach Adobe software classes. Available in either ACTP classrooms or on site, the ACE program is the best way to master Adobe products. For Adobe Certified Training Programs information, visit the Partnering with Adobe Web site at partners.adobe.com.

The Adobe Web site Can be viewed by choosing File > Adobe Online if you have a connection to the World Wide Web.

Lesson 1

1 Preparing Images for Print or Web

By Laura Dower

In this lesson, you will prepare a photograph of a painting for a printed exhibition postcard and for an online image on the gallery's Web site. You will learn correction techniques common to both media, as well as specific tips to make your image look its best in print and on the Web.

In this lesson, you will perform some basic editing to prepare an image for printing and a Web page. Then you will perform specific steps for each medium. You will learn how to do the following:

- Set image dimensions and resolution for print and Web images.
- Correct tonal range and color balance using adjustment layers.
- Remove scanning debris using the Dust & Scratches filter.
- Restore brush detail using the Unsharp Mask filter.
- Simulate an underpainting effect by adding a glaze of color.
- Choose color palettes, compression, optimization, and file formats for Web images.
- Customize color for Web images using the Saturation and Replace Color commands.

This lesson assumes a basic knowledge of monitor calibration, setting color management options for print and Web images, and proofing and printing CMYK images. These features and techniques are not detailed here. See your Photoshop documentation for procedures unfamiliar to you.

Getting started

Before beginning this lesson, restore the default application settings for Adobe Photoshop. For instructions, see "Restoring default preferences" on page 3.

You'll start the lesson by viewing the final Lesson file to see the photograph image that you will create.

1 Restart Adobe Photoshop.

2 Choose File > Open, and open the 01End.psd file, located in the Lessons/Lesson01 folder on your hard drive.

3 Click Cancel to dismiss the color management dialog box that appears. In the Profile Mismatch dialog box, click Don't Convert. (For information on setting up a color profile, see "Setting up a color profile" on page 182.)

4 When you have finished viewing the file, either leave the End file open on your desktop for reference, or close it without saving changes.

For an illustration of the finished artwork for this lesson, see the color section.

Now you'll open the start file.

5 Choose File > Open, and open the 01Start.psd file, located in the Lessons/Lesson01 folder on your hard drive. In the Profile Mismatch dialog box, click Don't Convert.

6 Choose File > Save As, rename the file **Paint.psd**, and click Save.

Basic image editing for both print and Web images

Whether your image will be printed on paper, or appear on a Web page or in another online document, some basic editing steps apply to both media. In this lesson, you will start by cropping and resizing the image and proceed to color and tonal corrections. You will then work on restoring some of the original brushwork detail from the painting that was lost in the scanning process. After completing these basic corrections, you'll perform procedures specific to print and Web publishing.

Cropping and resizing

Early in the retouching process, you should crop only the area of the image that you'll use, and throw away unneeded data to speed up editing and printing time. For the printed (4-inch by 6-inch) postcard, you'll use a crop of the image that is 2-inches by 3 inches at 266 ppi resolution. For the Web image later in this lesson, you'll resample down the image even more.

You'll make color corrections first on the high resolution version so that the print and Web images will be as consistent as possible.

🄴 If you are unsure what resolution you need for your specific printing conditions, see Chapter 3 in the Photoshop 5.0 User Guide or "Getting Images into Photoshop" in Photoshop 5.0 online Help.

1 Double-click the crop tool in the toolbox. In the Crop Tool Options palette, select the Fixed Target Size option, enter 2 inches for width and 3 inches for height. Leave the Resolution field blank.

Note: Leave the resolution blank when cropping to avoid inadvertently resampling up the image to match the value. Inadvertent resampling can occur when cropping in tightly on an image, if the original image was scanned at too low a resolution. The image's resolution may have been high enough at the original dimensions, but not enough to reproduce a small section of the image at an enlarged dimension.

2 Drag the crop tool to encompass the image area shown in the following illustration; zoom in on corner handles to align the area precisely. Double-click inside the border to apply the crop.

Before cropping   *Result*

It is a good habit to apply the crop, and then check the new resolution in the Image Size dialog box. You can then decide to resample down, or rescan the image at higher resolution if necessary.

3 Choose Image > Image Size and check the resolution. It should still be more than 300 ppi. Because your card will be printed with a line screen of 133 lpi, you need a resolution of only twice that number.

4 Enter **266** ppi for Resolution, make sure that Resample Image is selected, and click OK.

5 If necessary, reset the view to 100%.

6 Save your changes.

Adjusting tonal range and color balance

This image is a photograph of a painting, scanned in CMYK mode from a 35mm slide. The photography and scanning have caused the color to shift considerably from the original painting. The image has an overall gray-green cast, and the painting's intense blues have been lost.

You'll change the levels and color balance using two separate adjustment layers. These layers let you edit or remove adjustments at any time without permanently altering the file.

Scanned image   *Desired appearance*

1 In the Layers palette, choose New Adjustment Layer from the palette menu. In the dialog box, choose Levels for Type, select Group with Previous Layer. Click OK. The Levels dialog box appears.

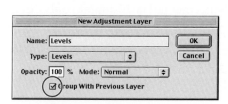 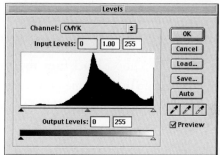

Levels adjustment layer

By adjusting the histogram of individual channels in the image, you can precisely control the tonal range of each ink color. Because primarily the blues in the original painting were lost in the scanning process, you will start by adjusting the Cyan channel.

2 Choose Cyan from the Channel pop-up menu. Notice that the histogram does not extend fully from shadows to highlights. All cyan color is concentrated in the midtones, resulting in a very limited tonal range.

3 Drag the left Input slider (the shadows) to the right until the value reads 115. Drag the right Input slider (the highlights) to the left to 217. Make sure that the Preview option is selected, and you will see a noticeable improvement in the image; the bright blues and reds have been restored and the grayish tone is gone. Note in particular how the blue brushmarks in the face have been brought out.

4 Now choose Magenta from the Channel pop-up menu. Drag the left Input slider (the shadows) to the right to 34. Drag the right Input slider (the highlights) slider to the left to 243. As you increase magenta in the shadows, the reds become more intense in the bottom part of the image.

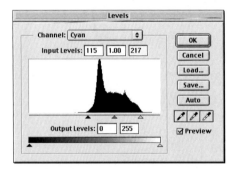
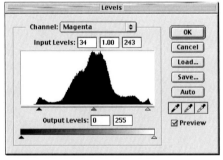

Adjusting Cyan channel levels   *Adjusting Magenta channel levels*

5 As a final step, choose Black from the Channel menu. The histogram only extends from the highlights into the midtones; no black appears in the shadow areas. Drag the left Input slider (shadows) to the right, and notice the change in contrast. You don't want to darken the image too much, however, so drag the slider to 30.

Before adjusting   *Result*
channel levels

6 In the Levels dialog box choose the composite CMYK channel, or press Ctrl/Command+Tilde (~). Compare the new composite histogram to the original. As the following illustration shows, the color distribution from shadows to highlights is more even.

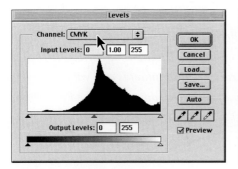
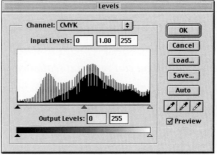

Unretouched CMYK histogram   *Adjusted CMYK levels*

7 Click OK. Toggle once between Undo and Redo (Ctrl/Command+Z) to compare the improvement.

This adjustment definitely improves the overall contrast in the image and eliminates the grayish appearance of the original scan. Next, you'll work with the Color Balance controls to alter the image a bit more.

8 Choose New Adjustment Layer from the Layers palette menu. Choose Color Balance for type, select Group With Previous Layer, and click OK.

9 In the Color Balance dialog box with the Midtones option selected, increase Red by dragging the Cyan/Red slider to the right to +50.

10 Click the Highlights option, and increase Yellow by dragging the Yellow/Blue slider to the left to –10. Click OK.

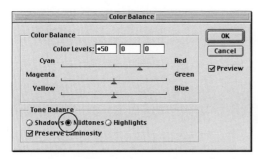
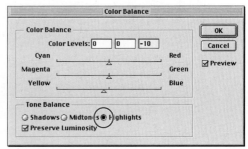

Color Balance adjustment layer, Midtones selected   *Adjusting Yellow highlights*

The advantage of applying these changes to adjustment layers is that after seeing your color proofs, you can go back and fine-tune the values you last set, which wouldn't be possible if you applied the settings directly to the image layer. You can also view individual adjustment layers—a very helpful tool in understanding which adjustments control which effect in the composite image.

Photographs shot on the same roll of film and scanned under the same conditions may exhibit common color problems in a batch of images. To save time correcting each image individually, you can record a sequence of correction commands and values using the Photoshop Actions palette. For more information, see Chapter 16 in the Photoshop 5.0 User Guide or "Automating Tasks" in Photoshop 5.0 online Help.

Retouching scanning debris

You may have noticed the distracting speck of dust on the shoulder of the figure. This piece of hair or dust was on the slide when it was scanned. One option for correcting flaws like this is using the rubber stamp tool to clone texture or color from a surrounding area to cover the flaw. In this case, the Dust & Scratches filter will give better results, and you will never have to touch a brush to your image.

Retouching many dust spots on an image can be very time-consuming. You'll save lots of time by carefully cleaning off slides and photos before scanning, so that the debris never appears in the digital image. Be sure to use a small air pump for this purpose. Blowing on a slide to clean it can introduce moisture on the transparency and cause a permanent flaw.

1 In the Layers palette, click the Background to make it active.

2 Zoom in on the speck in the image, and select the area containing the dust. (See the following illustration for details.).

Isolating the area improves results by focusing the controls on just the problem area of the image—rather than on detail in the entire image—and speeds up the time it takes to preview and apply the filter settings.

3 Choose Filter > Noise > Dust & Scratches. Make sure that Preview is selected. Usually, there is a trade-off between the Radius and Threshold settings. You can experiment with other images by adjusting both settings in opposite directions until you get a desired result. For this image, I adjusted the Radius slider to 7 and the Threshold to 15. Click OK.

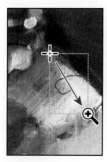 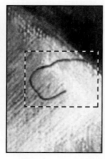 

Zooming in　　　　　*Selecting*　　　　　*Retouching dust*

4 Deselect the image.

5 Reset the view to 100% by double-clicking the zoom tool in the toolbox.

6 Save your changes.

💡 *On your own images, a higher Threshold value may remove a flaw better, but it may create a stark contrast between the softening of the selected area against the hard edge of the unaffected area. If a contrast occurs, feather the selection before applying the filter to create a more gradual transition.*

Preparing an image for print

Monitor calibration and accurate proofing are key to quality print reproduction. If you have produced printed material from digital images, you know that a monitor can display colors very differently than do inks on paper. Save yourself the frustration of realizing this on press by calibrating and proofing your artwork before printing final film.

❓ To ensure that your printed image will look like the one you've spent weeks composing and editing on your monitor, make sure that you have followed the steps in Chapter 5 in the Photoshop 5.0 User Guide or in "Calibrating your monitor" in Photoshop 5.0 online Help.

Restoring surface detail

Photographing artwork typically discards some textural detail from the original. Even more can be lost in the scanning process, as happened with this image. The basic focus of the image is OK, but the original painting's brushwork and surface texture is missing. To restore the brushwork and texture, you will use the Unsharp Mask filter.

1 Choose Filter > Sharpen > Unsharp Mask. Make sure that Preview is selected. Set the Amount to 100% and the Radius to 2 pixels. Click OK.

 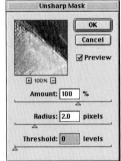 

Before sharpening   *Result*

You can also apply sharpening to individual channels. Depending on the kind of detail contained in that channel, sharpening it can give a more controlled result.

2 In the Channels palette, click the Cyan channel to make it active. By default, a grayscale version of the detail in the Cyan channel appears. To view the composite CMYK image while still working on just the Cyan channel, click to display the eye icon in the left column next to the CMYK channel. The Cyan channel remains highlighted and active.

 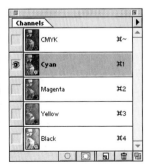 

Active Cyan channel in Cyan view only (left) and in CMYK composite view (right)

3 Reopen the Unsharp Mask dialog box by pressing Alt+Ctrl+F (Windows) or Option+Command+F (Mac OS). Set the Amount to 100% and the Radius to 2.

The thumbnail preview in the dialog box displays the effect on just the Cyan channel, but the image preview is of the composite CMYK channel. The sharpening effect is more subtle than the previous, but the brushwork has been further accentuated.

4 Select and deselect the Preview option in the filter dialog box to see the difference. Click OK.

Sharpening tends to look more dramatic on-screen than it will in the final printed piece. You may want to sharpen the image further after seeing your first proof. You may also want to compensate for resampling an image, which also softens detail. You will apply the Sharpen filter again later in the lesson when you prepare the Web version of this image.

Making additional color corrections for print

Often color corrections are subjective, and the standard procedures for improving color and contrast may not be enough. That is when you can use Photoshop's tools creatively—using layer modes, adjustment layers, and so on, to restore color to the original or alter it in a pleasing way. To keep final color changes between the printed piece and the Web version as consistent as possible, it is a good idea to work on the high-resolution CMYK print version first. CMYK colors convert well to RGB mode, but RGB colors won't convert back well to CMYK.

Adding a glaze of color

The original painting started with an orange-yellow underpainting that gave all the colors above it a warm glow. This glow was lost somewhere in the transition from paint on canvas to film and finally, a digital file. Some of the color can be restored using a new layer filled with a solid color. Rather than lay the color under the painting, you will layer it on top.

1 In the Channels palette, click the CMYK name to reset the composite CMYK channel as the active channel. It is not necessary to click the view icons.

Next you will create a New Layer in which to apply the color.

2 In the Layers palette, click the Color Balance adjustment layer at the top of the palette; then click the New Layer icon at the bottom of the palette.

3 In the Color palette, mix a yellow CMYK color. I used 41% magenta and 75% yellow.

4 Press Alt+Backspace (Windows) or Option+Delete (Mac OS) to fill the layer with the color. In the Layers palette, adjust the layer opacity to about 30%, and set the mode to Overlay.

New layer with solid color glaze, 30% Overlay mode

5 Save your changes.

💡 *To apply the same color correction techniques to a batch of images, automate the task by recording the procedures using Photoshop's Actions palette.*

Restoring shadow detail

Adding the color glaze dulled the overall contrast a bit. To darken just the blackest areas of the painting without darkening other colors, you will adjust the levels on just the Black channel of the image.

1 In the Layers palette, double-click the Levels adjustment layer to open the Levels dialog box.

2 Choose Black from the Channel pop-up menu (or press Ctrl/Command+4). Drag the Shadows slider, which should still be at 30 from the previous adjustment, to 75. Click OK.

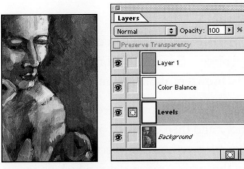 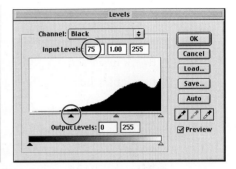

Increasing shadows in black channel

3 Save your changes.

Printing and proofing

Printing a color composite proof or film separations for a color laminate proof is the next step if you are planning to go to press with this project.

1 Save your changes in the Photoshop format.

Saving the original, layered file in the Photoshop format preserves the layers for future editing. The TIFF and EPS file formats flatten the image into a single layer.

The sample artwork on the opening page of this lesson shows a copy of the image you just prepared, saved in the TIFF format, and placed in Adobe Illustrator 8. In Illustrator, type was added, the file was color-separated, and then proofed as a single piece.

You could perform the same steps to prepare a color proof, and then return to the Photoshop version with the adjustment layers, edit them, and then use the Save As TIF command to overwrite the placed image in Illustrator. You could also keep working in Photoshop if you did not need to place the image in a page layout or illustration program.

2 Choose an option for continuing the lesson:

• To print and proof your artwork, see Lesson 6, "Color Management and Distribution."

🔲 For information on setting up color management in Photoshop, see Chapter 5 in the Photoshop 5.0 User Guide or "Reproducing Color Accurately" in Photoshop 5.0 online Help.

- To continue with this lesson, keep the file open and skip to the next section, "Preparing an image for the Web," to learn how online images differ from those destined for print.

Preparing an image for the Web

An advantage of preparing images for Web display is that you compose and edit your artwork in the same medium as the final piece—on an RGB monitor. You proof the image for variables such as different platforms, browsers, modems, and monitors.

Preparing an image for the Web involves the basic steps covered in an earlier section, "Adjusting tonal range and color balance," and then choosing optimization settings to create a more efficient file. *Optimization* refers to how the selected file format, color palette, and compression settings affect the quality and speed at which an image will download and preview.

Web images need a resolution of only 72 ppi; so they are quicker to edit and prepare initially. But once the image is posted on your Web site and downloaded for preview on other systems, even small images can take a long time to display. (*Download* refers to the amount of time an image takes to preview on a user's system when your Web page is accessed, as well as the amount of time it takes to select and save that image to a local hard drive.) Minimizing that time is critical when preparing and saving your files.

In general, there is a trade-off between download (preview) speed and image quality. Some images, such as those with textural or uneven detail, are quite forgiving and will display well under maximum compression settings. In this lesson, the photo of an oil painting has a wide range of textures and colors, without any hard edges or type. The photo's optimization settings differ greatly from those appropriate to a logo, graphic illustration, or image with smooth gradations of color.

Optimizing your files for the Web changes the range and display of color in your image. Be aware of these limits before spending a lot of time fine-tuning color that may not display with the compression or color palette settings you choose. You can make additional adjustments to an optimized image, but they are limited to the format in which you have saved the file. Although the JPEG format supports most color editing, the GIF format only lets you use controls available for indexed-color images. Even if you get your image to display just the way you want it on your system, it is impossible for you to fully control the variables in how others view the same image.

Note: *Any photo or digital image can be displayed on a Web page. If you have an illustration that was created in a vector-based program, such as Adobe Illustrator, just export it in Photoshop format so that the line art is converted, or rasterized, into pixel data.*

Saving the image in RGB mode

You will start by converting the CMYK image to RGB mode, the format in which it will appear on the Web.

1 If necessary, reopen the Paint.psd file, with all the color corrections you have done so far in the lesson.

2 Choose Layer > Flatten Image.

3 Choose Image > Mode > RGB Color to convert the image to RGB mode.

4 Choose File > Save As, rename the file **Paint1.psd**, and click OK.

Setting up display options for cross-platform viewing

Windows and Mac OS operating systems display color images slightly differently. For example, the same image generally appears darker on a Windows system than on a Mac OS system. Photoshop has an option for simulating either platform, so that you can interchangeably preview what the image will look like on both. Here, where you're still making basic corrections, it is a good idea to preview the image without special compensation.

1 Choose View > Preview.

2 Make sure that the default option of Uncompensated Color is selected.

Cropping and resizing for the Web

For this project, you will apply color and compression settings first, and then return to Photoshop to use a few tricks to retrieve some of the intense color that could not be reproduced in the print version.

You will use a different crop of the image for the Web page than for the printed postcard. Because images for the Web only need a resolution of 72 ppi, you will start by cropping and resizing the artwork.

In the program you're using to design your Web pages, such as Adobe GoLive™ or Adobe ImageReady, determine the image's dimensions in pixels. For this project, the dimensions will be 144 pixels by 432 pixels.

1 In the Crop Options palette, enter 144 pixels for width, 432 pixels for height, and 72 pixels/inch for resolution. Make sure that Fixed Target Size is selected.

2 Drag the crop tool over the image and adjust the borders as shown in the following illustration.

3 Double-click inside the border to apply the crop. Downsampling softens the image detail a bit.

Cropping image by 144 x 432 pixels   *Result*

4 Choose Filter > Sharpen > Unsharp Mask, and enter 31% for Amount and 3 for Radius. Click OK.

 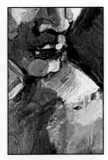

Downsampled detail   *Sharpening applied*

5 Save your changes.

Setting color compression and optimization for the Web

The key to preparing images for the Web is to keep file size to a minimum without compromising too much in image quality. To optimize your image means to choose compression settings that keep down file size, and thus download and display time, while choosing color settings that work best for your particular image. Photoshop 5.5 lets you experiment with various color and compression settings while previewing the outcome against the original image, as well as how it will look on different browsers and platforms.

Note: You can also view and modify optimized images in the document window of ImageReady 2.0. Because you're not using features specific to Image Ready, such as slicing or creating rollovers, you'll stay in Photoshop.

1 Choose File > Save for Web. This window lets you choose and preview various color and compression settings before applying the optimized combination to your image.

2 Click the 4-Up tab. This palette lets you preview your original image while experimenting with three variations on optimization settings.

The continuous-tone image of this painting is perfectly suitable for JPEG compression. To see why, you will start by looking at a few GIF settings.

3 Click the second image from the left to make it active. From the Settings pop-up menu (beneath the Cancel button), choose JPEG high. This preview looks close to the original, but you'll set a couple more options before making comparisons.

Note: Depending on your monitor size, the previews may appear vertically or horizontally.

4 Click the third image from the left to make it active, and choose GIF Web palette from the Settings menu. You should see a shift in the more limited color palette.

5 Finally, click the fourth image, and choose GIF 128 Dithered from the Settings menu.

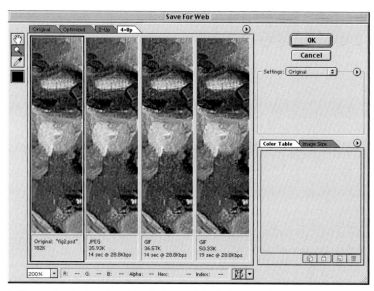

4-Up preview in Save for Web window with both JPEG and GIF optimization settings

Now you'll look at the set and consider the trade-offs. Since this image is highly textural, the differences may seem subtle. But this is good training in spotting how different settings affect color and detail.

6 First, zoom in to take a closer look at the image, by choosing a magnification level of 200% from the pop-up menu at the bottom left corner of the window.

Look at both the appearance of the image and the file size and download times listed beneath each. The GIF version at the far right doesn't look too far off from the original, although you should see a shift in color, particularly in the blues around the mouth. The file size is bigger than the other versions and the download time is 19 seconds, not something most users would want to wait out. The GIF Web palette version will download a little faster at about 14 seconds, but the color trade-offs don't make it a good option. The JPEG version at High quality looks truest to the original; you can probably shave a bit more off the file size and download time of about 15 seconds by compressing it even further.

7 Click the third image, and choose JPEG Medium from the Settings menu.

8 Click the fourth image, and choose JPEG Low. You can start to see the image soften in some areas, but it is not bad, and remember that you are still zoomed in. At a file size of 10K and a download of about 4 seconds, this is a pretty good choice.

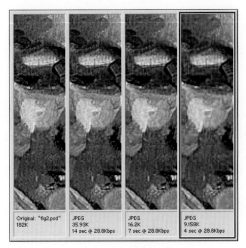

Original image compared to three JPEG versions

9 Zoom out to 100% view using the zoom tool in the dialog box or the pop-up View menu, and look again.

💡 *If image file size is your primary constraint on a project and you are unsure how to configure the various optimization settings in the most efficient way, try using the Optimize to File Size command. Click the Optimize Menu button next to the Settings pop-up menu, and choose the command from the menu.*

Previewing an image on multiple platforms and browsers

Images display a bit differently on Windows and Macintosh systems due to differences in color gamut on each platform. The main concern if you are preparing your image on a Macintosh, is not making your images too dark, as they will display even darker on Windows, and vice versa. Both Photoshop and ImageReady have options for simulating each platform.

1 Click the Preview button in the upper right corner above the rightmost image, and choose either Standard Windows Color or Standard Macintosh Color from the pop-up menu. Use the same pop-up menu to compare the differences in download time according to the modem speed used.

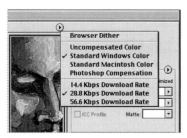

Monitor color and download preview options

Displaying the image as it will appear on each platform does not change the information in the file; it is simply a way to preview. Browser settings also affect the way images display.

2 If you have more than one browser installed on your system, preview how your image will look in each by choosing it from the Select Browser pop-up menu.

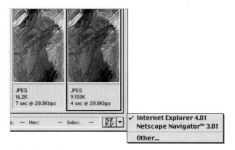

Selecting a browser preview

Saving optimization settings

If you create a custom set of optimization settings that you could apply to other images, save the settings so that they are available by name in the Settings menu.

1 With the fourth image selected, click the pop-up Optimize menu button next to the Settings button, and choose Save Settings.

2 Name the settings, and click Save. The set now appears by name in the Settings menu.

 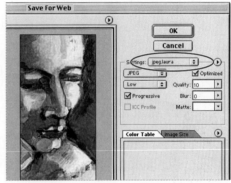

Saving optimization settings

💡 *To optimize a batch of images using the same compression settings, create a droplet in ImageReady to automate the task.*

If you plan to edit the image after saving it in an optimized format, as you will in this lesson, the following step is important.

3 Hold down the Alt/Option key, to change the OK button to Remember. Click Remember. This embeds all optimization settings with the file; if you make changes later, simply choose Save and you will bypass the Save As window.

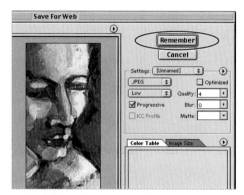

Holding down Alt/Option displays Remember button

4 Release the Alt/Option key to redisplay the OK button. Click OK. In the dialog box that appears, name the file **Fig.jpg**, choose a destination folder for the Web-optimized file, and click Save.

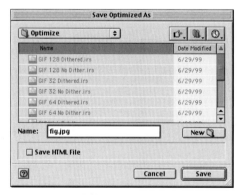

Saving optimized file

Increasing color saturation

After optimizing your image in JPEG format, you can still use some of Photoshop's color editing tools. An advantage of displaying an image on a Web page is that you can boost the intensity of colors in an image so that they really pop—something you cannot do with conventional process color inks on press or on a color printer.

1 In Photoshop, open the Fig.jpg image that you saved in the previous section.

2 Choose Image > Adjust > Hue/Saturation.

3 With the Master channel selected, drag the Saturation slider to the right to +36. The colors intensify, which is the effect you want, but the yellows look too extreme.

4 Choose Yellows from the Edit menu, and drag the Saturation left to –38.

 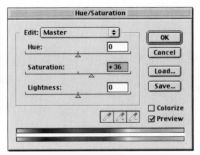 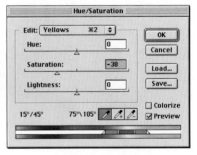

Adjusting saturation

5 Click OK.

6 Save your changes. Your image remains in optimized JPEG format, and you do not need to return to the Save for Web window.

Note: If you did not select Remember before saving the file in the Save for Web dialog box, the JPEG dialog box reopens and prompts you to choose new JPEG settings. Follow the instructions in "Saving optimization settings" on page 29.

Replacing color

In several isolated spots in the image, the color still looks darker and duller than in the original painting. Although it might be impossible to reproduce the desired color on press, the Web version is a perfect place to try, without adjusting the balance of other colors in the image.

1 Start by drawing a rectangular selection around the lips.

2 Zoom in to a 200% view.

3 Choose Image > Adjust > Replace Color.

4 Using the eyedropper tool in the dialog box, click the dark pink area of the lower lip in the image. Adjust the Fuzziness slider until the shape of the lower lip is somewhat defined in the black-and-white preview in the dialog box. Depending on where you clicked with the eyedropper tool, the Fuzziness value will vary. I used 40; you may need to push it as high as 80.

5 To replace the original color with a brighter pink, drag the Hue slider to +11, Saturation to +77, and Lightness to +26. (The color you get depends on the exact area you sampled.) Click OK.

Using the Replace Color command

6 Zoom out to a 100% view, and deselect the image.

7 Save changes to your file.

8 Close any open files, and quit Photoshop.

You've completed the lesson. Your image is ready to be posted on your Web page using Adobe GoLive or Adobe ImageReady.

Lesson 2

2 | Shading and Blending

By Laura Dower

This lesson gives you an overview of the shading and blending tools and techniques available in both Adobe Illustrator and Adobe Photoshop. You'll learn how to choose which program, and tools, are best suited for the effect you want.

In this lesson, you'll learn how to do the following in Adobe Illustrator:

- Give depth and shading to flat objects.
- Create shadows and shading using reflective color.
- Learn expert tips on the use of gradient and gradient mesh tools.
- Use the Gradient Editor to create a custom six-color gradient.
- Create depth and shading on flat images.
- Learn how to blend elements visually in a collage.
- Use painting tools and fade out options to blend edges.

This lesson assumes a basic knowledge of the gradient and gradient mesh tools in Illustrator, and the gradient and painting tools in Photoshop.

For more information on these tools, see Chapter 9 in the Photoshop 5.0 User Guide or "Painting" in Photoshop 5.0 online Help; and Chapter 8 in the Illustrator 8.0 User Guide or "Using Gradients, Blends, and Patterns" in Illustrator 8.0 online Help.

This lesson will take about 1-1/2 hours to complete.

If needed, remove the previous lesson folder from your hard drive, and copy the Lesson02 folder onto it.

Choosing Illustrator versus Photoshop

It is important to choose the right tool for the right job. Some styles of artwork are typically associated with either Illustrator or Photoshop, but sometimes overlooked are features and effects possible in both applications. In this lesson you will experiment with some tricks you may not be familiar with, as well as explore the advanced capabilities of the standard tools.

In general, Illustrator's strength is in its tools for drawing and editing individual shapes. If you want a crisp, hard edge and full editing control over contours and scaling, Illustrator is probably the right choice. Sometimes overlooked is Illustrator's capability for storing and editing colors by name, giving you a simple, efficient way to edit a single color that appears throughout your artwork. For instance, you may have used a dark blue in solid fills and in type, or as a color in gradients and shadows. Simply changing the color mix of that one blue color will automatically update all objects or gradients containing that color, without having to select or recreate a single one.

Photoshop's strength is its ability to blend photographic images along with illustrative elements, visually integrating them by adjusting color, shading, transparency, and lighting. If you want to combine images from separate sources, create soft faded edges or painterly effects, then Photoshop is the tool for the job.

You can always move your artwork between Illustrator and Photoshop, taking advantage of the most powerful tools and features available in each program. For the BBQ Betty illustration in this lesson, for example, I first drew all shapes in Illustrator and then brought them into Photoshop where I used scanned patterns to fill the shapes and adjusted the shading to create dimension and light. (I describe more about how I created the artwork at the end of the "Shading and blending in Photoshop" lesson.)

Some commonly used tools and features are available in both programs. In Photoshop, you can draw shapes using the pen tool and its Paths palette. In Illustrator, you can achieve Photoshop-like painterly effects without ever launching the application by rasterizing your drawing in Illustrator and apply a Photoshop filters, like Blur.

Getting started

Before beginning this lesson, restore the default application settings for Adobe Photoshop and Adobe Illustrator. For instructions, see "Restoring default preferences" on page 3.

In addition, make sure that you have enough memory allocated to complete this lesson. For more information, see "Memory requirements" on page 2.

You'll start the lesson by viewing the final Lesson file to see the image that you will create.

1 Restart Adobe Photoshop. Click Cancel to exit the color management dialog box that appears.

2 Choose File > Open, and open the 02End.psd file, located in the Lessons/Lesson02/02PSD folder. Click Don't Convert in the Profile Mismatch dialog box.

The image is composed of many separate shapes on different layers. Scanned patterns and photos were clipped to the drawn shapes. An old roadside cafe photo will be used as the background. Now, the elements look flat and disconnected. You will follow a series of techniques in Photoshop to blend these elements and add shading and definition.

The end file has been flattened into a single layer, so you will still have to follow the steps in this lesson to see how each layer and effect were created!

Start file (left) compared to final artwork (right)

3 When you have finished viewing the file, either leave the End file open on your desktop for reference, or close it without saving changes.

For an illustration of the finished artwork for this lesson, see the color section.

Shading and blending in Photoshop

The first project in this lesson will be done in Photoshop. The basic elements in the BBQ Betty artwork have already been drawn or scanned. Now you will integrate them visually.

Now you'll open the start file and begin the lesson by viewing the background.

1 Restart Adobe Photoshop. Click Cancel to dismiss the color management dialog box that appears.

2 Choose File > Open, and open the 02Start.psd file in the Lessons/Lesson02/02PSD folder on your hard drive. In the Profile Mismatch dialog box, click Don't Convert. (For information on setting up a color profile, see "Setting up a color profile" on page 182.)

3 Choose File > Save As, rename the file **BBQ.psd**, and click Save.

4 In the Layers palette, scroll to the bottom of the list and click the leftmost column to make the Background visible. (The view was turned off by default.) You will start by subduing this image so that it is not so dominant. You will first lighten the image by reducing its opacity.

5 Set the Layers palette opacity to 45%.

Background set to
100% opacity

Background set to
45% opacity

The bottommost layer is now semitransparent and reveals the default checkerboard pattern, a display option that indicates layer transparency. It is a little distracting.

6 Turn it off by choosing File > Preferences > Transparency& Gamut and choosing None for Grid Size. Click OK.

 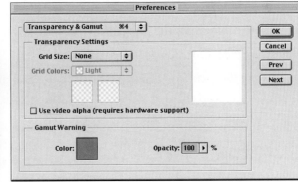

Transparency grid set to None

Creating a six-color gradient

Now you will create a custom gradient to apply over the background photo, using colors sampled from areas in the artwork.

1 In the Layers palette, make sure that the Background is still active. Create a new layer by clicking the New Layer button at the bottom of the palette.

2 Double-click the linear gradient tool in the toolbox to open the Gradient Options palette. From the Gradient pop-up menu, choose Yellow, Violet, Orange, Blue. You will use this four-color gradient as a base, and replace its colors with those from the artwork.

3 Click Edit to open the Gradient Editor dialog box.

4 Click Duplicate, and name the gradient **Photo Gradient**. Click OK.

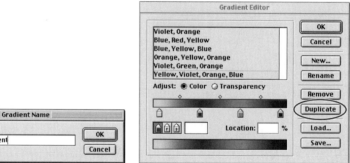

Four-color gradient duplicated as Photo gradient

You'll incorporate colors from the image into the gradient, first selecting a gradient stop in the Gradient Editor.

5 Start by clicking the second gradient stop from the left, beneath the gradient bar. (The triangle on top of the stop changes to black, indicating that it is selected.) You'll keep the Gradient Editor open as you work.

6 In the image, move your pointer over a dark purple in Betty's skirt (it changes to an eyedropper tool); click to transfer the color to the gradient stop.

7 Now click the far left gradient stop in the Gradient Editor, and in the image, sample a bright green color from the salad leaves in the BBQ bowl.

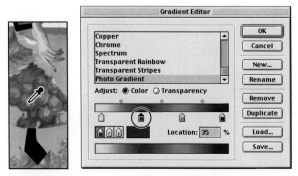

Purple color sampled from image and added to gradient

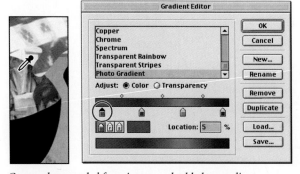

Green color sampled from image and added to gradient

You will add key colors from the image elements to the background gradient to integrate the image's foreground and background.

8 Click the third gradient stop from the left, and sample a strawberry red from Betty's mouth or hair ribbon. Then click the far right gradient stop, and sample a bright corn yellow color from her boots.

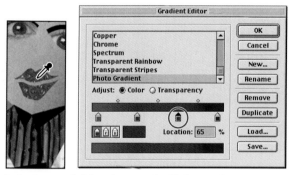

Red color sampled from image and added to gradient

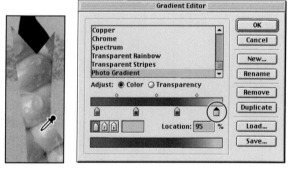

Yellow color sampled from image and added to gradient

Next, you will add two more colors to the gradient. To envision how this gradient will look on the image when it is created, it's helpful to think about the order in which the colors will be applied. The starting color of the gradient is the bright green at the far left. When you create the gradient, you'll start at the bottom of the image and drag upward, so that the green will fall at the bottom of the image and the yellow will fall at the top.

You can easily adjust the position where each color appears in the gradient by dragging the color buckets right or left along the bar. For instance, rather than have all colors equidistant from one another, instead you may want to position them relative to details in the underlying image. Often this is apparent only after you see your initial gradient applied to the image.

In this case, just choose Undo or delete the contents of the layer; then edit the gradient and reapply it. Don't worry if this is too much to visualize. You'll walk through it in the next section.

9 Still in the Gradient Editor, click beneath the gradient bar between the purple and red color stops to add a fifth color. With the new gradient stop selected, in the image, sample a bright blue color from Betty's BBQ mitt.

10 To create the sixth color, hold down the Alt/Option key, and drag the purple gradient stop to the far right edge of the gradient bar (to the right of the yellow).

I also made some adjustments to the position of the color and midpoint sliders. Note the following setup if you want to match the effect as closely as possible.

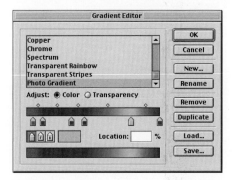

Final gradient setup

11 Click OK to close the Gradient Editor.

12 Save your changes.

Applying the gradient to the image

That's enough color editing. Let's see what this gradient looks like on the image.

1 In the Gradient palette, make sure that the Photo Gradient you just edited is selected in the list. Set the mode to Normal and the opacity to 100%. (You'll adjust these using Layer options after the gradient is created.)

2 Using the linear gradient tool, drag from the bottom of the image to the top. By default, the gradient will look opaque and block out the background image.

3 In the Layers palette, make sure the gradient layer (Layer 1) is selected, and set the Opacity to 30% and the mode to Multiply.

Six-color gradient applied; layer opacity set to Multiply at 30% opacity.

You adjust the opacity and painting mode in the Layers palette instead of the Gradient palette so that you can edit these values again later on, without having to re-create the gradient. If you created the gradient at 30%, for example, you could never increase the opacity beyond that.

4 If you want to adjust the position of colors in the gradient before continuing, start by choosing Select All on the layer, and pressing Delete. Use the Gradient Editor to adjust the gradient definition, and then use the gradient tool to drag the gradient across the layer. You can skip this step if you are satisfied with the effect.

> ### Gradients in Photoshop and Illustrator
>
> *Depending on how you create them, gradients in Illustrator may not look the same as those created in Photoshop. Gradients created in Illustrator and placed in Photoshop also tend to look different. You can use two techniques to make gradients from Illustrator (in both Illustrator and Photoshop) look better and more consistent.*
>
> *Many two-color gradients fade from black to another color. In Illustrator, setting up a gradient that fades from black to (for example) red will result in a good-looking gradient on-screen. But when it prints, the gradient will actually appear to get lighter in the center. What you want, of course, is for the gradient to gently change from black to red. If you think about it, however, what you really want is the gradient to change from a really really dark red to red. The end result is dramatically different; the red-to-black gradient has a pasty, pink-gray center, while the "dark" red-to-black gradient has a medium-dark red center.*
>
> *To create the really, really dark-red to red gradient, start with a gradient that is red (or whatever color you're using) on both ends. Then add 100% black to the gradient (if you're working in RGB, switch to CMYK for this step to make it easier, and then back to RGB after you've made the color change). This results in a much more pleasing fade than a simple red-to-black gradient. Adding color (or colors) to a black results in a "rich black," a term used to describe black generated by adding various amount of other CMY colors to 100% black.*
>
> *Bringing gradients into Photoshop occasionally produces banding or a gradient that looks too "computery." Fix this by creating a new layer and applying 999 (maximum) noise to it; then reduce the opacity of the layer to 10%. Apply the Soft Light mode to the layer for an even smoother appearance.*
>
> *—Ted Alspach*

Adding depth by darkening the edges of objects

Here is a great way to select just the borders of each object and shade the edges to create depth.

1 Select the Skirt layer.

2 Alt/Option-click the eye icon next to the Skirt layer to display only that layer.

3 Choose Select > Load Selection, and for Channel choose Skirt Transparency.

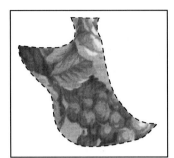 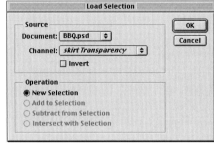

Skirt selected

4 Now choose Select > Modify > Border, enter **10** pixels, and click OK.

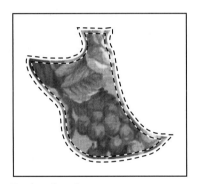 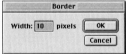

Border selected

5 Feather the selection 3 pixels (choose Select > Feather).

6 Hide the selection edges by pressing Ctrl/Command+H.

7 In the Layers palette, make sure that Preserve Transparency is selected.

8 Choose Image > Adjust > Levels to darken the selected area. I adjusted the skirt border by dragging the middle (midtone) slider to the right to an Input Levels of 0.15.

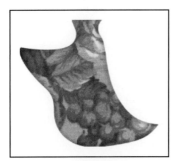 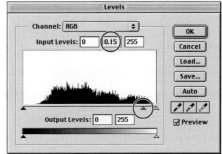

Border selection darkened using Levels

When you have feathered a selection border, you can use a variety of tools or commands to darken the edges. You can fill the area with a darker color, or use one of the painting tools within the selection for a less uniform shadow. You can also experiment with layer effects on your own images, because these controls simultaneously create a highlight and shadow. However, for the softer and more painterly effect you are after here, the border selection and Levels adjustment work best.

9 Save your changes.

Lightening the inside area of an object

You can use a similar procedure to define a shape further by lightening its inner area.

1 Select the object again by choosing Select > Load Selection, and Skirt Transparency for Channel.

2 This time choose Select > Modify > Contract, enter **10** pixels, and click OK. The selection shrinks to the inside edges of the object.

3 Feather the selection again by 3 pixels (press Ctrl+Alt+D in Windows or Command+ Option+D in Mac OS). Then lighten the area using Levels (Ctrl/Command+L). This time, drag the midtone slider left to 1.50. Click OK.

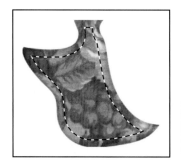
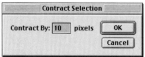
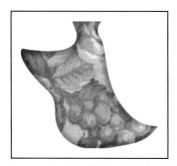
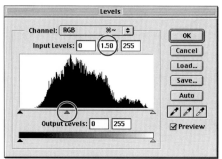

Contracting the selection and then lightening the area using Levels

Increasing contrast with the Saturate sponge

A final step in this modeling sequence is using the Saturate sponge to increase the color contrast between the dark edges you've just created and the lighter interior.

1 Deselect the inner shape.

2 In the toolbox, position the pointer on the burn tool and drag to select the sponge tool from the hidden tools. Double-click the sponge tool to open its Options palette, and choose Saturate from the pop-up menu.

3 In the Brushes palette, choose a large soft brush (I used 35). Begin scrubbing the sponge along the edges of the skirt, at the transition from dark to light.

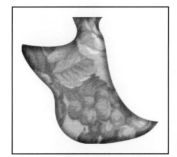
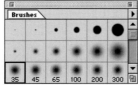
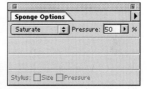

Saturate sponge applied to edges of skirt

4 In the Layers palette, Alt/Option-click the eye icon next to the Skirt layer to redisplay all layers.

5 Repeat the steps from this and the previous two sections for darkening edges, and lightening, saturating inside shapes for other layers in the artwork, such as Betty's shirt, boots, face and BBQ mitt.

6 Save your changes.

Shading objects with the burn and airbrush tools

Now you'll practice some techniques for adding shade beneath objects.

1 In the Layers palette, make the Background active.

2 Select the burn tool, and in its Options palette set the Midtones exposure to 100%. Use a large soft brush (I used 45) and trace around the edges of Betty to create a shadow. The first marks you make with the brush will be subtle.

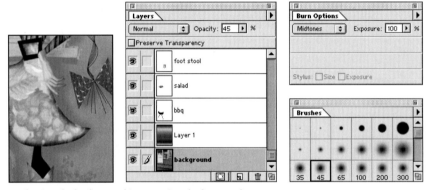

Darkening the background image using the burn tool

3 Continue working, dragging the burn tool over areas until you've achieved the desired level of darkness. Use the edges of the various shapes such as her boots, the footstool, her skirt, and so on, as a visual guide. You are actually editing the background image.

4 Save your changes.

💡 *Because this image already contains many layers, I won't have you create a copy of the Background for this project. Note that you are permanently altering the Background when painting with the burn tool. It is generally a good idea to keep a copy of the original, in case you want to revert back to the unretouched version.*

Creating modeling effects using radial and linear gradients

Now you'll add depth to the barbeque using gradients.

1 In the Layers palette, make the BBQ layer active. Alt/Option-click the eye icon next to the BBQ layer to make only that layer visible. Make sure that the Preserve Layer Transparency option is selected.

2 In the toolbox, reset the foreground and background colors to their defaults of black and white. (Press D on the keyboard.)

3 Select the radial gradient tool. In the Gradient Options palette, for Gradient choose Foreground to Background at 100% opacity. Click the Reverse option so that the gradient will fill from white to black (instead of black to white).

4 Position the gradient tool in the upper left corner of the BBQ. Drag down to the lower right edge of the bowl. Do not drag all the way down across the legs.

Because the Preserve Transparency option was checked on the layer, the gradient fills only areas on the layer that already contain image data and does not affect the transparent background.

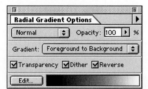

Creating radial gradient for BBQ bowl

You will create linear gradients across each of the legs. You must first select a leg so that the gradient does not affect other objects on the layer.

5 Use the lasso tool to roughly select one leg.

6 Select the linear gradient tool. Use the same settings from the radial gradient (set in step 3) in the palette.

7 With the gradient tool, drag a short horizontal line across the leg to fill it. Because the shape is thin, the direction and distance you drag the tool is sensitive. It may take a few tries to get the fill you want.

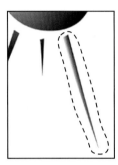
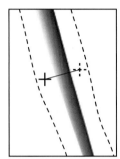

Leg selection   *Close-up of how to create gradient*

8 With the leg still selected, switch to the move tool (press Ctrl/Command), and move the leg into position against the bottom of the barbeque bowl, as shown in the illustration.

9 Repeat steps 7 and 8 for the other two legs.

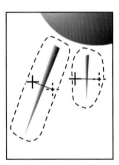

Linear gradient created for each leg

10 View all layers by Alt/Option-clicking the eye icon next to the BBQ layer.

11 Deselect the image.

12 Save your changes.

Creating cast shadows using the airbrush tool

Using the Fade setting on the airbrush tool, you can create nice shadow effects to emphasize the light source on an object.

1 If necessary, set the foreground color to black.

2 In the Layers palette, make sure that the BBQ layer is active. Deselect the Preserve Transparency option.

3 Select the airbrush tool. In its Options palette, set the Fade rate to 50 steps and the Pressure to 40%. Select Fade to Transparent. Choose Behind from the pop-up menu so that the shadow will be painted only behind the legs already on the layer.

4 Select a small soft brush in the Brushes palette. Zoom in on the legs.

5 Click once with the airbrush tool at the bottom of the leg; then hold down the Shift key, and draw a straight line to the right until the brush mark fades to transparent.

6 Repeat step 5 for the other legs.

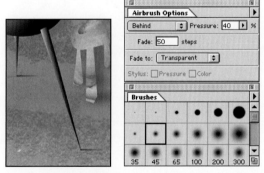

Cast shadows created for legs using airbrush and Fade setting

You can create similar shadows for the footstool legs by making the Footstool layer active, and then choosing a larger brush, lighter pressure, and shorter fade-out. I used a size 45 brush, with 15% pressure and a fade of 10 steps. Be sure to select the Behind option so that you do not paint shadows over the foreground elements.

7 Save your changes. Close the file and quit Photoshop.

Okay, that's it for the Photoshop portion of this lesson. Take a break; then come back to see what you can do with shading and blending in Illustrator.

(Although it is outside the scope of this lesson, the way this drawing was created is sort of interesting (well, to me). I started with a hand-drawn sketch that I scanned and placed on a template layer in Illustrator. I drew individual shapes in place using the pen tool, and then pulled them apart like puzzle pieces and filled them with black. I set up the old roadside cafe photo in Photoshop on a background layer, and then copied and pasted each shape from Illustrator into Photoshop, each one landing on its own layer. I reassembled each shape in place, and made sure the layers were in the right stacking order. Then I used clipping groups to fill individual shapes with scanned patterns and photos.)

Customizing Actions in Photoshop and Illustrator

Illustrator and Photoshop ship with a large number of actions, each of which can be customized in any way to suit your needs. Customizing actions can be an excellent way to familiarize yourself with them, and to learn how to take advantage of their capabilities.

For example, in Photoshop, a handy action installed with the application is Cast Shadow (type), which creates a cast shadow in front of the current text layer. But you can use this action to create cast shadows for any layer, not just text layers (try it on a brush stroke or odd shape that sits alone on a layer). In addition, you can easily modify the direction of the cast shadow from the in-front position to any place you desire, by placing a stop at the right point in the action. Open the action (click the triangle in the Actions palette to the left of the Cast Shadow (type) action), and click in the second column next to Transform Current Layer. When you run the action now, it will stop with the transformation matrix ready for your adjustments. Make your adjustments, and then press Enter. The action will continue, but the cast shadow is in the position you set for it!

In Illustrator, you can modify the Cast Shadow (type) action as well. Place stops at the Shear and Scale actions, and a dialog box will appear when it's time to change those settings. When modifying the Scale value, be sure to change only the vertical scale, not Uniform or Horizontal.

—Ted Alspach

Shading and blending in Illustrator

You will do the second part of the lesson in Illustrator. You may want to reread the introduction, "Choosing Illustrator versus Photoshop" on page 36, for an overview comparing the shading and blending strengths of Illustrator versus Photoshop. If you have not already restored the default Illustrator settings, do so now. For instructions, see "Restoring default preferences" on page 3.

1 Restart Illustrator.

2 Choose File > Open, and open the 02End.ai file, located in the Lessons/Lesson02/02AI folder.

3 When you have finished viewing the file, close the End file without saving changes.

Because Illustrator files containing lots of gradients and gradient mesh objects can be memory intensive, I suggest closing the file as you work through the lesson.

For an illustration of the finished artwork for this lesson, see the color section.

Creating reflected color effects using the gradient mesh tool

A feature long associated with Photoshop, but sometimes overlooked in Illustrator, is the ability to sample colors directly from your artwork using the eyedropper tool. By selecting from the palette of colors already present in your artwork, you'll be able to create more painterly and realistic effects.

02Start image   *02 End image*

1 Choose File > Open, and open the 02Start.ai file, located in the Lessons/Lesson02/02AI folder.

2 Choose File > Save As, rename the file **Bee.ai**, and click Save. In the Illustrator Format dialog box, choose 8.0 for Compatibility, and click OK.

3 Select the round head shape, and fill it with black and stroke it with None.

4 Choose Object > Create Gradient Mesh. Enter **6** for both Rows and Columns. For Appearance, choose To Center, and enter 35% for Highlight.

 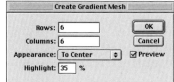

Gradient Mesh created for head

5 Zoom in close. Deselect the object. Then use the direct-selection tool to select a single anchor point along the bottom edge. You will add a turquoise highlight to the point to give the appearance that turquoise from the flower center is reflecting on the chin of the bee.

6 With the point selected, use the eyedropper tool and click the turquoise area of the flower center. Another option is to click Turquoise in the Swatches palette list. (Choose Name from the Swatches palette menu if swatches aren't listed by name.)

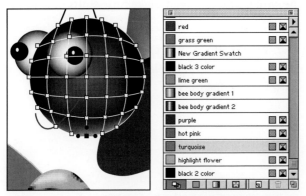

Mesh point selected, and turquoise color sampled from Swatches palette

The advantage to choosing the color by name is that if you decide you want to alter the turquoise color in your artwork later, all points or shapes painted by name will be automatically updated.

7 Hold down Alt/Option key to change the pointer to the paintbucket too. Click on a couple more points to spread the turquoise a little farther along the edge of the shape.

8 Repeat steps 6 and 7 further up the left side of the bug's head by sampling the hot pink color in one of the flower petals.

I used the same technique to paint the edges of the wings with color reflected from the body.

If you have a placed image or photo in your artwork, you can also sample colors from it to help blend elements visually. This technique lets you get a good color match when adding Illustrator type to a placed Photoshop image.

Managing color changes on gradient mesh objects

One of Illustrator's real strengths is the ability to edit colors throughout the artwork without ever having to redraw or paint a single shape. This allows incredible control over last minute changes, such as when your proofs come back, and the yellow you've been using is way off, or when your client changes its corporate color from green to red.

1 Make sure that all objects are deselected in your artwork.

2 In the Swatches palette, double-click the name Turquoise. This color was saved as a global process color, and was used to paint different objects in the artwork. By consistently choosing colors by name, you'll find it easy to make little shifts in color that you otherwise would have avoided.

3 Adjust the CMYK color sliders by dragging the Cyan slider to 100% and the Magenta slider to 20%. Make sure that the Preview option is selected so that you can see the effect of the color shift in your artwork before clicking OK.

 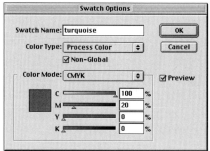

Color in artwork changed automatically by editing its color definition

Note: *If you want to be able to sample colors and know that they are referenced by the exact same name, be sure to select colors by name from the Swatches palette list. It's possible to sample a CMYK mix, and not a named color, if the points you sampled were originally painted using the eyedropper tool over a color gradation (such as by clicking between mesh lines on an object) or over a gradient fill.*

4 To darken the purple shadow along the edge of the flower center without selecting any points, double-click the name Purple in the Swatches palette list, and edit the color by adding 30% black. Click OK.

Creating shapes along a path using the Divide command

Now you'll use the Divide command to create the bee's body.

1 Zoom out and scroll to the right of the main artwork, to a copy of the bug's body and some curved paths. You'll use these to create individual segments that follow the curve of the bug's body, and then fill each with an alternating gradient.

2 Select the curved lines and the body shape.

3 In the Pathfinder palette, click the Divide command. A set of 10 individual shapes following the contour of the bee's body are the result.

Selecting lines and selecting the Pathfinder Divide option

4 Save your work.

Creating custom linear gradients

To add dimension to curved body segments, you will fill each with its own gradient, and then adjust the gradient's direction. This will create the illusion of curvature and playful stripes of green and purple. You will start by organizing the shapes to make selecting and editing easier.

1 Select every other shape in the body and cut them to the Clipboard.

2 Marquee-select the remaining shapes, choose Object > Group to group them; and fill them with Bee Body Gradient 1 from the Swatches palette list. The shapes are filled with a linear, green-to-white gradient.

3 Choose Edit > Paste in Front, and choose Object > Group to group the set. Fill these with Bee Body Gradient 2 by clicking the swatch name in the Swatches palette list.

Shapes filled with gradient 1 –   Shapes filled with gradient 2

4 Select a segment, and drag the gradient tool to change the direction of its gradient. Repeat for the remaining segments, adjusting the distance and direction of each according to the width of the shape and the illusion of curve that you want to create.

Direction of gradient fill on various shapes

5 Save your changes.

Managing color edits in gradient fills

It can sometimes be difficult to know how to store edits in the named swatch so that the objects in the artwork are updated with changes. Here's the procedure.

1 Make sure that the Color palette, Swatches palette, and Gradient palette are visible.

2 Deselect all objects in the artwork.

3 In the Swatches palette, click the swatch named Bee Body Gradient 2 (don't double click it; you don't want to open the dialog box). The Gradient palette displays the current gradient.

4 In the Gradient palette, choose Show Options from the palette menu. Click one of the purple gradient stops. All the colors in these gradients were created with named colors to facilitate easy editing throughout the artwork. To replace the gradient color with a new one, drag the color Turquoise from the Swatches palette list, and release it over the purple stop in the Gradient palette.

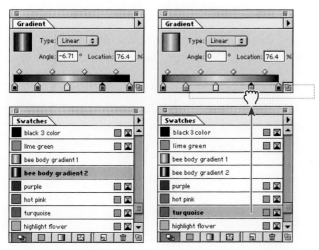

Gradient 2 selected by name   *Dragging color swatch to gradient stop*

5 Repeat step 4 for the other purple stop, replacing it with turquoise. Do not drag from the Color palette. You must drag the actual color by *name* from the Swatches palette list.

Now here's the most important part. Notice that nothing in your artwork has updated yet, even though you've edited the color in the gradient. (You shouldn't have any artwork selected at this point.)

6 Save the color change by holding down the Alt/Option key, and dragging the gradient swatch from the Gradient palette to the original name in the Swatches palette. Make sure that the name Bee Body Gradient 2 is highlighted before you release the mouse.

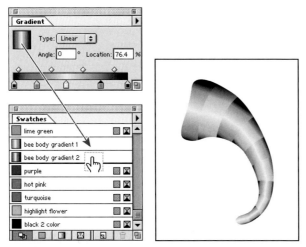

Replacing saved swatch with new gradient updates the artwork.

All shapes painted by that gradient name should now be updated with the new color.

7 Experiment with different color gradients by repeating steps 2 through 5 for either bee body gradient. Your end file may vary from mine depending on the color combinations you choose. (I liked the original green-and-purple combo, and stayed with that.)

8 Select the original solid blue body and delete it.

9 Select all the new gradient shapes and drag them into position under the head. Choose Object > Arrange > Send to Back to place the body behind the other parts.

10 Deselect the artwork. Save your changes.

11 Close any open files, and quit Illustrator.

That's it. You are ready to go out and do some shading and blending on your own.

Lesson 3

3 | Acquiring Digital Images

By Glen Janssens

This lesson explores the process of acquiring images in digital form in a number of different ways—from print, the Web, video, and a few places besides. In each form of acquisition, the lesson highlights potential pitfalls that can crop up, and gives you some techniques to use to correct inherent anomalies.

In this lesson you will learn how to acquire images from several different sources for use and manipulation in Adobe Photoshop. You'll learn how to:

• Follow general guidelines for image acquisition.

• Acquire images by flatbed scanning.

• Acquire images from digital photography.

• Acquire images from Photo CD or Image CD and stock libraries.

• Acquire elements from the Web and resample images up.

• Capture screen elements.

• Acquire frames from analog and digital video.

Each acquisition source is presented as a mini project. You will walk through the basic steps involved and learn general steps in Photoshop to help prepare your images for various forms of output.

The lesson will focus on basic information and tools associated with each acquisition method, but does not cover the numerous hardware and software configurations that make many of these acquisitions possible.

This lesson will take about 1-1/2 hours to complete.

If needed, remove the previous lesson folder from your hard drive, and copy the Lesson03 folder onto it.

General tips for acquiring images

All forms of image acquisition share several steps in common. This lesson covers basic guidelines you should follow when bringing digital images into Photoshop, including:

• Acquiring an image with enough resolution.

• Using target resolutions for different output media as a guide for image resolution.

• Optimizing shadow detail when capturing digital media.

• Identifying the final image's desired resolution before acquisition.

• Understanding how altering the image resolution affects the file size and image dimensions.

• Avoiding digital artifacts from the acquisition process.

Acquiring an image with enough resolution

The first, and most basic rule of image acquisition deals with content. Whenever possible, always acquire an image with at least 25%—and preferably 100%—more pixel resolution than your final project demands.

How much resolution should you begin with? If you know your final target resolution, double it when acquiring an image to provide enough resolution for your project. This is true irrespective of your final output medium. Acquiring at a higher resolution gives you greater flexibility when manipulating the image, particularly if it requires scaling, rotating, or filtering.

A good example of maintaining flexibility is in creating a vertical image for a magazine. If the original photograph was shot in landscape, or horizontal mode, you may have to both crop and zoom-in on the image. You'll be able to perform these tasks without creating information that doesn't exist in the original if you work with an image with twice the resolution desired for the final.

Original image

Zoom and crop area

Final cropped image

Identifying target resolutions for different output media

To determine how much resolution to begin with when acquiring an image, you can start with the final target resolution, which varies by different output media. (See the following table.) Then double this target resolution.

TARGET IMAGE RESOLUTIONS FOR DIFFERENT OUTPUT MEDIA

Medium	Image resolution range (in pixels/inch)
Newsprint	144 – 300 ppi
Magazine	166 – 1200 ppi
Black-and-white flyer	100 – 300 ppi
CD-ROM	72 ppi
DVD	72 ppi
Projected presentation	72 ppi
NTSC D1 digital video	72 ppi
PAL D1 digital video	72 ppi
Web site	72 ppi
35mm slide	1600 – 2800 ppi
Computer screen shots	72 ppi

Optimizing shadow detail when capturing digital media

Detail in digital imagery—particularly shadow detail—is very difficult to simulate or re-create properly.

You'll get far better results by adjusting your scanning software to optimize the scan's detail before manipulating your image in Photoshop, rather than trying to make up the information after the fact. (Some packages offer shadow detail adjustments, while others achieve the same effect through levels, gamma, or brightness algorithms.) Once again, your result is only as good as the image you begin with.

Identifying the final image's desired resolution before acquisition

It is critical that you begin with a target image's resolution in mind before acquiring images from any source. This will help dictate a logical starting point for your acquisition of images for your project.

Image resolution refers to the number of pixels displayed per the image dimensions, usually measured in pixels per inch (ppi). These factors plus the color depth of an image (8-bit with 256 colors, 16-bit with thousands of colors, or 24-bit with millions of colors) and the compression scheme of the file format (JPEG, PICT, TIFF, Photoshop, and so on), determine the image's file size.

It's important to realize that computer and video screens display imagery at 72 ppi. Even if an image has a higher image resolution, you will see it only if you zoom in. Other devices, such as an offset printing press or a laser printer, can output at much higher resolutions than a computer monitor—in fact, our eye demands that they do, as we have become accustomed to continuous-tone printing after years of exposure to it.

Note that an image can be expressed in several different image resolutions, while the file size remains constant. (In the following table, compare the pixel dimensions of the first three files.) But changing the image resolution can drastically affect the file size. (In the following table, compare the final file's dimensions and file size with the other three files.)

FILE SIZE DETERMINED BY IMAGE DIMENSIONS X IMAGE RESOLUTION

File name	Width		Height		Image resolution	File size
	Inches	Pixels	Inches	Pixels	Pixels/inch	(K)
03Starta.pct	5.944	428	4.125	297	72	373
03Startb.pct	2.972	428	2.063	297	144	373
03Startc.pct	2.000	428	1.388	297	214	373
03Startd.pct	2.972	856	2.063	594	288	1460

How altering the image resolution affects the file size and image dimensions

To illustrate how changing the image resolution can drastically affect file size, you'll explore the effects of altering a file's image resolution in Photoshop. You'll also see how changing the file's physical size affects resolution.

Before beginning this lesson, restore the default application settings for Adobe Photoshop and Adobe Illustrator. For instructions, see "Restoring default preferences" on page 3.

1 Restart Adobe Photoshop. Click Cancel to exit the color management dialog box that appears.

2 Choose File > Open, and open the 03Starta.pct file, located in the Lessons/Lesson03/03a folder on your hard drive. Click Don't Convert in the Profile Mismatch dialog box. (For information on setting up a color profile, see "Setting up a color profile" on page 182.)

You'll start by changing the image resolution.

3 Choose Image > Image Size to see information on the image resolution.

4 Deselect Resample Image, to maintain the original file size. (The file size appears next to Pixel Dimensions at the top of the dialog box; here it is 373K.)

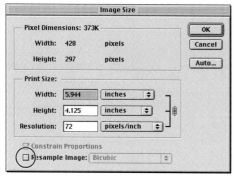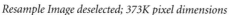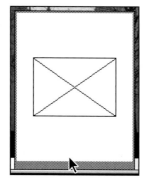

Resample Image deselected; 373K pixel dimensions   *72 ppi print size (6" x 4")*

5 For Resolution, enter **144**. Note that the width and height are halved in the Print Size area, but remain unchanged (373K) in the Pixel Dimensions area. Click OK.

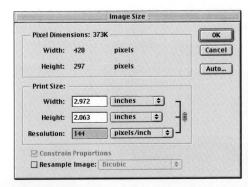 

Resolution doubled; pixel dimensions constant (373K)

144 ppi print size (3" x 2")

The resulting image appears the same on-screen, but will print with more detail because it has greater image resolution. (The 428 horizontal pixels have been compressed into half the distance, or 2. 972 inches, from the original 5.944 inches, to achieve twice the image resolution.)

Now you'll change the image's print size (its physical dimensions) to see the effect.

6 Choose Image > Image Size.

7 In the Print Size area, enter a width of **2** inches. The image resolution jumps to 214 ppi, but the pixel dimensions again remain the same. Click OK.

The resulting image appears smaller on-screen when viewed at 100%, yet will print with even greater detail because it has greater image resolution. (The 428 horizontal pixels are now confined to only 2 inches, producing an image resolution of 214 ppi.)

8 Close the file without saving changes.

Avoiding digital artifacts in the acquisition process

You can trick your scanning device to avoid moirés and other patterns in scanned imagery. Most nonphotographic printed materials are created through patterns of dots. When viewing a newspaper through a magnifying glass, dot patterns are very apparent. Scanners and some digital cameras convert analog media to data in a similar fashion— through patterns of pixels. When a dot pattern from a printing process is scanned using a pixel pattern, the combination of the two can result in a pattern referred to as a moiré.

Before scanning, simply rotate your printed media slightly to avoid undesirable moirés.

Poorly scanned print (moiré present)   *Detail area*   *Dot pattern detail*

Acquiring images via flatbed scanning

All flatbed scanners and their scanning software differ slightly. Most, however, contain basic functions that aid in the acquisition process. This project uses Agfa's Fotolook software to digitally scan a photograph. Your scanning software may differ, but its basic components should work in the same fashion.

Once the photograph has been scanned, you will correct the following in Photoshop:

• Color correction using the Levels.

• Dirt removal using the clone feature of the rubber stamp tool.

• Hue and saturation adjustment using the HSL filter.

In my experience, most scans from prints tend to be dense. This part of the lesson focuses on corrections to salvage a dark scan with dirt and other difficult scanning artifacts, which commonly appear when using a flatbed scanner.

In this part of the lesson, you will work with a scanned photograph to be included on a CD cover. The cover will be printed with a 133-line screen. Using a multiple of 2, the target resolution will be 266 ppi. (It's common practice to multiply the print line screen by 2 or 3 to arrive at a target resolution.) The final target size will be 2.5 inches wide by 3.5 inches tall.

Scanning the photo

Most scanning software lets you preview your scan in either grayscale or color. In this case, the photo was scanned from a 4-inch by 6-inch print. To ensure that you scan the image with enough resolution to work with, see "Identifying target resolutions for different output media" on page 68.

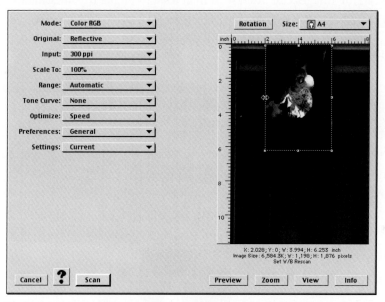

Previewing the scan and cropping

Checking the scan for problems

You'll start by rotating the scan and checking for problems using Levels to preview the image.

1 Choose File > Open, and open the 03Endb.psd file, located in the Lessons/Lesson03/03b folder. Click Don't Convert in the Profile Mismatch dialog box.

2 When you have finished viewing the file, either leave the End file open on your desktop for reference, or close it without saving changes.

For an illustration of the finished artwork for this lesson, see the color section.

Now you'll open the start file and begin the lesson by rotating the scan.

3 Choose File > Open, and open the 03Startb.pct file, located in the Lessons/Lesson03/03b folder. Click Don't Convert in the Profile Mismatch dialog box.

4 Choose File > Save As, and rename the file **Girl1.pct**.

5 Choose Image > Rotate Canvas > 180° to rotate the image. Scans are often oriented incorrectly; this can either be corrected in Photoshop or in your scanning utility.

Even if you're careful, images can often scan in at a slight angle. If your scan appears slightly askew, the easiest way to correct it is by using the free transform tool. In Photoshop, simply open the skewed scan and select all of the image; choose Edit > Free Transform, and rotate the image until it appears correctly aligned.

6 Choose Image > Adjust > Levels to open the Levels dialog box. Make sure that the Preview option is selected in the lower right corner. Position the dialog box on-screen so that you can view the image as you make changes.

7 Check the scan by selecting the highlight control (the white triangle at the right of the histogram) and dragging it to the extreme left to about 30. This will limit the dynamic range of the image and will reveal a blue streak at the left edge of the photograph. It will also reveal a number of dirt specks in the scan.

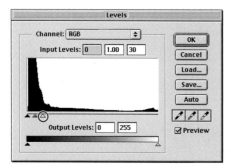 

Using Levels preview to check for problem areas   *Scanning artifact and dirt*

8 Click Cancel to leave the photo unchanged and exit the Levels dialog box.

Adjusting the foreground levels

In most cases, it is undesirable to adjust an image's Levels settings more than once. Each adjustment discards information. But in this case, it's not possible to correct both the extreme density of the photograph and the blue streak left by the scanning process in one adjustment. Thus, you will correct the subject first, the background second, and then the blue streak.

You first need to isolate the subject from the background so that you can adjust its levels slightly differently than for the background. The goal is to have the subject pop in the photograph without appearing abnormal.

1 Select the lasso tool. In the Lasso Options palette, set the Feather to 20.

2 Zoom in to 67% or 100% depending on your monitor's resolution. Scroll until the girl's face is mid-frame.

3 Draw an outline around the edge of her head, arms, and body. In many cases, your selection may be very loose or a best guess around the edge of the subject.

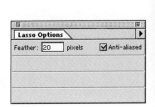

Feather of 20 *Subject selected*

4 Save the selection by choosing Selection > Save Selection. Name the selection **Foreground**, and click OK. Your selection will be saved for later reference.

5 Save your changes.

6 With the selection still active, choose Image > Adjust > Levels. Position the Levels dialog box so that you can see the image.

7 In the Levels dialog box, make the following adjustments using the Input Levels fields or sliders beneath the histogram:

• With the RGB channel selected, drag the highlights (white triangle) and midtones (gray triangle) to the left, setting the Input Levels values to 0, 1.92, and 139. Don't click OK yet. These adjustments brighten the subject considerably.

• Choose Blue for Channel (or press Ctrl/Command+3). Warm up the image by setting the Blue channel midtone to 0.82. Many scans tend to come in on the cool side, or more blue. This is a simple way to compensate.

• Finally, adjust the green levels in the Levels dialog box by choosing Green for Channel (or press Ctrl/Command+2). Set the Green channel's midtone to 0.95.

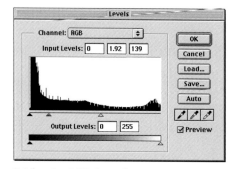

Brightening RGB channel

8 Click OK. Do not deselect.

Adjusting the image's background levels

To adjust the background levels, you will isolate the background from the foreground subject. When isolating an image's foreground and background, the edge between the two areas becomes critical. It is helpful to overlap that edge slightly to blend the two areas better.

First, you will contract the saved foreground selection.

1 Choose Select > Modify > Contract, enter **2**, and click OK to reduce the selection by 2 pixels on all edges.

Now you'll add an additional feather before adjusting the adjacent background levels.

2 Choose Select > Feather, enter **5,** and click OK. The new selection is slightly smaller and softer than the previous one.

3 Choose Select > Inverse to invert the selection from the foreground to the background. You are now ready to adjust the image's background levels.

4 Choose Image > Adjust > Levels (or press Ctrl/Command+U), and set the RGB input levels to 0 blackpoint, 1.05 midtone, and 151 highlight.

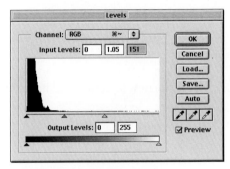

Adjusting background RGB levels

5 Next, adjust the blue levels in the Levels dialog box by switching to the Blue channel (press Ctrl/Command+3). Set the Input Levels midtone for the Blue channel to 0.93.

6 Finally, adjust the green levels in the Levels dialog box by switching to the Green channel (press Ctrl/Command+2). Set the Input Levels midtone for the Green channel to 0.97.

7 Click OK to apply the changes.

8 Deselect the image.

9 Save your changes.

Correcting the scanning artifacts with levels

As you discovered in "Checking the scan for problems" on page 73, a large blue streak appears at the left edge of the image. This type of artifact is not uncommon in flatbed scanning. It can be corrected using a combination of the right selection, and a levels and a saturation adjustment.

1 Select the lasso tool. In the Lasso Options palette, make sure that the feather is set to 20.

2 Expand the image window so that you can see the entire subject.

3 Select the blue area of the image using the lasso tool.

Blue streak selected

4 Choose Select > Feather, enter **50**, and click OK. The new selection will have a very soft edge, making a Levels blend less obvious.

5 Choose Image > Adjust > Levels.

It is sometimes helpful to view the adjustment without the selection outline turned on. Within the Levels dialog box, press Ctrl/Command+H to hide the selection. Outside of the dialog box, choose View > Hide Edges.

6 In the Levels dialog box, adjust the Input Levels:

• Set the RGB midtone to 0.93.

• Press Ctrl/Command+3 to switch to the Blue channel. Set the midtone to 0.90.

• Press Ctrl/Command+2 to switch to the Green channel. Set the midtone to 0.94.

7 Click OK. Do not deselect yet.

Notice that the left side is slightly more saturated than the rest of the image.

8 Choose Image > Adjust > Hue/Saturation. Desaturate the selection by decreasing the saturation level to –10. Click OK.

Saturation reduced to –10

9 Deselect and save your changes.

Removing dirt from the scan

Now that the image's levels are set, the dirt in the scan should be more visible. Varying amounts of dirt show up in most scans as anomalous or different colored pixels, and can be easily removed using the rubber stamp tool.

1 Select the rubber stamp tool, and set its opacity to 70% in the Rubber Stamp Options palette.

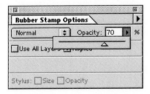

Rubber stamp clone option, 70% opacity

2 Select a small, soft-edged brush from the Brushes palette.

3 Zoom in to 100% or higher where dirt is apparent by pressing Ctrl/Command+spacebar, and then clicking the area.

4 In the image near some dirt, select a nearby area to clone that has the same character-istics by Alt/Option-clicking the desired location. Your goal is to try to match the dirt with the pixels that would have been present had there been no dirt.

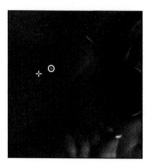

Selecting a good clone source

5 With a clone source selected, drag over the dirt.

As you drag, the plus sign represents the clone source and the circle represents the clone brush. Essentially, you are duplicating pixels beneath the plus sign and transferring them to the circle area in the shape and size of the selected brush.

6 Repeat steps 4 and 5 to remove the dirt, scrolling around the entire image to locate problem spots. It is helpful to zoom in and out occasionally to check your work.

7 Save your changes.

Blurring the background

Next, you will defocus the background by blurring it, and then change its hue so that the subject seems to pop out of the image more.

1 Select the Foreground selection by choosing Select > Load Selection. Click OK.

💡 *Load the selection quickly by making the Channels palette active, and Ctrl/command-clicking the Foreground channel.*

It is important to not blur the edges of the foreground subject. To maintain the edges, you will expand your saved selection and then invert it.

2 Choose Select > Modify > Expand. Enter **15**, and click OK to expand the edge of the selection by 15 pixels.

3 Choose Select > Feather. Enter **50**, and click OK to produce a very soft edge.

4 Invert the selection by choosing Select > Inverse.

5 Choose Filters > Blur > Gaussian Blur. Set the blur level to 9 pixels and click OK to defocus the background.

Background selected   *Gaussian Blur filter*

6 Deselect your selection and save your changes.

Changing the hue of the background

To complete the image editing, you will shift the hue of the background to a bright green, which contrasts with some of the foreground colors.

1 Load your previous foreground selection by choosing Select > Load Selection and invert it by choosing Select > Inverse. Your changes will apply to the background.

2 Choose Image > Adjust > Hue/Saturation. Adjust the Hue to +70 or by dragging the slider or entering the value. Saturate the green by adjusting the Saturation to +50. Click OK.

You'll crop the image to complete your work.

3 Using the rectangular marquee, drag a rectangular selection for the image crop.

4 Choose Image > Crop to crop the image.

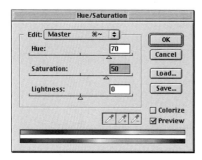

Hue +70, Saturation +50

Final cropped image

5 Save your changes.

The image is finally ready for the CD cover (were you to complete the hypothetical project). What is that pill she's holding? And why is she wearing wings? Who is this band anyway?!

6 Close the file.

Acquiring digital photography

Now, you will learn how to acquire a digital photo and make adjustments for common levels problems. Digital cameras can at times exaggerate certain aspects of color and saturation. You need to make adjustments to balance out these anomalies.

In the next several steps, you will prepare the image for inclusion in a hypothetical online birthday announcement that will be delivered as a PDF document.

Importing a digital image

Most digital cameras work in a similar way in their acquisition mode, which includes software that resides in the Import/Export folder in the Adobe Photoshop Plug-Ins folder. (This software generally comes with an automatic installer that places the acquisition plug-in into the appropriate folder.)

Note: *If you don't have a digital camera, you can complete this section using the Lesson file indicated, or you can skip to the next section, "Acquiring Photo CD images" on page 86.*

1 Choose File > Import > Olympus (or your camera's software). The acquisition software appears.

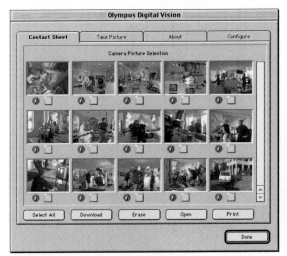

Olympus Digital Vision software   *Original digital photograph*

Note: *If you don't have a digital camera, choose File > Open, and open the 03Startc.pct, located in the Lessons/Lesson03/03c folder on your hard drive. You can also skip to the next section, "Acquiring Photo CD images" on page 86.*

An image of a red-jacketed girl with sunglasses appears. This image was acquired using an Olympus Stylus D-300L and the Olympus 1.1 plug-in software.

2 Select and open the image you want to acquire, following the instructions for your acquisition software. For instructions, see your product's documentation.

3 Save the image as **Girl2.psd**.

Adjusting common color and saturation problems

The initial image has a few subtle color and saturation issues that can be corrected in Photoshop. First, you need to correct the flat dynamic range in the image.

1 Choose Image > Adjust > Levels. Position the Levels dialog box so that you can view the image.

The histogram reveals large unused areas in the shadows and highlights of the image. Data exists across the Red, Green, and Blue channels in 256 levels each. Generally, adjusting the input levels so that the image's darkest point is set at the left edge of the histogram and its highlight is at the right makes the image more vibrant.

2 In the Levels dialog box, make the following adjustments using the Input Levels fields or sliders beneath the histogram:

• Set the image's shadow point to 35 (drag the black triangle right, to the left edge of the histogram).

• Set the image's highlight point to 231 (drag the white triangle left, to the right edge of the histogram).

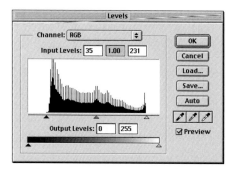

RGB histogram with highlight and shadow points adjusted

The image's color and shadow detail appears to pop out more as a result. You have moved all data (256 shades of gray in the Red, Green, and Blue channels) into the area under the histogram, spreading shadow and color information across the full range of the image.

If necessary, warm up the image using individual channels. For instructions, see "Adjusting the foreground levels" on page 75.

Besides a flat dynamic range, often digital photographs and their corrected shadows exhibit oversaturated color.

You'll bring the image's overall saturation back into acceptable ranges in areas such as the red jacket and lavender pants.

3 Choose Image > Adjust > Hue/Saturation. Drag the Saturation slider to –3.

After levels, saturation adjustment

4 Save your changes.

Cropping the image

At times it can be difficult to grab the exact corner of an image with a selection tool. A good way to do that is to increase the size of your image window, and then begin making your selection outside of the image itself. This technique ensures that you select the pixels closest to the edge or corner. You'll try it now.

1 Click the Info palette to make it active (choose Window > Show Info if it's not visible on-screen). If the units aren't set to pixels, choose Ruler Units from the palette menu, and choose Pixels.

2 View the image at 100% by selecting the percentage value in the lower left corner of the image window, typing **100**, and pressing Enter or Return.

3 Drag the lower right corner of the image window down and to the right to increase the frame around the photo. (See the following illustration.)

4 Select the rectangular marquee tool, and position it below the lower right corner of the image, in the gray area of the image frame. Drag the cursor up and all the way to the left until the selection is as wide as the image and 428 pixels high.

5 Choose Image > Crop to crop the photo.

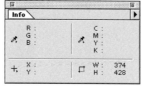

Expanded image window   *Height measuring 428 pixels*   *Cropped image*

Note: *The illustration of the original image appears more saturated and denser than your working version. The difference results from the screen capture software, which requires correction. For more information, see "Capturing an image, dialog box, or menu from your screen" on page 97.*

6 Choose File > Save As. For Format, choose PICT, for inclusion in a photo layout that will become a PDF; or JPEG (Medium-6 for maximum quality and minimum file size) for use as an e-mail attachment. Rename the file, and click Save.

The image is ready to use as an online birthday announcement, delivered in a PDF document (should you so choose).

7 Close the file.

Acquiring Photo CD images

Kodak's Photo CD format has become a popular way to digitally access and archive photographs. Photo CD comes equipped with viewing software to allow you to preview your images and to use them as a screen saver by setting them in a Slide Show mode.

This part of the lesson will cover the following topics:

• Previewing images using Kodak's Slide Show software (Macintosh only).

• Selecting the right image resolution for your project.

• Opening images in Photoshop for enhancement and adjustment.

- Prepping an image for a printed publication.

- Making a selection using Color Range.

- Setting the final target resolution of the image.

Previewing images in Kodak Slide Show (Macintosh only)

Every Photo CD comes with Slide Show, Slide Show Viewer, and photos in five sets of resolutions. (The Picture CD format has fewer choices in resolution, but works in a similar fashion.) Photo CDs also come with an insert card printed with thumbnails of each scan on the disc. If you cannot locate your image from the thumbnails, the next best tool is Kodak's Slide Show, included in the Lesson03 Photo CD folder.

Sample Photo CD window

1 Choose File > Open, and open the Photo CD folder in the Lessons/Lesson03 folder on your hard drive. Double-click the Slide Show. It automatically launches the Viewer, which features small (192-pixel by 128-pixel) previews of the images.

Slide Show images

2 Navigate through the images on the CD either by using the Right and Left arrows to page through each photo, or by pressing the spacebar to cycle through all of the images on the CD. The previews include the image number burned in the upper left corner. For this lesson, you will work with image 02, prepping it for a print publication.

3 Quit the SlideShow Viewer.

Selecting the right image resolution for your project

Photo CDs' five resolutions work best with scanned transparencies (slide film). The consumer format, Image CD, works well with scanned negatives (print film).

POTENTIAL USES FOR DIFFERENT PHOTO CD RESOLUTIONS

Width	Height	PPI	Possible uses
192	128	72	Previews, convert to GIF for the Web.
384	256	72	Convert to GIF/JPEG for the Web, presentations.
768	512	72	Convert to JPEG for the Web. Presentations, still-image composites, video stills, motion graphics elements.
1536	1024	72	Print imagery, still-image composites, motion graphics elements, visual effect elements, film title elements.
3072	2048	72	Print imagery, still-image composites, motion graphics elements, visual effect elements, film title elements.

In this part of the lesson, you will use Image 02 as a background in a print layout that requires a final target resolution of 3.75 inches wide by 2.50 inches tall at 400 ppi. Thus, math dictates that the starting image will require at least 1500 pixels in width (3.75 inches by 400 ppi) and 1000 pixels in height (2.50 inches by 400 ppi). This points to either of the two highest resolutions, 1536 pixels by 1024 pixels, or 3072 pixels by 2048 pixels, as the only candidates.

For this lesson, assume that Image 02 was composed specifically for the final layout and that no cropping will be required. Thus, the 1536 x 1024 resolution would be the best choice to work with because it is four times smaller in size (when opened) than the next larger size, and will be much quicker to work with.

Opening Photo CD images in Photoshop for editing

Opening an image on a Photo CD is the same as opening an image on a hard drive or CD.

1 Choose File > Open, and select the Photo CD folder in the Lessons/Lesson03 folder on your hard drive. Click Open to see its contents.

The contents of this folder are set up exactly like the Photos folder on a Photo CD.

2 Select the 1536 x 1024 folder, and click Open. Select 02, and click Open to open Image 02 of the Slide Show at a resolution of 1536 x 1024. (Alternatively, open the 03Startd.pct file, located in the Lessons/Lesson03/03d folder on your hard drive.)

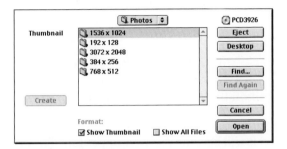

3 Choose File > Save As, rename the file **Dome.psd**, and click Save.

Prepping the image for a print layout

Next, you will prep the image for inclusion in a print layout. A goal of the layout is to draw out the reds in the image.

Photo CD scans tend to represent fairly well the contents of the transparency. This translates into a good distribution of information across the Red, Green, and Blue channels, which will be visible in the image's histogram.

1 Choose Image > Adjust > Levels. Position the dialog box so that you can see the image. The histogram shows that the levels distribution is fine in the RGB space.

In this case the image was shot in flat light with very slow film (50 ASA). The resulting photo has a tight grain structure, but suffers from a blue-gray cast over the image.

2 In the Levels dialog box, make the following adjustments using the Input Levels fields or sliders beneath the histogram:

• First, adjust the blue levels by switching to the Blue channel (press Ctrl/Command+3). Set the Blue channel's shadow point to 12, and the midtone point to 0.84. This will warm up the image slightly.

• Adjust the green levels by switching to the Green channel (press Ctrl/Command+2). Set the Green channel's shadow point to 9, and the midtone point to 0.84.

- Finally, adjust the red levels by switching to the Red channel (press Ctrl/Command+1). Set the Red channel's shadow point to 0, the midtone point to 1.11, and the highlight point to 239. The image will warm up more.

3 Click OK.

Making a selection using Color Range

You will make the reds in the image even more prominent using the Color Range feature.

1 Choose Select > Color Range. Position the dialog box so that you can easily see the image.

2 Move the pointer onto the image. It will become the eyedropper tool. Position it over one of the red iron girders and click to sample the color red in this image.

3 Drag the Fuzziness slider to 140 or more, and click OK. This will expand the selection to most of the red girders and other red areas of the image.

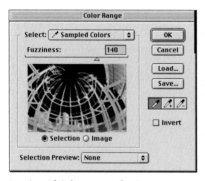

Preview of Color range selection   *Red selection in image*

4 Choose Image > Adjust > Hue/Saturation. Set the Saturation to +70 and click OK to make the reds very prominent in the image.

Final image

Setting the final target resolution of the image

As a final step, you'll change the image's resolution for the page layout.

1 Choose Image > Image Size.

2 In the Image Size dialog box, deselect Resample Image.

3 Set the Resolution to 400. The Print Size changes to 3.84 inches by 2.56 inches. Click OK. During page layout, you could crop the final image to fit the 3.75-inch by 2.50-inch target.

4 Save your changes.

5 Close the file.

Acquiring elements from the Web

Now, you will acquire an image from the Adobe Web site. In the process, you will explore different image formats and perform typical tasks to prepare the image for other uses.

The process of acquiring an image from a Web page is similar in Netscape Navigator's and Internet Explorer's browser. I created this lesson using Netscape Navigator 4.6 and Microsoft Internet Explorer 4.5.

Getting permission before using an image

An important note about copyright issues: many of the images contained on Web sites are protected under copyright laws. Beyond the moral issues surrounding the support of fellow artists, from a legal standpoint it is critical that permission be obtained for use of any copyrighted image. This includes imagery contained on Web pages. Most of the graphics and photos on the Internet are protected, copyrighted materials.

The images contained on the Adobe site are protected under copyright law. Permission is granted for use of the front page graphic on the Adobe site for learning purposes in this lesson. If you're ever in doubt about copyright issues, it's a good idea to ask permission.

Acquiring an image from a Web page

You'll start by logging on to the Adobe Web site and acquiring the main image on the page.

1 Log on to Adobe's site at www.adobe.com using either Netscape Navigator or Internet Explorer. Your image will look different than the one shown here.

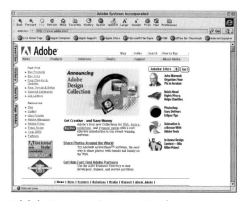

Adobe's Home page in Internet Explorer 4.5   *Adobe's Home page in Netscape Navigator 4.6*

2 Position your pointer over the image. Right-click (Windows) or hold down the mouse (Mac OS) to display a pop-up window.

3 Choose Save Image As (Windows) or Save this Image As (Mac OS).

Saving an image in Netscape Navigator 4.6

4 In the Save As dialog box, navigate to the Lessons/Lesson03/03e folder, name the file **Web.jpg**, and click Save.

Saved JPEG image

About Web image formats

The Web uses a number of different formats for imagery and animation. Some of the most popular formats and their uses include the following:

• GIF (.gif) is a compact, fast-loading file format popular for animated sequences. An 8-bit format, GIF thus handles some images poorly.

• JPEG (.jpg) features different levels of compression from 0 to 12. The 24-bit format is excellent for maintaining quality while reducing file sizes of photographic imagery and graphics.

- PNG (.png) stands for Portable Network Graphic. This 24-bit format features an alpha channel for transparent overlays and better compression than GIF. The format was created as an alternative to a rumored "GIF tax" in 1995.

- Flash (.swf) is the defacto vector-graphic standard (images are created from math, not pixels). It features very compact file sizes, and is great for animation and audio syncing.

Increasing image resolution

In most cases, I would not recommend trying to create resolution that does not exist in the first place. That said, if you're in a pinch and absolutely have to—as in the case of a low-resolution image from the Web that you need to incorporate into a presentation— here are some methods that will greatly increase your chances of success.

In this section, you will use Bicubic image resizing and some filters to double an image's resolution.

1 Return to Photoshop, and open the Web.jpg file that you just saved, in the Lessons/Lesson03/03e folder on your hard drive.

2 Choose Image > Image Size. Make sure that the Resample Image and Bicubic options are chosen (these are the default settings).

Bicubic is the preferred resize algorithm for most photographic and composite graphic imagery, because the 24-bit (millions of colors) format handles subtle gradations well.

3 Change the Resolution to 144 pixels/inch. Notice that the pixel dimensions change, and the file size quadruples. Click OK.

Stair-stepping after Bicubic resizing

Cleaning up the image

Scaling a JPEG or compressed image can result in digital artifacts. Applying the Median filter smooths most of the artifacts.

1 Choose Filter > Noise > Median. Position the dialog box so that you can view the image.

2 Set the Radius to 1 pixel, and click OK. The Median filter produces a slightly soft or blurred image. You'll correct that by sharpening the image.

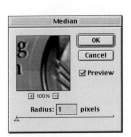 

Blurring with Median filter   Result

3 Choose Filter > Sharpen > Unsharp Mask. This filter lets you selectively enhance sharpness on the image.

4 Drag the sliders interactively to achieve a crisper look. Zoom in on the image preview, using the dialog box controls. Pay special attention to avoid digital artifacts such as stair-stepping or ragged edges. Click OK.

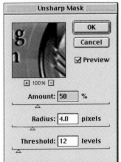 

Sharpening with   Result
Unsharp Mask filter

5 Save your changes.

6 Close the file.

You have now successfully doubled the resolution of this image to make it satisfactory for presentation level printing.

Capturing screens

Screen capture is one of the most basic and critical steps for preparing training and presentation materials. In this section, you will learn about screen resolution; acquiring (called capturing) an image from your screen, including a dialog box or menu; and increasing a screen capture's resolution.

About screen resolution

The monitor resolution you are able to view is determined by your display card's capabilities and your monitor settings (Display control panel in Windows; Monitors control panel in Mac OS). Many older display cards display less than 24-bit color (SVGA on the PC, Millions on Macintosh computers).

This limitation affects only what you can see, not the captured screen's bit depth (also known as the color depth). The computer application you are acquiring from is generating an image with millions of colors, but the VGA display is only capable of displaying that same image in thousands of colors. Thus, capturing a screen on a Windows system that displays only 16-bit color (Thousands of colors), actually captures a 24-bit image.

For example, the following illustrations show two screen captures acquired at different display resolutions—one from a 16-bit monitor and the other from a 24-bit monitor. They appear identical because they are both 24-bit images.

Acquired by a 16-bit monitor   *Acquired by a 24-bit monitor*

Capturing an image, dialog box, or menu from your screen

Most system software has a command that lets you capture the entire resolution of your computer screen at 24-bit color.

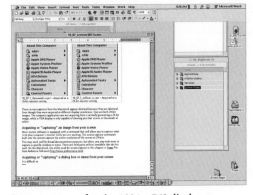

Screen capture of entire 1024 x 768 display area

If you only want to capture a specific window or menu, you can save time using a third-party utilities capable of capturing menus, windows, and dialog boxes in various formats. Many of these utilities include options of palette, resolution, or even offer the ability to record the actions of your cursor into a movie format.

• On a PC, press the PrtScn key (formerly Print Screen) on your keyboard, to capture the screen in RAM. Open any image-editing application (for example, choose Start > Accessories > Paint to open a simple image editor available on most PCs), and paste the screen capture. Save the file.

• On the Macintosh, press Shift+Command+3 to capture a screen. Screen capture for this lesson was done with the Snapz Pro utility from Ambrosia Software (www.ambrosiasw.com).

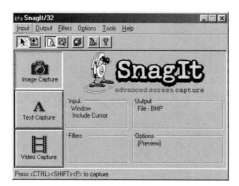
SnagIt for Windows

Snapz Pro for Mac OS

These options are a tremendous time saver when creating training materials such as the Classroom in a Book you are reading.

Snapz Pro's Palette options   *File format options*

Increasing a screen capture's resolution

Screen images are aliased, with unsmooth—that is, non-anti-aliased—edges. The best way to increase a screen image's resolution (for a printed publication, for example) is to use the Nearest Neighbor algorithm, which increases resolution by duplicating nearby pixels. To demonstrate the improvement, in this section you will try all three algorithms offered in Photoshop.

1 Choose File > Open, and open the 03Startf.pct file in the Lessons/Lesson03/03f folder on your hard drive.

2 Choose Image > Image Size to display the image resolution and dimensions. Make sure that Resample Image and Bicubic are selected (the defaults). Enter **288** in the Resolution text box and click OK.

The resulting image will be four times larger in resolution (it will contain 640 pixels in its width as opposed to its original 160). It will also appear blurry. This is because the Bicubic scaling algorithm anti-aliases edges, to make them appear smoother, producing a soft, mushy effect.

3 Revert the file to its original state by choosing Edit > Undo. Now you'll repeat step 2.

4 Next, choose Image > Image Size to re-open the Image Size dialog box. Choose Bilinear from the Resample Image pop-up menu. Enter **288** for Resolution, and click OK.

The resulting image also appears blurry, as the Bilinear scaling algorithm also anti-aliases edges to make them look smoother.

5 Choose Edit > Undo to revert the file to its original state.

This time, you will resize the file using the Nearest Neighbor algorithm.

6 Choose Image > Image Size. Choose Nearest Neighbor from the Resample Image pop-up menu. Enter **288** for Resolution, and click OK.

Bicubic resizing with blurring   *Nearest Neighbor with crisp edges*

This is the best result because the image appears crisp. The Nearest Neighbor scaling algorithm does not anti-alias edges, thus making them appear as clean as the original.

7 Close the file without saving changes.

Acquiring frames from video

Now you'll learn about video basics with respect to graphics—including the differences between digital and analog-digital video files—and see how to extract an image from a stream of existing video. I will walk you through the clean up often required in working with video imagery for print or screen use, including selecting a frame for use as in another application, such as Illustrator; removing field information; and cleaning up the image.

To complete this and the next section, you must have QuickTime 3 or higher and the QuickTime Player installed on your computer. (For more information, see the instructions in "Viewing a QuickTime movie" on page 102.)

This section does not cover capturing analog video nor the numerous configurations and technical issues involved. If you are equipped with digitizing hardware and software, see their documentation for specifics about video capture.

About digital and analog-digital video files

When working in digital form with an acquired digital file and with video that was originally shot in analog form, differences are subtle.

A file that is acquired digitally is generally shot with a digital camera onto digital tape. Digital acquisition formats include DV, DV-CAM, Mini-DV, Digital Betacam SP, and High Definition Digital. The digital tape looks very similar to its analog cousin, but differs slightly in composition.

Files in digital and analog form differ in these ways:

• Essentially, files shot in digital form are one generation cleaner than those shot in analog form; digitization from analog causes some information and image quality to be lost. The loss in image quality may seem trivial, but can produce a noticeable difference in the image quality of your final piece.

• A digitally acquired image is automatically recorded in pixel form; the image is composed of pixels. Analog video must be converted to pixels to be viewable in digital form.

• Many digital cameras provide the option of shooting in frames, as opposed to fields. Fields must be removed before digitally altering a final image—particularly in the case of creating digital visual effects.

General video issues affecting graphics

It is helpful to think of video (digital or analog) as a series of still images. Each image differs slightly from the last; in shots containing moving imagery, the path of movement becomes apparent looking at a series of stills.

Series of still images

In its native form, all analog video differs from film, because each frame is separated into fields. Two fields together comprise a full frame of video. This convention was developed to produce smoother motion in video broadcasts.

 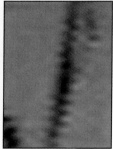

Close-up view of fields

Video operates in different standards around the world; by far the most popular are NTSC and PAL. Each is entrenched in different areas of the world (NTSC is the North American standard; PAL is the European standard). If you are interested in more information about each standard, several Web sites are devoted to the topic, which you can find by searching for either standard.

NTSC AND PAL VIDEO STANDARDS

	Frame rate (frames per second)	Pixel dimensions	Bit depth	Image resolution
NTSC video	29.97 fps	720 x 486 (D1)	24-bit	72 ppi
	29.97 fps	640 x 480 (standard)	24-bit	72 ppi
PAL video	25 fps	720 x 576 (D1)	24-bit	72 ppi

Acquiring frames from analog video

In this part of the lesson, you will work with a file that was acquired by a DV camera with the frame mode set to a 16:9 aspect ratio.

Most analog video that has been digitized contains fields. The most important point about creating graphics from digitized analog video is that you must eliminate these fields before you can convert the analog video frame to a still graphic.

Viewing a QuickTime movie

You'll start by viewing the movie in QuickTime.

1 From the Windows desktop or the Mac OS Finder, locate the file 03Startg.mv in the Lessons/Lesson03/03g folder on your hard drive.

2 Double-click the file to open it and launch QuickTime. (If you have not already installed QuickTime, you will be prompted to do so. If your system is not equipped, log on to the Apple site at www.apple.com/quicktime/ and download the current version.)

Viewing a QuickTime movie

Viewing a digital movie in QuickTime is similar to viewing a movie in any other digital player. QuickTime operates as an architecture for several different compression algorithms, and is not itself a compression format. In QuickTime, you can play back files in an uncompressed mode to various levels of compression, from Animation Compressed (a lossless algorithm) to Sorenson (a very efficient low-bandwidth algorithm) to MJPEG-B (a common form of motion JPEG that highly compresses moving imagery).

3 Press the play button (large right arrow) located at the bottom of the frame. The movie will play back, but will likely appear jerky, depending on your computer's processor.

Note: Most digital video files are played back with the help of dedicated hardware (JPEG or MPEG). Recently, software playback of full-screen MPEG files has become more efficient when coupled with fast processors on new computers.

4 In QuickTime, choose Movie > Get Info to open the Info palette.

5 Choose Movie from the left pop-up menu, and Time from the right pop-up menu. The Info palette will display the precise frame number that you are viewing.

The QuickTime Info palette

6 Position the Info palette on-screen so that you can see it as you view the QuickTime movie.

7 In the movie, drag the current frame indicator on the playbar to the far left or to the beginning of the movie.

Grabbing a frame

Now you will select the frame to import into Photoshop. You'll work with a low-resolution frame.

1 Step through the movie frame-by-frame using the Right arrow key or the playbar. Select frame 02:08, using the Info palette for reference.

Note: The person depicted in this movie is none other than the editor of this book, Luanne Cohen.

Field artifacts appear in most frames; you will remove the fields in the next part of the lesson.

2 When you have selected the frame, choose Edit > Copy to copy the frame into RAM. Leave the QuickTime movie open in case you need to refer to it again.

Removing field information and cleaning up the image

In general, still images acquired from digitized analog video appear undersaturated on a computer screen. This is mainly due to the underlying broadcast specifications of the NTSC and PAL standards. Both standards feature a color gamut that is considerably smaller than what computer monitors are capable of displaying. In particular, the white point of most NTSC or PAL files tends to fall somewhere near 230 on the scale of 0 to 255; as a result, images often appear muddy when brought into Photoshop.

You will prepare the image for tracing in another application. Precise color balance is less important than contrast at the subject's edges. Your goal in this part of the lesson will be achieving a contrast that lets you easily define the edges of the parachutist.

1 Start Adobe Photoshop. Create a new file by choosing File > New.

2 Set the width to 640 pixels, the height to 480 pixels. Name the file **Jump.psd**, navigate to the Lessons03/03g folder, and click OK. A blank Photoshop document will open.

3 Paste the selected frame into the Photoshop document by choosing Edit > Paste. It will appear as a selected new layer in your document.

4 Delete the Background by dragging it to the Trash button at the bottom of the Layers palette.

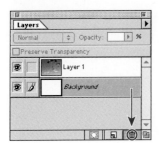

Deleting the Background

Next, you will remove the fields from the file. All video that is field-separated has what is referred to as a dominant field. This field dominance is determined by the video digitizing hardware, or the capture card. While most cards capture video with field 1 (often referred to as the upper, or odd, field) as dominant, some capture with field 2 dominant (the lower or even field). The video that you opened in QuickTime was captured with a field 1 dominant card.

Note: *If you don't know whether your file was captured upper field dominant or lower, don't worry. If the following results are unsatisfactory, undo your action and simply try the other form of field dominance to see if it yields a better result.*

5 Choose Filter > Video > De-Interlace. You will select even fields to remove because most of the file's image information is in the upper, or odd, fields.

6 Select Even Fields to remove the even fields in the file. Make sure that Interpolation is selected, and click OK.

Interpolating to create new picture information for continuous-tone images is always preferable. That method creates data between every other field by looking at the pixels above and below to determine what should fall in between.

Some parts of the image may have appeared clearer before interpolation. This phenomenon sometimes occurs when different elements in a frame are moving at a different rate. It can also be created by the angle of the optics on the camera, whether the camera was moving during the shot, and so on. These and other factors all influence how a particular compression algorithm converts an analog signal into a digital one.

 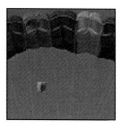

Field artifacts

If an area of the image has a lot of field artifacts, try switching the field dominance to the opposite direction. The goal is to get the image prepared with clean edges for tracing in Illustrator. You must decide what works best for you.

Adjusting the frame's levels

Next, you will adjust the image's levels so that it will be easier to use the image as a template for tracing.

1 Choose Image > Adjust > Levels.

2 Click Auto to adjust the levels automatically. The usable RGB information is spread over the full spectrum of 0 to 255, and the histogram extends fully. Click OK.

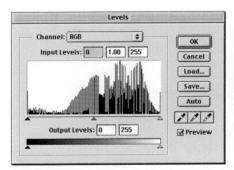

Restoring full gamut with Auto levels   *Result*

3 Save and close the file.

You can now use this file in another application, such as Illustrator. (This image reappears in Lesson 11, in "Project 1: Adding vector graphics to a raster image" on page 335.)

Acquiring frames from digital video

Now you will learn how to extract an image from a stream of existing digital video and clean up the common problems from acquired digital video. This time, you'll work on a high-resolution frame, using techniques similar to those for the low-resolution frame.

Viewing a QuickTime movie

You begin by viewing the movie and selecting a frame.

1 From the Windows desktop or the Mac OS Finder, locate the file 03Starth.dv in the Lessons/Lesson03 folder/03h folder on your hard drive.

2 Double-click the file to open it and launch QuickTime. (If you have not already installed QuickTime, you will be prompted to do so).

Because this movie is in its original acquisition format (DV-NTSC), it will appear blocky if you do not have the DV-NTSC codec installed with QuickTime. This will not affect your ability to perform the procedure.

3 In QuickTime, choose Movie > Get Info to display the Info palette.

4 Choose Video Track from the upper left pop-up menu, and choose Format from the upper right pop-up menu to display the file's pixel dimensions, color depth, and the data format.

Displaying file dimensions,
color depth, and data format

5 Now choose Movie from the left pop-up menu, and choose Time from the right pop-up menu. The Info palette will display the precise frame number that you are viewing.

6 Position the Info palette on-screen so that you can see it as you view the QuickTime movie.

Grabbing a frame for use in a multimedia presentation

Now you will locate and grab a frame to use.

1 In the movie, press the play button (large right arrow) at the bottom left of the frame. The movie will play back, but will likely appear jerky, depending on your computer's processor.

2 Drag the current frame indicator on the playbar to the far left or to the beginning of the movie.

3 Step through the movie frame-by-frame using the Right arrow key or the playbar. Select frame 02:01, using the Info palette for reference.

Locating an exact frame

4 When you have selected that frame, choose Edit > Copy to copy the frame into RAM. Leave the QuickTime movie open in case you need to refer to it again.

Cleaning up the image

To clean up the frame, you'll follow the same technique as you did for the low-resolution frame.

1 In Photoshop, create a new file by choosing File > New.

2 If the size is not automatically set to 720 pixels wide and 480 pixels high, specify those dimensions. Name the file **Sail.psd**, and click OK.

3 Choose Edit > Paste to paste the selected frame into the blank Photoshop document as a new layer.

4 Delete the Background.

The acquired file

The file will come in with black edges on the right and left side of the frame. This is an artifact of the 16:9 digital conversion that happens in the camera.

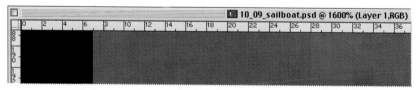

7-pixel black line on left side

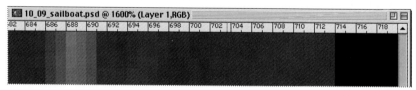

6-pixel black line on right side

5 Double-click the rectangular marquee tool. In the Marquee Options palette, choose Fixed Size for Style, and enter **640** pixels for Width and **480** pixels for Height. These will be the final dimension of the multimedia presentation.

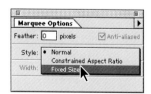

Selecting a fixed-size marquee

6 Click the image with the marquee tool. A 640-pixel by 480-pixel selection will appear. Position it so that the composition is pleasing.

7 Choose Image > Crop to crop the image.

Adjusting the frame's levels

Because NTSC and PAL have smaller color ranges than RGB computer monitors, most digital-video capture hardware and camera equipment create images that appear cooler and washed out when viewed on a computer monitor. You'll use levels to add density to the RGB channel, and then warm the color in the individual channels.

1 Choose Image > Adjust > Levels.

2 In the Levels dialog box, make the following adjustments using the Input Levels fields or sliders beneath the histogram:

• In the RGB composite channel, drag the black point to the right to a value between 10 and 20. This will add density to the image.

• Switch to the Blue channel (press Ctrl/Command+3). Drag the black point to the right until the black triangle is aligned with the left edge of the Blue channel's histogram.

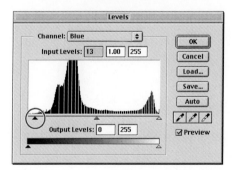

Aligning black point at left edge of the Blue channel's histogram

• Switch to the Green channel (press Ctrl/Command+2). Drag the black point slightly to the right (less than 10 points); avoid dramatically pushing the file too far to red.

• Switch to the Red channel (press Ctrl/Command+1). Drag the black triangle to align it with the left edge of the Red channel's histogram.

The final image

3 Click OK.

4 Save your changes.

5 Close the file, and quit Photoshop.

You can now incorporate the image in a multimedia presentation.

Lesson 4

4 | Advanced Masking

By Jen Alspach

Masking uses a shape over other shapes to cut away parts that you don't want—like a cookie cutter. Masking in Adobe Illustrator and Adobe Photoshop produces similar results, following different methods. In Illustrator, creating the mask is straightforward, and the mask can be edited at any time. In Photoshop, you can choose various ways to create the mask, but editing the mask can be a bit cumbersome.

In this lesson, you'll create two separate pieces of artwork as you experiment with masking.

In Illustrator, you you'll learn how to do the following:

• Use the Pathfinder palette to cut away sections.

• Use compound paths with masks.

• Assemble masked objects into complex artwork.

• Add outside components to the masks.

In Photoshop, you'll learn how to do the following:

• Use the Extract command to create a mask.

• Use the pen tool to makc an accurate selection for a mask.

• Fix edge artifacts of a mask by defringing.

• Erase the background.

• Create a selection with Color Range and then make a layer mask.

• Use Quick Mask mode to fix the edges and save the selection as a channel.

• Put the image together with layers, transformations, and text.

This lesson will take about 1-1/2 hours to complete.

If needed, remove the previous lesson folder from your hard drive, and copy the Lesson04 folder onto it.

Getting started

Before beginning this lesson, restore the default application settings for Adobe Photoshop and Adobe Illustrator. For instructions, see "Restoring default preferences" on page 3.

In addition, make sure that you have enough memory allocated to complete this lesson. For more information, see "Memory requirements" on page 2.

You'll start the lesson by viewing the final Lesson file to see the corporate image that you will create.

1 Restart Adobe Illustrator.

2 Choose File > Open, and open the 04End.ai file, located in the Lessons/Lesson04/04AI folder on your hard drive.

3 When you have finished viewing the file, either leave the End file open on your desktop for reference, or close it without saving changes.

For an illustration of the finished artwork for this lesson, see the color section.

Masking in Illustrator

In this part of the lesson you'll work with layers to move objects in front or behind other objects. You'll put together various illustrations and mask areas to create an eye-catching piece for a Web page.

Masking in Illustrator can be done in various ways depending on the complexity of the image. For complex shapes that you want to cut around—like blends, or gradient mesh objects—the Mask function works great. In Illustrator, you put the mask on top of the objects to be masked and with all parts selected, you choose Create Mask. At any time in Illustrator you can edit the mask's path to change the mask or edit the masked objects.

For simple images that won't need editing later, a little-used masking technique is to use the Pathfinder's Divide or Minus Front options to cut away the pieces that you don't want.

Using the Pathfinder palette to cut away sections

You'll use the Divide feature of the Pathfinder palette to fit your objects into the shape you want without distortion. This is a very quick way to "mask" objects. Divide works great with any filled shape, but it has a few drawbacks. It doesn't work with shapes that only have a stroke, and because it deletes objects rather than hiding them, you can't edit the objects that you are masking.

Now you'll open the start file and begin the lesson by creating a four-section graphic for a corporate publication piece.

1 Choose File > Open, and open the 04Starta.ai file, located in the Lessons/Lesson04/04AI folder on your hard drive.

2 Choose File > Save As, rename the file **Quadrant1.ai,** and click Save. In the Illustrator Format dialog box, select version 8.0 of Illustrator and click OK.

3 In the Layers palette, Alt-click (Windows) or Option-click (Mac OS) the eye icon next to the Building layer to turn off the other layers. You won't use them yet.

4 Press Ctrl+A (Windows) or Command+A (Mac OS) to select all of the shapes.

Note: *If you use this procedure with other artwork, remember that the masking shape must be on top of the other shapes.*

5 To view the Pathfinder palette, choose Window > Show Pathfinder. Click the Divide button.

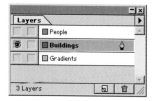
Hiding unneeded layers

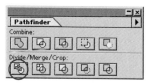
Pathfinder palette, Divide option

6 Deselect the objects by clicking in an empty area of the illustration.

7 With the direct-selection tool, select the parts of your image that you want to remove. Press Delete to remove them. Also remove the quadrant outline; you used this shape only as a cutter.

It's a good practice to get rid of excess pieces and keep a cleanly drawn illustration, to make it easier to print or to edit the illustration later.

8 Alt-click (Windows) or Option-click (Mac OS) the eye icon next to the Building layer to display all of the layers to see the whole quadrant.

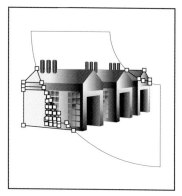
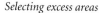
Selecting excess areas

Result with all layers visible

9 In the Layers palette, choose Flatten Artwork from the Layers palette. Double-click the layer name and change it to **Quadrant 1**.

10 Save your changes. Keep the file open.

Using compound paths with masks

Now you'll create the second quadrant of the piece using compound paths. Compound paths let you create holes in an object so that you can see through it. You'll try this technique now.

Note: *Type that has been converted to outlines must then be converted to a compound path before you can mask the type.*

1 Choose File > Open, and open the 04Startb.ai file, located in the Lessons/Lesson04/04AI folder on your hard drive.

2 Choose File > Save As, rename the file **Quadrant2.ai**, and click Save.

3 In the Layers palette, Alt/Option-click the eye icon next to the World layer to turn off all other layers.

4 Use the direct-selection tool to select the slightly curved, pie-shaped quadrant outline. You'll use this later as the masking object. Choose Object > Hide Selection (Ctrl/Command+ 3) to hide the outline so that you won't accidentally select this piece when you create the compound path.

The land is missing some important lakes. You'll add them to the land masses by creating a compound path.

5 Click one of the land pieces. Choose Edit > Select > Same Fill Color.

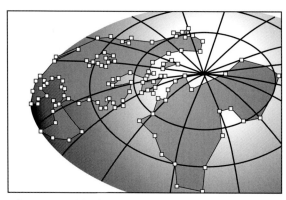

Selecting same fill color

6 Choose Object > Compound Paths > Make. This makes a compound path from the selected areas that have the same fill color, and changes the fill color to that of the backmost object in the stacking order (in this case, a gradient).

7 Deselect. You'll notice that the two inside pieces did not create holes. You'll fix that by changing the direction of one of the paths.

8 Select the inside pieces of the land that didn't create holes.

If you have a hard time locating these paths in Preview mode, choose View > Smart Guides. When the pointer is positioned over the path, it is highlighted.

9 Choose Window > Show Attributes. In the Attributes palette, click the dimmed direction path to reverse the path's direction. Now you can see the holes through the land.

In a compound path, one path must go clockwise and the other counter-clockwise. Glitches occur if both paths go in the same direction.

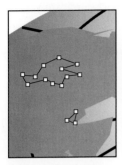

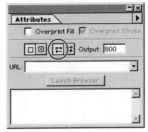

Compound path holes selected

Holes revealed when path direction changed

Reverse Path Direction button in Attributes palette

10 On the left side of the globe, use the selection tool to select the latitude and longitude lines, and choose Object > Arrange > Bring to Front to move the land and water behind the black lines.

11 Choose Object > Show All or press Alt+Ctrl+3 (Windows) or Option+Command+3 (Mac OS) to view the quadrant outline. This will be the masking object.

12 With the object still selected, choose Object > Arrange > Bring to Front.

13 Press Ctrl/Command+A to select all of the pieces that you are going to mask and the mask. Choose Object > Masks > Make (Ctrl/Command+7).

14 Deselect the lines to see the results of your mask.

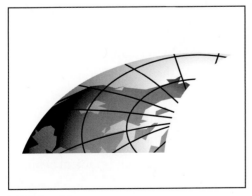

Masked world

15 Save your work.

Creating a compound mask

You'll continue by masking additional objects in the second quadrant artwork. (To save your work incrementally, you can save and rename your artwork separately as you complete each mask in this section. Then you can save the final file in the last step.)

1 In the Layers palette, turn off the World layer and turn on the Computers layer to mask the next area.

2 Select all of the artwork (press Ctrl/Command+A). Choose Object > Masks > Make (Ctrl/Command+7). Deselect.

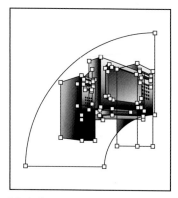

Masked computer   *World layer turned off*

3 In the Layers palette, turn off all layers but the Background.

4 In the artwork, select the black quadrant outline, and copy it to use later.

5 Press Ctrl/Command+A to select all. Choose Object > Masks > Make (Ctrl/Command+7) to create the mask.

6 Choose Edit > Paste in Front (Ctrl/Command+F) to restore the quadrant outline. Choose Object > Arrange > Bring to Front to make the shape the frontmost object on this layer, so that you can use it as a mask.

7 Press Ctrl/Command+A to select the rectangle and the clouds to be masked by the background shape. Press Ctrl/Command+7 to make the mask.

8 Choose Edit > Paste in Back, to place the copied background gradient behind the mask.

9 In the Layers palette, Alt/Option-click the eye icon column to view all layers. Choose Flatten Artwork from the palette menu. Rename the layer **Quadrant 2**.

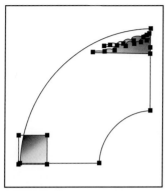
Masking object

Result

10 Save your changes, and keep the file open.

Putting the four quadrants together

Now you'll put together all four quadrants to make a circular shape of the images.

1 Choose File > Open, and open the 04Startc.ai file, located in the Lessons/Lesson04/04AI folder on your hard drive.

2 Choose File > Save As, rename the file as **Circle.ai**, and click Save. You will assemble the artwork in this file.

I like to keep my illustrations organized with layers. You'll end up with four quadrant layers that form a circle.

3 Make the Quadrant1.ai file active.

4 In the Layers palette, choose Paste Remembers Layers from the palette menu.

This command is a toggle and remains set for subsequent files until you deselect it. Paste Remembers Layers retains the layering order of objects you paste.

5 Press Ctrl/Command+A, and then press Ctrl/Command+C to copy all of the artwork to the Clipboard. Close the Quadrant1.ai file.

6 Make the Circle file active, and paste the selection (Ctrl/Command+V).

7 With the artwork still selected, grab a corner of the quadrant and move it until it snaps to the guide. Deselect the artwork.

8 In the Layers palette, move the Quadrant 1 layer down so that it is just above the Quadrant 3 layer.

9 Save your file.

Positioning quadrant and adjusting the layer order

10 Repeat steps 3 through 9 for the Quadrant2.ai file, positioning the Quadrant 2 layer in the Layers palette beneath Quadrant 1, as shown in the following illustration.

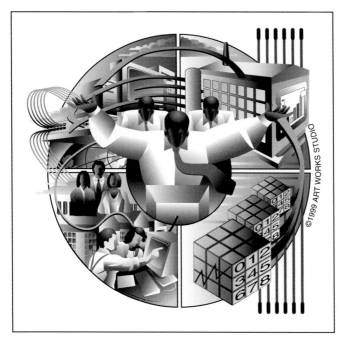

All four quadrants in position and final layer order

11 Save the file.

Creating masks with the pen tool

To finish the logo of the company's Web page, you'll need to do a bit more masking to complete the illustration. Now you'll use the pen tool to draw a mask.

1 In the Layers palette, turn off the Building layer and the People/Blocks layer.

2 Zoom into the upper part of the circle. Using the pen tool, create a shape to mask the top line and its shadow, making the edges around the computer accurate. Rough out other parts of the path.

3 Select the mask and the lined object with its shadow, and choose Object > Mask > Make or Ctrl/Command+7.

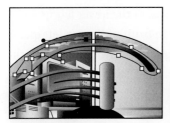 

Drawing top line and shadow mask   *Masked line*

4 Mask the top three lines that are in front of the computer. Draw the path accurately along the side of the computer and rough it out for the other areas.

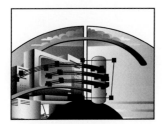

Masking lines in front of computer

(Refer to the final artwork in the following illustrations for placement of the lines.)

5 Create a mask path by drawing the line in front of the monitor and behind the gray horizontal hard drive. Draw the angle along the side of the hard drive accurately, and rough out the rest of the path.

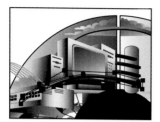

Masking lines in front of hard drive

6 Using the pen tool, draw a mask for the curved wires in the lower left quadrant, following the cloud shape closely. These lines will be in front of the top left quadrant and behind the clouds in the bottom left quadrant. Using the selection tool, select the curved wires coming out of the hard drive.

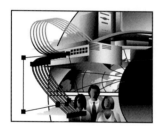

Masking curved wires

7 Select the cylinder shape and choose Object > Arrange > Bring to Front.

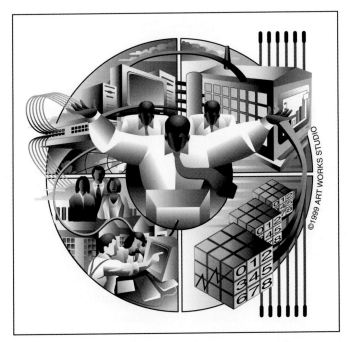

Final illustration

8 Deselect the artwork.

9 Display all the layers in the Layers palette.

10 Save the file.

11 Close all open files and quit Illustrator.

Masking in Photoshop

Photoshop lets you create a mask many ways—using the Extract, Add Layer Mask, Paste Into, and other features like Quick Mask. In Photoshop, you create a border around your image to serve as the cutting edge. In a sense you are creating a frisket, but much more accurately and easily. However, editing a mask in Photoshop can be cumbersome.

A mask is only as good as your selection—the more accurate and detailed, the better. How you make a selection depends on the type of art you are masking. For simple images you can erase the background from your image easily using the Extract command, background eraser, or magic eraser. For more complex images, with unclear edges, you can use various selection options to create your mask.

But even if the mask isn't perfect, you have many ways to clean up the edges. The Add Layer Mask function is the quickest way to create a mask without losing any of the original image and offers the easiest editing because you still have the whole original image.

Getting started

In this lesson, you'll take flowers from different images and arrange them in a bouquet using various masking techniques.

You'll use a variety of means to select different flowers and create masks. You'll then arrange the flower selections to create a business card for a flower store.

1 Restart Adobe Photoshop. Click Cancel to dismiss the color management dialog box.

2 Choose File > Open, and open the 04End.psd file, located in the Lessons/Lesson04/04PSD folder on your hard drive. Click Don't Convert in the Profile Mismatch dialog box. (For information on setting up a color profile, see "Setting up a color profile" on page 182.)

An image of a group of flowers has been created to make a beautiful business card. When you have finished viewing the file, either leave the file open on your desktop for reference, or close it without saving changes.

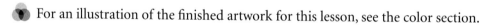 For an illustration of the finished artwork for this lesson, see the color section.

Extracting a mask

You'll start by using the Extract command to remove the background from the flower. Extract works great with an unclear edge, and it is so easy to use. You use the edge highlighter tool to mark the edge between the flower and the background. You then choose what area to keep, then preview. If the image isn't quite right, then you can reset and change the settings, or accept the image and alter with other tools in Photoshop.

1 Choose File > Open, and open the 04Starta.psd file, located in the Lessons/Lesson04/04PSD folder on your hard drive.

2 Choose File > Save As, rename the file **White.psd,** and click Save.

3 Choose Image > Extract. With the zoom tool, click in the center of the flowers to enlarge your view.

4 In the Extract dialog box, select the edge highlighter tool. Trace around the edges of the two large flowers, including pixels inside and outside the edges.

5 Select the fill tool. Click the inside of the flowers to indicate the area you want to keep.

Edges highlighted

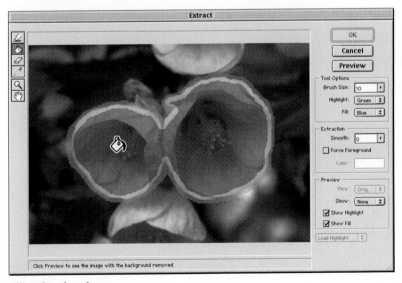

Filling the selected area

6 Click Preview. If the mask is to your liking, click OK. Otherwise, repeat steps 3 through 5.

Extracted flowers

The file has a checkerboard background, indicating that the background is transparent. Some artifacts may still appear. But you can clean up the stray pixels using the eraser tool with a soft-edged brush (in case you get close to the flowers), or you can use any of the selection tools to select the stray pixels and delete them.

7 Press Ctrl/Command+A to select all of the flowers, and then copy them. Close the file.

8 Choose File > Open, and open the Card.psd file, located in the Lessons/Lesson04/04PSD folder on your hard drive.

9 Choose File > Save As, rename the file **Card1.psd**, and click Save.

10 Paste the flower, and name the layer **White Flower**.

11 Display the Info palette.

12 Press Ctrl/Command+T to activate the Free Transform command. You'll scale down the flower before adding more flowers to the arrangement.

13 Shift-drag the top corner square around the flower inward, to scale it down and keep the flowers proportionate. Use the Info palette to determine when you've scaled it about 42%. Press Enter to apply the new size.

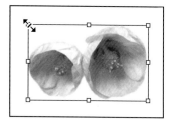

Scaling down flowers

14 Save the Card1.psd file.

Masking with a path

Now you'll use the pen tool to create a mask from a very accurate path, turn it into a selection, and then convert the selection into a mask.

Working with and saving paths gives you more options for saving your file. Saving a selection as a channel limits how you can save the file.

The pen tool is a very elegant, accurate way of tracing over parts of an image. Once you master the nuances of the pen tool, you can use it in many programs including Adobe Illustrator. For more information and lessons on the pen tool, see Lesson 8, "Mastering the Pen Tool."

1 Choose File > Open, and open the 04Startb.psd file, located in the Lessons/Lesson04/04PSD folder on your hard drive.

2 Choose File > Save As, rename the file **Pink.psd**, and click Save.

3 Double-click the hand tool to zoom in on the flower.

4 Select the pen tool (press P), and start tracing around the flower.

Click to make a corner point at the intersection of the petals, and drag to create a smooth point around the curve of the petals. Don't try to get the flower perfect the first time. You can use the direct-selection tool to edit the path.

5 When a small circle appears beside the pen tool icon, indicating that you're over the start point of the path, click to connect the end point with the start point.

Corner and smooth points   *Closing the path*   *Adjusting the path*

I intentionally drew some of the petals incorrectly to show you how to fix the path using the anchor points and direction lines.

6 Press A to select the direct-selection tool. (It's a hidden tool, located under the pen tool.) Then adjust the lines:

• Click a point to activate the direction lines, and then drag the direction line handles to alter the shape of the path.

• Drag an anchor point to move the whole point. In this case we are moving the whole point to adjust the path.

7 When the path is as accurate as you'd like, click the Paths palette tab to make the palette active.

8 Double-click the Work Path in the Paths palette, or choose Save Path from the Paths palette menu. Name the path **Flower**, and click OK.

9 Convert the path to a selection by choosing Make Selection from the Paths palette menu. Click OK.

10 If the path is still visible beneath the selection, deselect it by clicking in the palette below the path name.

11 Choose Select > Feather and enter a Feather Radius of 1 pixel to soften the edge of the selection around the flower. Click OK.

12 Copy the selection, and then close the file.

13 Make the Card1.psd file active, and choose paste (Ctrl/Command+V) the selection.

14 Name the new layer **Pink Flower**.

You'll notice that there is a slight dark edge around the flower. We need to fix this so it blends nicely into any background.

Defringing a selection

Now that you've created your selection, you'll check for edge artifacts (stray pixels around the edge of the flower). Then you'll fix the edge using the Defringe command.

1 Zoom in on the flower to see it better.

2 Choose Layer > Matting > Defringe. Enter 1 pixel for the amount. Click OK.

Notice the difference between the flower with and without Defringe. After defringing, the dark outline is gone. You can choose Edit > Undo and Edit > Redo to compare the results.

3 Save the file.

Edge artifacts   *Defringe applied*

Making a layer mask from a Color Range selection

The Color Range function lets you easily make a selection from an area that is similar in color. For example, sometimes it is easier to select the background, and then select the inverse. For this exercise you'll use Color Range to select a flower and mask it with a layer mask.

1 Turn off all other layers except Yellow Mum. Make sure that it is the active layer.

2 Double-click the hand tool to enlarge the image.

3 Choose Select > Color Range. Adjust the Fuzziness to 75 for a soft edge.

4 Use the Color Range eyedropper to click an area of the yellow flower in the image.

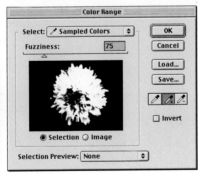

Selecting with Color Range eyedropper

Now you'll add to your selection.

5 Select the eyedropper-plus tool in the Color Range dialog box. In the image, click other yellow areas to add them to the selection.

6 When the yellow flower appears white in the Color Range dialog box, click OK to see your selection.

I didn't select the inside green parts to this flower because it would select too much of the background greens. You'll grab those few pixels with the lasso tool.

7 Select the lasso tool in the toolbox. Shift-drag around the center of the flower to add to the selection, and drag and get the rest of the pixels in the flower. Alt/Option-drag around any selected areas outside the flower to deselect them.

8 Choose Select > Modify > Contract. Enter 1 for the pixel value. This pulls in the selection by 1 pixel and ensures that the flower doesn't have an edge.

Selecting remaining yellow pixels

9 Click the Add Layer Mask button in the Layers palette. The selection is now a mask for the Yellow Mum layer.

10 With the layer mask still active, touch up the edges with the paintbrush. Black will reveal more of the image and white will hide it.

11 Press Ctrl/Command+T to activate the Free Transform command, and scale down the flower so that it's not so large. Shift-drag the upper corner inward to scale down. Press Enter when the flower has been reduced to about 30%.

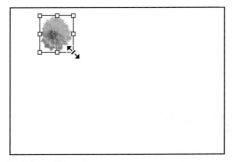

Resizing yellow mum

12 Save the file.

Using Quick Mask to fix the edges

After making a basic selection with any of the selection tools, you can fine-tune that selection using the Quick Mask mode. Quick Mask mode lets you edit a selection, pixel-by-pixel, using the paintbrush, pencil, or any of the selection tools. This painstaking process ensures accuracy in your mask.

1 Select the Sunflower layer. Alt/Option-click the eye icon to turn off all the other layers.

2 Double-click the hand tool to enlarge the image.

3 Choose Select > Color Range. Set the Fuzziness to **46**.

4 Click the eyedropper tool on the yellow petals of the large sunflower. Continue to Shift-click until you have a well defined edge around the flower. Don't worry about the inside of the flower. Click OK.

5 Use the lasso tool and Alt/Option-drag to deselect the areas outside of the flower. Shift-drag to select the areas inside the flower.

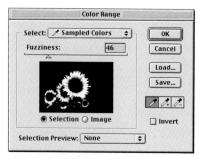 

Completing the selection

6 Click the Quick Mask mode button in the toolbox.

7 Double-click the Quick Mask mode button in the toolbox to edit the options. (I prefer to see the mask show the selected areas, so I would choose Selected Areas.) Click OK to accept the changes.

8 Zoom in to see the individual pixels.

9 Select the paintbrush tool in the toolbox. In the Brushes palette, select a small soft-edged brush.

10 Start painting in the missing areas. To remove the mask from the areas, paint with white. To switch the foreground and background colors, press X on the keyboard, or click the swap-arrow button in the toolbox.

Quick Mask mode   *Editing mask in Quick Mask mode*

11 Continue painting around the flower, removing and adding to the mask as needed.

12 When you're satisfied with the mask, click the Standard Mode button in the toolbox. Double-click the hand tool to zoom back out.

13 With the selection still active, click the Add Layer Mask button in the Layers palette.

Final Quick Mask selection   *Masked sunflower image*

💡 *Layer masks can be viewed and edited just like quick masks. To view a layer mask with the image, click the eye icon next to the layer mask name in the Channels palette. You can use any of the painting tools or filters on your layer mask.*

Putting it all together with layers

To make the flower arrangement, you'll make multiple copies of the flowers and arrange them by layers using the move tool. Some of them may also need to be scaled and rotated.

1 In the Card1.psd file, check to see that the layer names and layer match the illustration below.

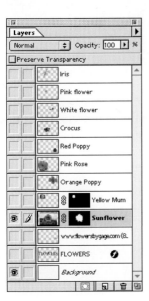

Now you'll select each layer in turn, and scale down the flower to the desired size relative to the other flowers.

2 Alt/Option-click the eye icon column next to the Iris layer to turn on all layers. Select the Iris layer to make it active.

3 Press Ctrl/Command+T. Shift-drag the corner inward to scale down the flower proportionately, and then press Enter to apply the transformation.

Using these flowers, you'll make copies of the layers and arrange the flowers in a nice horizontal way.

4 Use the move tool to reposition the Iris layer.

5 Repeat steps 2 through 4 for each hidden flower layer. Scale down the flower relative to the other flowers in size. Arrange the flowers to your liking.

6 Alt-drag (Windows) or Option-drag (Mac OS) the Sunflower layer to the New Layer button at the bottom of the Layers palette, to duplicate that layer. Name it **Sunflower1**.

7 Use the move tool to move the duplicate next to the original sunflower. Repeat the step as desired to make additional sunflower copies. Scale if desired.

8 Save the file.

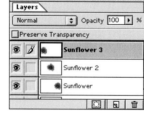

Duplicated flowers   *Duplicated layers*

9 Repeat steps 6 through 8 to make duplicates of the remaining flowers and arrange them to create a dense bouquet.

For variety, you can rotate and resize flowers, or alter their color.

Adding text and finishing the business card

Now that the flowers are arranged nicely, you'll finish the image by making a business card. You'll add text, a shadow, and fade out the flowers to make this card complete.

Typically you would use Photoshop to apply cool type effects, but you would use Illustrator to create the type for the address and other information. Illustrator's PostScript® type is much sharper than pixelized type in Photoshop. For this lesson, you'll create the type in Photoshop.

You'll start by merging the flowers, but retaining the white background for use later. Merging puts all visible or selected layers on one layer.

1 In the Layers palette, turn off the white Background by clicking its eye icon. Be sure that the two type layers also are turned off. Then select the topmost layer, and choose Layer > Merge Visible.

2 Rename the layer **Flowers**.

3 Choose File > Save As, rename the file **Card2.psd**, and click Save.

4 In the Layers palette, turn on all the other layers.

5 Move the Flowers layer below the www.flowers layer.

Another way of masking in Photoshop is to create a clipping group. You will use the FLOWERS type layer to mask the flower bouquet.

6 Make sure that the Flowers layer is selected.

In a clipping group, the bottommost layer, or base layer, acts as a mask for the entire group.

7 In the Layers palette, position the pointer on the line between the Flowers layer (the pointer changes to two overlapping circles). Alt/Option-click the line between the Flowers layer and the FLOWERS type layer.

Flowers clipping group masks type above it

Dotted lines between the grouped layers indicate the clipped layers. The base layer in the group is underlined, and the thumbnails for the overlying layers are indented.

8 Save your work.

As a final, and optional step, duplicate the Flowers layer, and drag it so it is just above the Background. Set its opacity to 24% for a faded effect.

Final file with background flowers

9 Save yourchanges. Close the file and quit Photoshop.

Lesson 5

5 | Advanced Compositing

By Karen Tenenbaum

With Adobe Photoshop and Adobe Illustrator, you can make complex composites using a variety of methods. Some of the prime tools in Photoshop are layer masks, blending modes, and clipping groups. Illustrator lets you use its functional layer hierarchy to structure complex type designs, plus use special tools such as the Pathfinder feature.

In this lesson, you will work on an ad for a fictional hair product company called Super Schoen. You'll learn how to do the following in Photoshop:

• Make layers in Adobe Photoshop by copying.

• Work with a variety of Photoshop layer masks.

• Learn when to apply Photoshop layer masks.

• Use Photoshop adjustment layers and clipping groups to control layer effects.

• Work with layer modes and layer effects in Photoshop.

• Export an Adobe Photoshop file to Adobe Illustrator.

In Illustrator, you will learn how to:

• Create complex type effects.

• Export an Illustrator file to Photoshop.

This lesson will take about 1 hour to complete.

If needed, remove the previous lesson folder from your hard drive, and copy the Lesson05 folder onto it.

Getting started

Before beginning this lesson, restore the default application settings for Adobe Photoshop and Adobe Illustrator. For instructions, see "Restoring default preferences" on page 3.

In addition, make sure that you have enough memory allocated to complete this lesson. For more information, see "Memory requirements" on page 2.

You'll start the lesson by viewing the final Lesson file to see the composited image that you will create.

1 Restart Adobe Photoshop. Click Cancel to exit the color management dialog box that appears.

2 Choose File > Open, and open the 05End.psd file, located in the Lessons/Lesson05 folder on your hard drive. Click Don't Convert in the Profile Mismatch dialog box. (For information on setting up a color profile, see "Setting up a color profile" on page 182.)

05End image

3 When you have finished viewing the file, either leave the End file open on your desktop for reference, or close it without saving changes.

For an illustration of the finished artwork for this lesson, see the color section.

Now you'll open the start file and begin the lesson by designing the composite image.

4 Choose File > Open, and open the 05Start.psd file in the Lessons/Lesson05 folder on your hard drive. Click Don't Convert to exit the Profile Mismatch dialog box. (For information on setting up a color profile, see "Setting up a color profile" on page 182.)

5 Choose File > Save As, rename the file **Hair.psd,** and click Save.

Beginning the design

To get you started with the design of the your ad, consider what type of output you will need. In this case you will create a low-resolution composite image (comp), measuring 8.5 inches by 11 inches at 72 ppi.

A digital comp is usually a low-resolution version of a design idea or proposal. Producing a low-resolution piece lets you spend more time generating different design ideas quickly.

For more information about resolution, see "Identifying target resolutions for different output media" on page 68.

Using layer modes to blend

Working with layers in Photoshop is one of the most effective and versatile ways to create composite images. Each layer can be edited as discrete artwork, allowing unlimited flexibility. Using layer modes, you can create blends from one layer to another, or adjust the tonality of an image. You will use layer modes to create a high-contrast version of the image.

1 In the Layers palette, copy the Background by dragging it to the New Layer button at the bottom of the palette.

2 Change the layer mode to Color Dodge, to get a very high-contrast version of the original image.

Creating high contrast   *Color Dodge mode*

3 Merge the layers down (press Ctrl/Command+E or choose Merge Down from the Layers palette menu).

You will use the new version of the photograph as the basis for your illustration. For the greatest flexibility in compositing, you will extract the image from its background.

The 05Start.psd file includes a premade selection of the woman and her hair.

4 Load the selection by choosing Select > Load Selection. In the Load Selection dialog box, for Document, choose Hair.psd; for Channel, choose Alpha 1. Click OK.

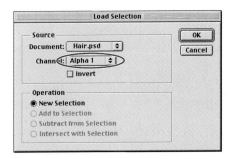

You need another copy of this extracted image for the most flexibility in blending the images or choosing other background colors for the entire composite.

5 Place a copy of the selected area on its own layer by choosing Layer > New > Layer Via Copy (or press Ctrl/Command+J).

6 In the Layers palette, delete the Background by dragging it to the Trash button.

7 Now, duplicate Layer 1 by Alt/Option-dragging it to the New Layer button at the bottom of the palette. Rename the layer **Hair 2**.

8 Rename Layer 1 as **Hair 1**.

9 Save the file.

Setting the layer transparency display to white

When working with layers, I get more flexibility by cutting each element from its background and placing it on a transparent layer. I used to add a bottom layer containing white, to replicate what I would get when I flattened my composite. But then I realized that I didn't need the extra layer, and could change the transparency display instead.

1 Choose File > Preferences > Transparency & Gamut.

2 For the Grid Size transparency setting, choose None. Click OK. You can immediately see the effects of this change.

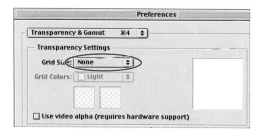

Blending with layer masks

Layer masks let you hide or reveal parts of the artwork on an individual layer. When you hide artwork, that part of the layer becomes transparent, and underlying layers show through. You can control how much artwork on a layer is hidden or revealed by making selections for the mask and by painting on the mask using black, white, or shades of gray.

To blend the two copies of your image, you will first offset one and then use a layer mask to hide a portion of the top image.

1 In the Layers palette, select the Hair 2 layer.

2 Offset it by choosing Filter > Other > Offset. For Horizontal, enter **40**, for Vertical, enter **0**. Click OK.

3 Use the rectangular marquee tool to select the right half of the Hair 2 layer (the selection does not have to be precise).

4 At the bottom of the Layers palette, click the Add Layer Mask button. Presto! You have a layer mask conforming to your selection.

Layer mask added to Hair 2 layer   *Layer mask thumbnail*

Often, you may create a layer mask that you would like to change in some way. Perhaps, as in this example, you would like the edges to be softer. Fortunately, you don't have to redo the mask or use a soft paintbrush to edit it, which might give you uneven results.

5 In the Layers palette, make sure that the Hair 2 layer mask is still selected.

6 Choose Filter > Blur > Gaussian Blur. Try a radius of 50, or choose another value if you wish. Click OK.

As you can see, a filter has just the same effect on a layer mask as on a regular layer. You'll try another filter for a textural effect.

You can work with layer masks as you would with any other layers. The only restriction is that masks reside in a world of black-and-white values only. So color adjustments won't affect layer masks, but Levels adjustments and most filters will.

You will add another filter effect to just the layer mask.

7 Choose Filter > Noise > Add Noise. Enter an amount of **50**, and choose Uniform distribution. (Leave Monochromatic deselected; this option won't affect the layer mask because it is a grayscale.) Try different settings to see the effect.

Gaussian Blur and Noise filters applied

The mask needs a little fine-tuning. Applying the two filters created a strange transition on the left side of the woman's mouth.

8 Select the paintbrush tool. In the Brushes palette, choose a medium-size soft brush.

💡 *To change the brush size—for example, if you would like a larger brush to edit a larger area or a smaller brush for more detailed work—press the Left Bracket or Right Bracket ([or]) keys to make the brush cycle through its smaller and larger sizes!*

9 Press D to select the default colors in your toolbox. White now becomes the foreground color, which will paint back in the original image on this layer.

10 In the Layers palette, make sure that the Hair 2 layer mask is still selected. Paint with 100% white on the layer mask, and paint out the second lip and nose.

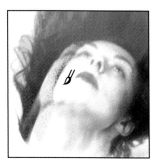

Painting out the duplicate lip and nose

11 Save your changes.

Using adjustment layers

Using adjustment layers, you can repeatedly apply color and tonal adjustments to a layer without permanently changing the pixel values in the image. For example, if you add a Color Balance adjustment layer to an image, you can experiment with different colors again and again, because the change occurs only on the adjustment layer. If you decide to return to the original pixel values, you can hide or delete the adjustment layer.

Colorizing with adjustment layers

To accentuate the idea of bright, beautiful hair, you'll now colorize both layers using adjustment layers. Any color or tonal change you make to an adjustment layer appears on all layers below it.

1 In the Layers palette, hide the Hair2 layer by clicking its eye icon, so that you can see the layer on which you'll work.

2 Select the Hair 1 layer. Choose New Adjustment Layer from the Layers palette menu, or choose Layer > New > Adjustment Layers.

A quick way to add an adjustment layer to a selected layer is to Ctrl/Command-click the New Layers button at the bottom of the Layers palette.

3 For Type, choose Hue/Saturation. Leave Group With Previous Layer deselected, to apply the adjustment layer to all layers beneath it. Click OK.

4 In the Hue/Saturation dialog box, select the Colorize option. Set the Hue to **38**, and the Saturation to **86**. Click OK to create a golden look.

To return to an adjustment layer at any point to change its effect, double-click the adjustment layer's name in the Layers palette.

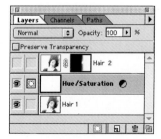

Hue/Saturation adjustment layer

Applying an adjustment layer to a single layer

Adjustment layers act as a veil through which all underlying image layers appear. You can confine the effects of an adjustment layer to a single layer or group of layers using either the Group With Previous Layer option or clipping groups. You'll try out the Group with Previous Layer option.

Grouping and clipping groups perform the same function. (In a clipping group, the bottommost layer, or base layer, acts as a mask for the entire group. The effect of an adjustment layer would end at the bottom of the clipping group.)

[?] For more information on clipping groups, see Chapter 11 of the Photoshop 5.0 User Guide or "Creating clipping groups" in Photoshop 5.0 online Help.

1 In the Layers palette, turn the Hair 2 layer back on, and select it.

2 Choose Layer > New >Adjustment Layers. For Type, choose the Hue and Saturation command. Select Group With Previous Layer. This ensures that the adjustment layer is only applied or "clipped" to the Hair2 layer and does not affect the Hair 1 layer. Click OK.

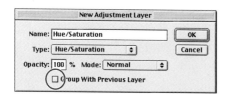

Group With Previous Layer selected

Note: *If you don't select Group with Previous Layer when you create the adjustment layer, you can confine the layer's effect later with a clipping group. Select the layer that will clip the layer directly under it, position the pointer between the two layers to be clipped, and Alt/Option-click. A dotted line appears between the grouped layers, and the base layer is underlined.*

Because the image already has a lot of red, you'll boost just the saturation here.

3 Choose +61. Click OK. You'll notice that the overall saturated colors work well for the hair and shirt, but not for the facial area, which is too yellow.

You'll block out the effects of the adjustment layer.

Applying an adjustment layer to parts of an image

You can selectively apply the effects of an adjustment layer by painting with black to hide part of the layer, and painting with white to reveal it. Use percentages of either for blends, directly on the adjustment layer itself. Unlike regular layers, adjustment layers come with "built in" masks and don't need to have one added.

1 Select black as the foreground color (press D to select the default colors and then press X to switch them).

2 Select the paintbrush tool and a medium-size soft brush.

3 Make sure that the Hue/Saturation adjustment layer is selected. Then dab out the effects of the adjustment over the woman's face, especially along the hairline.

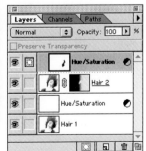

Clipped adjustment layer   *Painting in the facial area*

4 Save your changes.

Editing and managing masks

When working with layer masks or adjustment layers, 100% of black hides, 100% of white reveals, and percentages of either black or white provide blends. You can edit your mask in other ways, too.

Using brush modes to paint on masks

Typically, masks are adjusted using one of the paint tools in a Normal blending mode, or perhaps with some opacity applied. However, you can also use your brush tools in other blending modes.

Now you will now use the paintbrush in Dissolve mode to create more texture on your mask.

1 In the Layers palette, select the Hair 2 layer mask.

💡 *To move your selected layer from the adjustment layer to the Hair 2 layer, press Alt/Option+ Left Bracket ([) to move down one layer, or press Alt/Option+ Right Bracket (]) to move up a layer. Then select the mask itself by Ctrl/Command-clicking it. Wow—that's much easier. To select the layer image itself, press Ctrl/Command+Tilde(~).*

2 Select the paintbrush tool. In the Options palette, choose Dissolve for mode.

3 With the foreground color still set to black, start painting in the top area of the woman's hair to mask out more of the Hair 2 layer, but this time with a textural effect. Try painting with different opacity amounts to vary the effect.

💡 *If you don't like the effects you're applying, use the History palette to go back to where you started.*

Painting out hair in Dissolve mode

Merging layers

You will now merge the effects of your blended image.

A good way to work with layers is to work until you are happy with the results; save this version with all the layers, layer masks, and adjustment layers. Then merge as many layers or apply as many masks as you can, and begin working again.

1 Save your work so far. Remember that nothing has been permanently altered, because you've been working on layer masks and adjustment layers.

Merging layers that have layer masks associated with them automatically applies the masks. Merging an adjustment layer with a regular layer applies the effects permanently. But if you saved a layered version of your file before merging layers, you can backtrack.

2 Hide any layers that you don't want to merge in the Layers palette.

3 Merge all visible layers without flattening the image by choosing Layer > Merge Visible or Merge Visible from the Layers palette menu. (Or press Shift+Ctrl/Command +E.) This merges all layers that are displayed without flattening the image, and retains transparent areas of the layers.

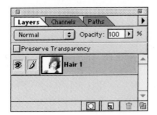

Merged layer in Layers palette

The Hair.psd file now has only one layer.

4 Save the new file as **Hair1.psd**.

This file still has transparency associated with it, displayed as white.

5 To view the transparent areas, Ctrl/Command-click the layer thumbnail in the Layers palette to load the layer transparency. Then deselect.

Using image adjustments on layer masks

Layer masks can be treated in the same way as layers. If you have a large area that you would like to fill in, use a selection tool such as the lasso to select the specific area; then fill it with white to reveal the image on the layer, or with black to hide it. In the same way, if you want a mask to have more or less contrast, use black-and-white image controls like Levels to adjust the effect on the image and mask.

Now you'll add a gradient to make the composite image fade along a diagonal from the bottom left to the top right. You'll use Levels to fine-tune the gradient's effect.

1 Add a new layer mask to the Hair1.psd image by clicking the Add Layer Mask button at the bottom of the Layers palette.

2 Change your colors to their defaults of white for the foreground and black for the background color (press D on the key board, if necessary).

3 In the Layers palette, make sure that the Hair 2 layer mask is selected.

4 Select the linear gradient tool, and in its Options palette, for Gradient choose Foreground to Background.

5 In the image, drag the linear gradient tool from the top right corner to the bottom left corner.

Gradient applied to the layer mask

Layer mask thumbnail with gradient

The gradient blends over the length of the image. For a more dramatic effect, you'll adjust the gradient using Levels.

6 With the layer mask still selected, choose Image > Adjust > Levels (or press Ctrl/Command+L). In the Levels dialog box, drag the white Input Levels slider to the left, to the center of the histogram, to build up contrast in the gradient mask blend. Then adjust the black and gray sliders, until the histogram resembles the following illustration.

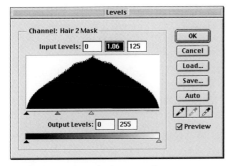

Applying Levels to the layer mask

Because Photoshop layer masks are essentially 8-bit channels, you can use any of the adjustment tools that you would normally use on a grayscale image. Applying Levels or Curves to a layer mask, for example, is a great way to create contrast.

Importing a Photoshop image into Illustrator

Working between Illustrator and Photoshop is easy and seamless—many key commands and overall principles are similar. Photoshop even has type layers now.

But Illustrator has a few special features that you need for this ad—type that follows a path, and the Pathfinder commands.

1 Save your changes.

2 Choose File > Jump To > Adobe Illustrator 8.0 Alias to open the Hair1.psd image in Illustrator. Illustrator starts automatically, and places your current Photoshop image on a standard Artboard.

[?] For information on creating an alias to switch between applications, see Chapter 3 of the Photoshop 5.5 User Guide Supplement or "Jumping between applications" in Photoshop 5.5 online Help.

3 Choose File > Documentation Setup. Select Landscape for orientation and click OK. Your horizontal page should be ready to go.

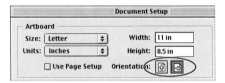

4 Choose View > Hide Page Tiling so that the page tiling doesn't distract you.

5 Choose File > Save As, rename the file as **Schoenad.ai**, and click Save.

Understanding layers in Photoshop and Illustrator

Illustrator and Photoshop both have layers and Layers palettes that seem to act in a similar fashion. But the very structure of layers (that is, what a layer is) in each program is very different. Understanding the differences is key to using layers effectively in each application.

Both Illustrator and Photoshop can be considered to be object-oriented products. Photoshop allows manipulation and precision control of objects at the pixel level (that is, changing the color and opacity of individual pixels), as well as of "sets" of pixels, which have been grouped into layers. Photoshop's layers are actually individual objects that can be moved and modified without affecting other layers. Illustrator allows manipulation of objects only at the object level. But because you work with so many objects at once, Illustrator offers many tools for modifying and organizing several objects at once. Layers, like groups and compound paths, are really "sets" of objects arranged primarily for organizational benefits.

Layers in Photoshop don't equal layers in Illustrator; rather, they equal individual objects in Illustrator. Layers in Illustrator are actually "sets" of objects, for which Photoshop has no comparable function. Knowing this, you might think that Illustrator's ability to export its layers as Photoshop layers doesn't make sense. In reality, however, while the layers in each application differ significantly, being able to separate layers from Illustrator into layers in Photoshop gives much more control over your artwork once it is in Photoshop. Photoshop has much more extensive opacity controls than Illustrator. (Illustrator allows objects to be fully transparent, opaque, or overprinted—a combination of the two). So bringing Illustrator layers into Photoshop can result in effects that just aren't possible otherwise.

—*Ted Alspach*

Using layers in Illustrator

Every Illustrator file contains at least one layer. Creating multiple layers in your artwork lets you easily control how artwork is printed, organized, displayed, and edited. Once you create your layers, you can work with them in various ways, such as duplicating, reordering, merging, flattening, and adding objects to them.

1 Notice that your file only has one layer, Layer 1. (If the Layers palette isn't visible, choose Choose Window > Show Layers.)

You'll start by creating layers for the photo image and trim marks.

2 In the Layers palette, double-click the Layer 1 name. In the Layer Options dialog box, name the layer Photo, select Lock, and click OK. You don't want to change this layer as you design the text.

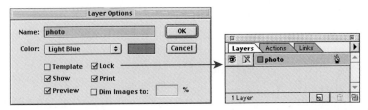

Locking the Photo layer

Because the ad will be full-page, it needs an area for the trim or bleed. To visually represent this trim, you will make a special layer to hide all elements that cross into the trim area. The advantage of making a trim layer in Illustrator is that you can design your type with the trim in mind, and also export it to Photoshop, where it will continue to visually represent the bleed for your reference.

3 Alt/Option-click the Create New Layer button at the bottom of the Layers palette to make a new layer. Name it **Trim**, and click OK.

To help you place the trim borders accurately, you'll add some guides.

4 Press Ctrl/Command+R to display rulers. Drag guides from the ruler and place them 1/4-inch from the top and bottom edges of your Artboard, and 1/4-inch from the right and left sides.

💡 *To change the ruler units quickly, right-click (Windows) or Control-click (Mac OS) the ruler to display a menu selection of units.*

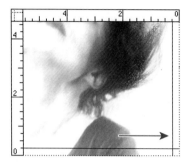

Adding guides

Now you'll add some rectangles that you'll use to set the trim marks.

5 Using the rectangle tool, draw a rectangle exactly the size and position of the photo image. Select the default colors (press D on the keyboard), and fill the rectangle with white and stroke it with black. The rectangle will cover the image temporarily.

6 Now draw a second rectangle 1/4-inch within all sides of the Artboard. Start to draw it using the inside 1/4-inch guides you created, dragging from the top upper left to the bottom right.

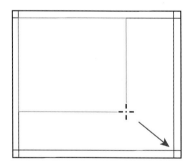

Dragging the second rectangle

7 Select both rectangles.

8 Choose Window > Show Pathfinder to display the Pathfinder palette. Click the Exclude button.

Exclude Pathfinder option

The photo now shows a 1/4-inch trim hidden all the way around the outer edge. This trim will help you gauge how to design the overall ad.

9 In the Layers palette, lock the Trim layer by clicking in the lock column to the right of its eye icon.

10 Create a new layer and name it **Type 1**. The new layer appears on top of the Trim layer. Drag the Type 1 layer beneath the Trim layer in the Layers palette.

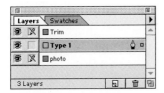

Type 1 layer repositioned

11 Save your work.

Adding type on a path

In this part of the lesson, you will add type to the image that follows a path. An advantage of working in Illustrator rather than Photoshop is the myriad type tools. With Illustrator's type tools, you can create horizontal or vertical type anywhere in your image, and make text flow into shapes or along the edge of an open or a closed path.

You can use a path already created for you, or create your own.

1 Choose File > Open, and open the Path.ai file, located in the Lessons/Lesson05 folder on your hard drive. Select all of the file (Ctrl/Command+A), and copy it. Close the file.

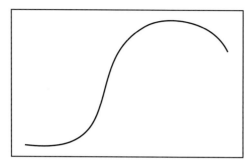

Path artwork

2 Make the Schoenad.ai file active, and paste the path into your file.

Note: By default, the pasted layer is pasted on the selected layer, Type 1. If you changed the default to Paste Remembers Layers, the path is pasted onto a separate layer.

3 Select the type tool, and position it on the path. The type tool automatically turns into a path-type tool. Click once and begin typing your text ("Super Schoen" in the example). You can use any font on your system. I used 45-point Myriad, all caps. (Press Ctrl/Command+T to display the Character palette.)

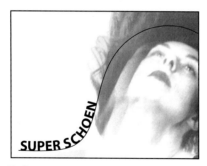

Path type

Now you will copy this type and place it around the head of the woman.

4 In the Layers palette, select the Type 1 layer and Alt/Option-drag it to the Create New Layer button at the bottom of the palette. Rename the new layer **Type 2**.

The new copied type is automatically selected.

5 Use the selection tool to move the path to a new position so that some of Type 1 and Type 2 overlap.

6 Reposition where the type begins on the path, by using the selection tool to drag the beginning of the type along the base of the path to its new position.

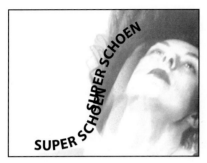

Type 2 layer repositioned   *Type moved along the path*

7 Add a few more overlapping type layers.

8 Repeat steps 4 through 7 until you have several more type layers. I created three more type layers for a total of five layers.

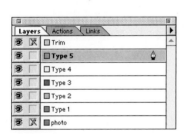

Multiple type layers in the Layers palette and image

Locking and hiding layers

As you can see, it is hard to distinguish one piece of type from the next, and especially difficult to select each piece of type. To work on the separate type elements, you must lock and hide individual layers. Layers that are hidden or locked (indicated by the crossed-out pencil icon) can't be edited.

1 Hide all layers except the Type 1, Photo, and the Trim layers, by clicking the eye icon next to the layer name to hide it.

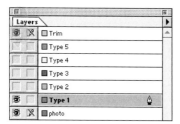

2 Choose Edit > Select All (Ctrl/Command+A) to select the type on Type 1 layer.

Changing type attributes

When the type's basic placement is set, you can explore changes to fonts, scaling, and color. Being able to lock and hide layers makes this task simpler.

1 Choose Type > Character to display the Character palette. Choose Show Options from the palette menu. Change the horizontal scale of your type. I chose to scale by 200%.

2 Using the type tool in the artwork, select a single letter, and change its size. I changed the *S* in *Super* to 100 points.

3 Now adjust your kerning. Select the *S* and *U* in the word *Super*. Kern the space between the larger *S* and *U* by changing the Tracking Value to **–50**.

In Illustrator, it is easy to select specific letters and change their individual colors. In Photoshop, this process takes several steps and is not available in the Type dialog box).

4 Continue to use the type tool in the artwork to edit letters and change their color. For the smaller letters, I chose gold. For the large *S*, I chose orange.

5 Continue to edit the line of type as desired.

💡 *You can also edit the path itself, and the type will conform to the new shape of the line!*

Editing and coloring type

6 Redisplay all of the layers again by Alt/Option-clicking the Type 1 layer twice. (The first click turns off all layers except the selected one; the second click turns on all layers.)

You'll select the next type layer in a different way.

7 In the Layers palette, Alt/Option-click the lock column next to the Type 2 layer. All other layers will lock automatically.

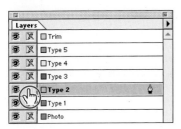

Locking all layers but Type 2

8 Now change the scale and color attributes of this type relative to the other type layers. Try using the eyedropper tool to select colors from the image to use on the type. Use the hiding or locking method to gain access to the objects you need.

9 Deselect.

10 Save your file.

Using the Pathfinder commands

The Pathfinder commands in the Pathfinder palette combine, isolate, and subdivide objects, and they build new objects formed by the intersections of objects. To use the Pathfinder palette, you click a button in the palette that corresponds to the desired result.

Right now, the Super Schoen company logo is made out of pieces of type. But what if you've been asked to jazz up the design? The Pathfinder command in Illustrator gives you great tools to make your piece more lively.

Before you can use the Pathfinder command, you must convert your type to outlines.

1 Choose File > Open, and open the Logo.ai file, located in the Lessons/Lesson05 folder on your hard drive.

2 Choose Edit > Select All (press Ctrl/Command+A), and then choose Type > Create Outlines. Your type turns into a set of compound paths that you can edit and manipulate as you would any other graphic object. But you can't edit the outlines as type.

Type logo as outlines

You'll convert the paths into one object.

3 If the Pathfinder palette isn't displayed, choose Window > Show Pathfinder. In the Pathfinder palette, click the Unite button.

4 Deselect.

5 Save your changes

By converting the type to a single object, you can now edit it as any other path—including filling it with a single color, gradient, or pattern.

Controlling the order of pasted layers

Illustrator copies and pastes a selected object on the currently selected layer, unless you specify otherwise. When you select the Paste Remembers Layers command, Illustrator copies the layer and pastes it as a new layer in your file.

1 With the Logo.ai file active, choose Paste Remembers Layers from the Layers palette menu.

2 Select all of the artwork (press Ctrl/Command+A), and copy it (Ctrl/Command+C).

3 Make the Schoenad.ai file active. Choose Edit > Paste.

When Paste Remembers Layers is selected, a named pasted layer is put at the top of the Layers palette; a layer that still has its default name (Layer 1, Layer 2, and so on) is pasted above other unnumbered layers in the palette.

4 In the Layers palette, rename the layer you just pasted as **Logo**. Then drag it just above the Photo layer.

5 In the artwork, position the logo at the very edge of the ad's left side, with part of the logo underneath the trim.

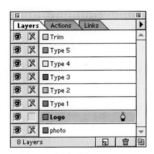

Repositioning logo   *All layers locked but Logo*

Returning to Photoshop from Illustrator

You are going to return to Photoshop to add some layer modes, soft drop shadows, and special effects to your type and logo.

First, you'll export your Illustrator file as a layered file.

1 Choose File > Export; for Format, choose Photoshop 5. Rename the file **Schoenad.psd**, and click Save. In the Photoshop Options dialog box, for Color Model, choose RGB; for Resolution, select Screen (72 dpi); and make sure that Anti-Alias and Write Layers are checked.

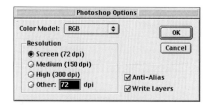

Now you'll return to Photoshop.

2 Close your file, and quit Illustrator, if desired.

3 Make Photoshop active. Choose File > Open, and open the Schoenad.psd file that you just saved in step 1.

Using layer modes and layer effects

You'll notice that all the layers that existed in Illustrator now appear as Photoshop layers. Photoshop also adds a Background.

1 In Photoshop in the Layers palette, delete the Background by dragging it to the Trash button.

You'll blend the type layers using layer modes and add a drop shadow.

2 In the Layers palette, select the Type 1 layer; for mode, choose Multiply.

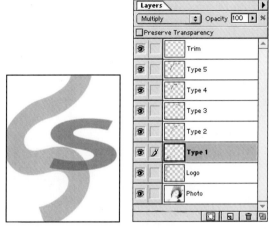

Type 1 layer selected with Multiply mode

3 With the Type 1 layer still selected, choose Layer > Effect > Drop Shadow.

4 In the drop shadow dialog box, adjust some of the settings to see the effect. I used 100% opacity, Angle of 120, Distance of 10 pixels, Blur of 10 pixels, and Intensity of 20%. Any changes you make will preview. Click OK.

It looks as if the shadow is blocking out the type. You'll fix that in the next part of the lesson.

5 Save your changes.

Creating layers from layer effects

If a layer has a layer effect along with a mode setting, the layer mode may seem to apply to the layer effect rather than to the image. In many cases, this isn't the look you want.

1 To see an example of the effect, select the Type 1 layer in the Layers palette. Double-click the Effects icon to the right of the layer to display the Effects dialog box. Turn off the Drop Shadow option by deselecting the Apply option.

Notice that the letters with the drop shadow applied are much darker than when the drop shadow is off. Click Cancel.

Drop shadow on   *Drop shadow off*

To keep the integrity of the selected mode and display the type with a soft drop shadow, you must first create layers from the effect.

2 Choose Layer > Effects > Create Layer.

In the Layers palette, a new drop shadow layer—with a blurred black copy of the image—appears beneath the Type 1 layer.

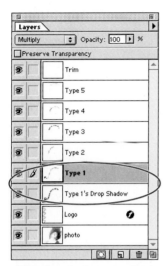

Adding drop shadow to newly created layer

Next, you need to mask the areas of the Drop Shadow layer that fall inside the type itself.

3 Start by Ctrl/Command-clicking the Type 1 layer in the Layers palette to load the transparency selection.

4 Next, select the Type 1 drop shadow layer.

The selection exactly matches the type. If you were to add a layer mask, it would contain the drop shadow information within the type area. But you want the drop shadow's blurred edges to appear only outside of the type. So you'll invert the selection.

5 Choose Select > Inverse.

6 To add a mask to the Type 1 Drop Shadow layer, click the Add Layer Mask button at the bottom of the Layers palette.

Layer mask added to Type 1 drop shadow

Voilà! You've created a drop shadow that retains the effect of the Multiply blending mode.

7 Continue to change modes or add layer effects to the other layers in the image.

When you've completed adjusting the type, you'll replace the Photo image with your edited artwork for the ad.

8 Choose File > Open, and open the Hair1.psd file in the Lessons/Lessons05 folder.

9 Drag the image to the Schoenad.psd file.

10 In the Layers palette, position the new image layer at the bottom of the palette. Then delete the Photo layer by dragging it to the Trash button.

11 Save your changes.

As a final step, save a flattened copy of this comp for your client.

12 Choose File > Save a Copy, and rename the file **Schoen_final.psd**. For format, choose Photoshop 5. Select Flatten Image to flatten all visible layers, and click Save.

13 Close any open files, and quit Photoshop and Illustrator.

You've completed your comp and are ready to show it to the client for approval.

Lesson 6

6 | Color Management and Distribution

By Rita Amladi

Adobe Photoshop and Adobe Illustrator let you specify colors in many different ways. At production, several issues can keep these colors from reproducing accurately. In this lesson you'll learn how to produce cross-application projects that maintain and model color appearance across several media.

Outputting to print media generally requires a larger color gamut than for most Web-based art. The approach I advocate in a print and Web publishing workflow is to work with source images with a sufficiently large color gamut—large enough to address all the media to which you plan to output your art. Working with such images gives more flexibility in your workflow, and allows you to use and re-use the original images in a variety of contexts. This is a major gain over the tried-and-true, device-dependent workflow that has traditionally been used for color matching or management.

In this lesson, you will follow an overall workflow that will help you set up color management for your files across several applications. As you produce two cross-application projects, you will color-manage images from scanner to on-screen viewing, from application to application, and to various destinations including inkjet proofs, printing press, and Web-published pages.

You'll learn to do the following in this lesson:

• Establish a color workflow for each project involving print and Web-based publishing.

• Set up appropriate color spaces in each application, and convert accurately from one color space to another.

• Import color-managed scans into Adobe Photoshop.

• Save files in the correct format with the necessary information needed for proper color management between applications and output media.

• Match the color appearance of objects created in different applications.

This lesson will take about 1-1/2 hours to complete.

If needed, remove the previous lesson folder from your hard drive, and copy the Lesson06 folder onto it.

Important: *For your results to match those in this lesson, you must use the latest application versions.*

🔲 Before proceeding with the rest of this lesson, it is recommended that you read "Color Management Basics," for additional background information. This PDF document is in the Lessons06 folder on the Advanced Classroom in a Book CD.

Color management basics

If your design and production workflow is fairly typical, color images can get passed along from input or digital capture devices to multiple applications and to the monitor for display purposes. From here, the electronic document can be printed or imaged to a variety of media. Without any color management in place, it can be downright impossible to predict the color integrity of the final images as they are scanned, displayed on the screen, and printed.

While the actual goals and workflow you employ in your own projects may vary from the workflow presented in this lesson, I hope you will come away with a better understanding of the principles of color management built into the various Adobe applications.

Production workflow for a printed postcard

In this lesson you will follow a color-managed workflow that will create two projects for a herbal tea company: a printed postcard announcing a seasonal event, and an accompanying splash page for the company's Web site.

Postcard

Splash page for Web site

To produce the printed piece, you will follow this workflow:

• Standardizing a comprehensive workspace for acquiring and editing images for all ensuing uses for the images.

💡 *In general, outputting to print media requires a more expanded color gamut than for most Web-based art. It's more efficient to acquire and save source images in a comprehensive color space that's large enough to address all the media to which you plan to output your art.*

- Setting up all the color spaces involved in the workflow. This will include the editing and output spaces.

- Assembling the artwork and performing any necessary editing tasks.

- Converting to the chosen output color space.

- Embedding the color space profiles in the saved image. When such color-managed files are placed in another color-savvy application, they can be displayed and printed consistently.

Getting started

Before beginning this lesson, delete the Color Settings file in the Adobe Photoshop 5.5 Settings directory. Also restore the default application settings for Adobe Photoshop and Adobe Illustrator. For instructions, see "Restoring default preferences" on page 3.

1 Restart Adobe Illustrator. You will open the final postcard image to see what you'll create.

2 Choose File > Open, and open the 06End.ai file, located in the Lessons/Lesson06/06AI folder on your hard drive.

3 When you have finished viewing the file, either leave the End file open on your desktop for reference, or close it without saving changes.

For an illustration of the finished artwork for this lesson, see the color section.

Creating the postcard

In assembling art for the postcard, you will import and color-manage the continuous-tone art in Photoshop. You will also create a color gradient as part of the postcard design. Later in Illustrator, you will match the type's color to the gradient, and add a vector-based illustration. As you build this project, you will learn to set up each application to color-manage the project consistently.

Choosing an appropriate workspace in Photoshop

Based on the strategy to use a multifunctional color space for this project, you will start by choosing an appropriate RGB color workspace in the RGB Setup dialog box. When you have completed assembling and editing the art, you will convert the color space to a unique CMYK color space that matches the color gamut of your final print medium.

It is important to set up all color workspaces that will be used in the workflow before beginning the project. This lets you proof the evolving document on-screen at any time.

Setting up the RGB workspace

First you will set up the RGB color space using the RGB Setup dialog box. This dialog box features several RGB work spaces, a couple of which are good choices for assembling and editing the postcard project artwork. These spaces are multifunctional because they contain most of the colors in the printer's CMYK space, and serve as a good starting point for Web-based art, another RGB display medium.

1 Restart Adobe Photoshop. Click Cancel to exit the color management dialog box.

2 Choose File > Color Settings > RGB Setup, to set up the RGB color workspace.

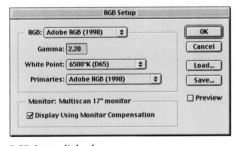

RGB Setup dialog box

This dialog box includes 10 built-in RGB workspaces. You can also load an ICC profile of an RGB workspace. The RGB workspace you select here must work for all the images involved in your workflow. It must also take into consideration the color space of the input devices (a scanner, in this case) and the color space of the output devices (a four-color offset press, and possibly a digital color proofer).

You could use a couple of the RGB color spaces to produce the postcard:

• The ColorMatch RGB space is based on the Radius PressView® monitor space. This space is closely calibrated to print work, and is a good choice especially if you are using a calibrated PressView monitor.

- Adobe RGB (1998) is another excellent RGB space for print work. It encompasses most of the colors in the CMYK gamut, which is a big bonus for working in an RGB space, because it gives you more flexibility in your production workflow.

3 Choose Adobe RGB (1998) from the RGB presets menu.

4 Leave the Gamma, White Point, and Primaries settings unchanged. You would change these settings if you planned to build a custom RGB workspace.

These values are associated with your selected workspace conditions and are independent of the same settings in your monitor space.

- Gamma indicates the brightness curve of the workspace.

- The White Point setting defines the white point of the chosen workspace. Although D50 or 5000° K is common while trying to match the color proofing standards in the US, this color can be a little too yellow for RGB spaces. Hence, it is configured for D65 or 6500° K.

- Primaries indicate chromaticities for the Red, Green, and Blue Primaries in the color space.

The bottom of RGB Setup dialog box lists your monitor profile. After you have used Adobe Gamma or other software to create an ICC device profile for your monitor, you must save the profile in the correct location on your hard drive. In Windows 95 and 98 and Windows NT, profiles are installed in the Windows/System (System 32 for Windows NT)/Color folder. In Mac OS using ColorSync 2.0-2.12, profiles are installed in the System folder/Preferences /ColorSync® Profiles folder. In Mac OS using ColorSync 2.5, they are installed into the System folder/ColorSync Profiles folder.

? For more information, see "Where CMS components are installed in your operating system" in the "Color Management Basics" PDF on the Advanced Classroom in a Book CD.

5 Select Display Using Monitor Compensation to use your monitor to preview the colors accurately in the chosen color space. When this option is selected, the color management system (CMS) immediately converts colors from the selected RGB work space (or CMYK color space) to the monitor's RGB space.

6 Click OK.

Setting up the CMYK workspace

Now you will set up the CMYK workspace for the postcard printing.

1 Choose File > Color Settings > CMYK Setup.

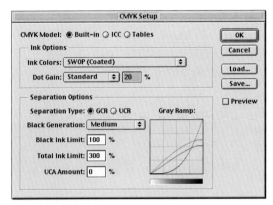

CMYK Setup dialog box

2 For CMYK Model, select the ICC option to perform the color conversion.

You can choose to convert a CMYK color space in three ways:

• The Built-In option uses the color separation engine that is built into Adobe Photoshop.

• ICC is a CMYK model that supports all components of an ICC-based color management system. This option lets you specify all the components of the color management system (CMS).

• Tables let you load any previously created color separation table, used with older versions of Photoshop, and lets you save ICC output profiles.

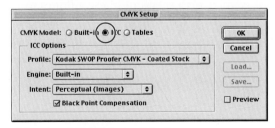

ICC option of CMYK Setup dialog box

3 For Profile, choose Kodak SWOP Proofer CMYK-Coated Stock. The postcard will be printed on a four-color offset press on coated stock.

4 For Engine, choose Built-In for the color-matching engine. This choice is similar to the Adobe CMS Engine in Illustrator.

5 For Intent, leave the setting as is for now. You will set Intent on a per-image basis prior to color separation.

Intent refers to a rendering intent, which is a translation method used in the conversion by the CMS. For most photographic images, you will choose the Perceptual intent, and choose the Relative Colorimetric intent when converting illustration art created in programs such as Adobe Illustrator.

6 Select Black Point Compensation, to reproduce details in the shadow tones.

This option maps the darkest value in the source color space (the Adobe RGB workspace, in this case) to the darkest value available to the chosen CMYK device—thus ensuring that a wider tonal range is available to reproduce the tones in the image.

Note: You would deselect the Black Point Compensation option if color separating an image (converting it to the CMYK mode) rendered the shadow details lighter on-screen. Lightening can occur if the black point of the chosen print device is not as dark as the black point of the monitor—for example, if the CMYK color space is Newsprint, if you are using certain inkjet paper stock with a high fiber content, and so on.

7 Click OK. You will refer to these settings later when you color-separate the file.

Setting up a color profile

The last, important step before opening this project's images is to set up the Profile Setup dialog box to determine how the CMS in Photoshop will handle images when they are opened in the application. It is well worth spending a few minutes to set up the profile correctly. Incorrect settings here can affect the color integrity of an image, as it is opened and saved in Photoshop.

1 Choose File > Color Settings > Profile Setup.

Profile Setup dialog box

2 For Embed Profiles, select all of the options to embed the corresponding workspace profile. Saving the file embeds (that is, tags the file with) the profile.

In general, it is recommended that you embed a profile so that another ICC-compliant application or device reading the embedded profile knows exactly how to represent the image's colors. But do not embed a profile if the image is intended for Web publishing; very few browsers currently have color management features.

3 For Assumed Profiles, choose Ask When Opening for all modes. This option lets you specify a profile to use when opening a file without an embedded profile or a legacy file (that is, a file saved in Photoshop version 4 or lower that did not support embedded profiles).

Next, you'll instruct Photoshop how to handle files without an embedded profile or one that doesn't match the color mode's workspace.

To make the best use of color management, convert any legacy or other untagged images to the workspace chosen for your workflow—with the exception of CMYK images, which are color-separated for output to a specific device. Previous versions of Photoshop used the monitor color space as the working space for RGB images. If you have a profile for your monitor handy and the only untagged files you will open are legacy files, set your monitor profile as the Assumed profile for RGB images.

4 Set the Profile Mismatch Handling:

• For RGB, choose Ask When Opening to display the Profile Mismatch dialog box for specifying a color space for the file conversion.

• For CMYK, choose Ignore. You do not want to assign a color space to these images other than the one for which they were color separated.

• For Grayscale, leave the default setting.

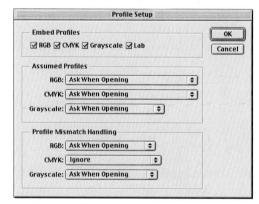

Profile Setup dialog box

5 Click OK.

You are ready to open and color-manage the postcard images.

Applying a color space profile to an image

Now you'll open the first image for the postcard, a legacy file. To use the image in your color-managed workflow, you must convert it to the chosen RGB workspace.

1 Choose File > Open, and open the Backgrnd.psd file, located in the Lessons/Lesson06/06PSD folder. The Missing Profile dialog box appears.

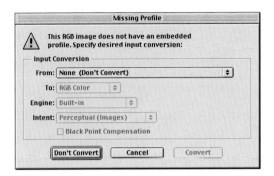

2 In the Missing Profile dialog box, set the following options:

• For From, choose the profile for your calibrated monitor, or choose the monitor standard that best matches your monitor.

• For To, choose RGB color as the color workspace.

• For Engine, choose Built-in.

• For Intent, choose Perceptual, because the image is a photograph.

• Select Black Point Compensation.

3 Click Convert.

The CMS in Adobe Photoshop converts the colors from the specified Monitor RGB space to the Adobe RGB (1998) space, and the Background image opens in RGB mode. (Don't worry if the image looks dark; it was made to look that way for design reasons.)

4 Choose File > Save As, rename the file **Backgrnd1.psd**, and click Save.

You have successfully completed the first step in color-managing your project.

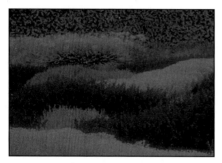

Background image

Editing the postcard image

Next, you will undertake a few editing tasks to produce the postcard. These tasks have little to do with color management, but are required nonetheless in every project.

You'll start by resizing the image to serve as the postcard's background. The postcard will measure 6.5 inches by 4.5 inches.

1 Resize the image by choosing Image > Image Size. Deselect Resample Image, so that you don't alter the pixel structure of the image. Enter a Width of 6.5 inches; the height will adjust accordingly.

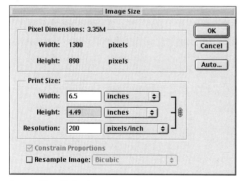

Image Size dialog box

2 Click OK.

Next, you'll add a colored gradient.

3 Choose View > Show Rulers (press Ctrl/Command+R). Drag a vertical guide, and position it 1 inch from the right edge of the postcard.

4 In the Layers palette, click the New Layer button to create a blank new layer.

5 Using the rectangular marquee, draw a selection in the rectangular space defined by the guide on the new layer (Layer 1).

6 Double-click the linear gradient tool in the tool palette. In the Linear Gradient Options palette, for Gradient, choose Foreground to Transparent, and choose the Normal mode.

To select a color from the millions of available colors, I decided to use a custom color library as a starting point.

Custom color libraries are yet another way to select color while in the RGB or CMYK color mode. For example, if you choose a color from a PANTONE® custom library while in the RGB mode, you are simply using a shortcut to choose from the vast quantity of available RGB colors. The resulting color will be defined by Red, Green, and Blue values, just like any other color in the RGB mode.

7 Click the foreground box in the toolbox to display the color picker. Click Custom, and select the PANTONE Coated color library from the list. Rapidly type **165** (the PANTONE swatch number) to choose a tangerine color. Click OK.

8 In the image, Shift-drag a linear gradient from the top of the image downward, inside the selection marquee.

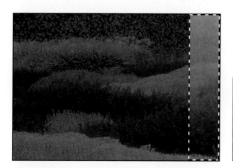
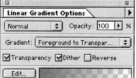

Foreground-to-background linear gradient added to Layer 1

9 Deselect the image.

10 Save your changes.

You've completed all the editing tasks for this image, and are ready to convert it to CMYK mode.

Color-separating an image

Your first step before color-separating an image is to specify a rendering intent for the image in CMYK Setup. This lets the CMS choose an appropriate color translation method for the image.

1 Choose File > Color Settings > CMYK Setup.

2 For CMYK Model, select ICC.

3 Make sure that the option displays the same settings you used previously—for Profile, Kodak SWOP Proofer CMYK-Coated Stock; for Engine, Built-in; for Intent, Perceptual (Images); and Black Point Compensation selected. (For details, see "Setting up the CMYK workspace" on page 181.)

4 Click OK.

5 Before converting the image to the CMYK color space, you can preview how colors will appear in CMYK mode, while still in RGB mode.

6 Choose View > Preview > CMYK. Notice that the vivid tangerine color you specified appears slightly different—less bright, even slightly brown. Because you used a swatch from the custom PANTONE Color Library to select the process tint, this is to be expected.

7 Choose Image > Mode > CMYK Color. Click Flatten at the prompt.

Because you selected the Display Using Monitor Compensation option in the in RGB Setup dialog box, the CMS converts the CMYK color data in the image to the RGB color space of your profiled monitor for display purposes. This gives you an accurate preview of the printed image in the CMYK mode.

8 Save your changes.

Matching colors in different applications

To match this tangerine color to other elements that will be added to the layout in Adobe Illustrator, you'll need to take a reading on the gradient.

1 Choose Window > Show Info.

2 Select the eyedropper tool. In its Options palette, select Point Sample for the sample size.

3 In the image, move the pointer to the very top of the gradient, where the tangerine color is the most saturated. Shift-click to set a color target. In the Info Window, note those CMYK values at the target (#1). (My reading was C=0, M=73, Y=87, K=0.) You will use these values later in, "Matching color and assembling the artwork" on page 196.

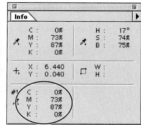

Color target showing CMYK values

4 When you have finished, choose File > Save as, rename the file **Backgrnd_CMYK.psd**, and click Save.

Opening a file with an embedded profile

Now you will open a second, scanned image with an embedded profile, so that you can add the image to the page layout.

1 Choose File > Open, and open the Lotus.tif file, located in the Lessons/Lesson06/06PSD folder on your hard drive.

Lotus image in CMYK mode

The CMYK image opens directly in Photoshop because the file was previously scanned and separated for the same print space set for the postcard project (Kodak SWOP Proofer CMYK-Coated Stock). Even with a different print color space, the CMYK image would open directly in Photoshop because you had specified that CMYK files be ignored in case of profile mismatch. (See "Setting up a color profile" on page 182.)

If you are unsure whether the CMYK image's color space matches the intended CMYK color space, it's better to rescan the original art to match the current CMYK profile or to match a large RGB color space such as the Adobe RGB (1998) space. If you cannot rescan the original art, convert the CMYK color space of the file to the chosen CMYK space using Image > Mode > Profile to Profile. This command converts between any two color spaces. As a general rule, avoid converting between two CMYK spaces, because each space is tied to a particular printer's color gamut, and may contain unique colors.

2 Resize the artwork by choosing Image > Image Size. Resize the image to match the resolution of the other images used in the postcard by deselecting Resample Image, and entering **200** ppi, the same resolution as the background image. Click OK.

3 Choose File > Save As, for Format choose Photoshop, and rename the file **Lotus_CMYK.psd**. Click Save.

4 Close the file and quit Photoshop.

Color management in Adobe Illustrator

The next part of the project must be produced in an illustration program such as Adobe Illustrator, because you will add vector-based artwork and type to the postcard design. You will then colorize them to match the tangerine color you specified in the first image.

Adobe Illustrator, like many other Adobe products such as Adobe InDesign™ and Adobe Acrobat®, includes several color management features. The Adobe CMS technology is integrated into all of its applications with a similar interface for the relevant dialogs.

A big difference in the way Photoshop and Illustrator manage color is in the RGB workspace. Because most images created and imported into Adobe Illustrator tend to be in the CMYK color space, the application lacks an RGB workspace that is independent of the monitor's RGB space. This lack only affects an RGB image opened in Illustrator: if the RGB image was created and saved in a color space different from the monitor's color space, the colors will display differently when opened or placed in Illustrator. Photoshop images saved for the postcard project aren't affected, because they were saved in CMYK mode.

Verifying CMS settings in Illustrator

You will first configure settings related to Illustrator's color management system (CMS).

Before you begin, make sure that you have restored the default preferences for Adobe Illustrator. For instructions, see "Restoring default preferences" on page 3.

1 For the CMS in Illustrator to work correctly, verify that these required files are on your hard drive:

• The Adobe CMS must be installed in the Adobe Illustrator folder; this file is named RB2Connection.win (Windows) or RB2Connection.mac (Mac OS). The color-matching engine (CMM) is an important component of the CMS in Illustrator. The Adobe CMS is similar to the Built-In CMM in Adobe Photoshop.

• The Color Conversion and Color Conversion Utilities plug-ins must be installed in the Plug-ins > Extensions folder. These two files are installed automatically by the Adobe Illustrator installer, but you should verify that they are installed correctly before proceeding.

2 Restart Adobe Illustrator.

Setting Illustrator color settings

In the next part of the lesson, you will choose color settings. Once they are correctly set, the CMS in Adobe Illustrator will automatically color-manage any Photoshop images correctly.

1 Choose File > Color Settings.

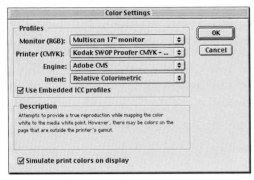

Illustrator Color Settings dialog box

2 In the Color Settings dialog box, for Monitor (RGB), choose your monitor device profile.

3 For Printer (CMYK), choose Kodak SWOP Proofer CMYK-Coated Stock—the profile that you selected as the CMYK color space in Adobe Photoshop.

4 For Engine, choose Adobe CMS.

5 For Intent, choose Relative Colorimetric. A brief description of this intent appears in the dialog box. This intent works particularly well for color illustrations that originate in Adobe Illustrator.

For more information on rendering intents, see Chapter 7 of the Illustrator 8.0 User Guide or "Changing color management settings" in Illustrator 8.0 online Help.

6 Select Use Embedded ICC Profiles. When this option is selected:

• Illustrator files are saved with the monitor and printer profiles. If you placed this file in another CMS-savvy application, it would know how to represent the file's colors.

• Any placed Photoshop file with embedded profiles, and any PDF, JPEG, or TIFF file with an embedded profile, will be color-managed accurately. If this option is deselected, no color management will occur, even on a file with embedded profiles.

7 Select Simulate Print Colors on Display. This option compares the print device's ICC profiles with the chosen monitor, and displays only those colors in the printer's gamut.

8 Click OK to save your changes.

Finalizing the artwork in Illustrator

You're now ready to open your illustration for the postcard design. As in Photoshop, you first must do a few necessary editing tasks on the image.

1 Choose File > Open, and open the Teapot.ai file, located in the Lessons/Lesson06/06AI folder on your hard drive.

2 Choose File > Save As, name the file **Teapot1.ai**, and click Save. For Format, choose Illustrator version 8.0, and click OK.

Teapot image

3 Select the teapot art. You will colorize the teapot art a lime green.

4 Fill the selection with either a process tint, a custom color, or enter CMYK values in the Color palette. I used the CMYK values of C=75, M=5, Y=100, K=0.

5 Save your changes. Keep the Teapot1.ai file open, so that you can drag the illustration into the next file you work on.

Now you are ready to assemble all the images you have worked on so far, in the postcard layout.

6 Choose File > Open, and locate the Postcard.ai file in the Lessons/Lesson06/06AI folder on your hard drive.

7 Choose File > Save As, rename the file **Postcard1.ai**, and click Save. For Format, choose Illustrator version 8.0, and click OK.

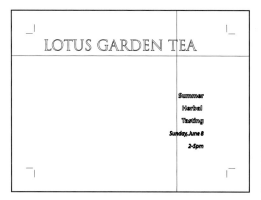
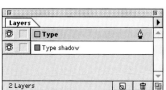

Art work view of Postcard1 image

8 In the Layers palette, create a new layer and name it **Background** layer. Drag the Background layer to the bottom of the layer stack.

9 Choose File > Place, and locate and place the Backgrnd_CMYK.psd. When the file opens in the Artwork mode, position the bounding box in the center of the rectangle formed by the crop marks.

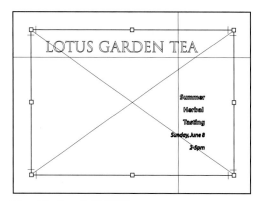
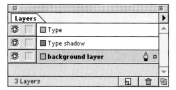

Placed Backgrnd_CMYK image

10 Preview the file.

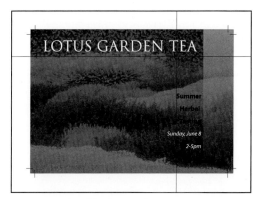

Previewing placed background

Next you will place the Lotus_CMYK.psd image in the layout.

11 In the Layers palette, create a new layer and name it **Lotus**. Position the Lotus layer directly above the Background layer.

12 Choose File > Place, and locate and place the Lotus_CMYK.psd.

13 Align the top left corner of the Lotus image to the guides, as shown in the following illustration.

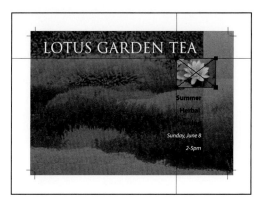
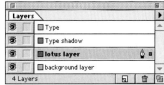

Positioning Lotus_CMYK image

Finally, you will add the Teapot1.ai illustration to the layout.

14 In the Layers palette, create a new layer and name it **Teapot**. Position the Lotus layer at the top of the layer stack.

15 Make the Teapot1.ai image active. Press Ctrl/Command+A to select all, and using the selection tool, drag the illustration to the Postcard1.ai file.

16 Choose Object > Transform > Scale. Select Uniform, and enter **80**%. Click OK. Center the illustration in the lower left rectangle formed by the guides.

Postcard1 image scaled 80%

Matching color and assembling the artwork

Next, you will match the type in the Type layer to the tangerine color of the gradient.

1 In the Layers palette, click the Type layer to make it active. Alt/Option-click its eye icon to lock all the other layers.

2 Press Ctrl/Command+A to select the contents of the layer. In the Color palette, enter the CMYK values for the tangerine color you had noted in Adobe Photoshop.

I entered C=0, M=73, Y=87, K=0—the values I noted earlier in "Matching colors in different applications" on page 188. The tangerine color of the type should match the most saturated color in the gradient.

3 Deselect the type. Unlock all locked layers.

Postcard1 with color-matched type and Lotus image

4 Save the file.

You are now ready to print the color-managed postcard to the CMYK standard you have chosen, Kodak SWOP Proofer CMYK-Coated Stock. After you set up the separation options you may print or save the file as a PDF document.

Setting separation options

The color separation options that you specify are saved with the color-separated file and contain printer-specific settings such as the halftone screen ruling, bleed specification, and so on.

1 Choose File > Separation Setup. (If you were to print the image directly, you could also choose File > Print, and then click Separation Setup in the Print dialog.)

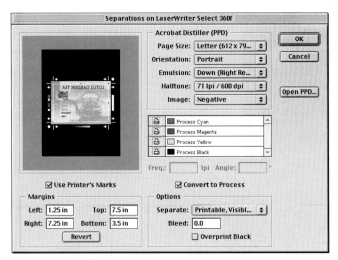

Separation Setup dialog box

2 Click Open PPD, and select the PPD file that corresponds to your printer or image-setter.

For more information on selecting PPD files, see Chapter 15 in the Illustrator 8.0 User Guide or "Selecting a PPD file" in Illustrator 8.0 online Help.

3 To specify which layers to separate, in the Options section of the dialog box, for Separate, choose Printable, Visible Layers.

4 Next to the color names, make sure that a printer icon appears for each CMYK color. By default, Illustrator creates a separation for each CMYK color in the artwork.

5 Based on recommendations from your print or prepress service provider, specify the Emulsion, Image (negative/positive), and Halftone settings.

6 Click OK.

You are ready to print or save your color-managed separations.

7 Choose File > Save, and navigate to where you will save the file. If you plan to print to a remote location, such as at your prepress or print provider, select Include Placed Files in the File. However, this creates a significantly larger file. Check with your print service provider to see whether a linked or embedded file is preferred.

8 Click Save.

You have successfully completed the color management tasks involved with creating and saving the postcard.

Preparing Illustrator graphics for use in other applications

You may want to place your color-managed art inside another ICC-compliant application such as Adobe InDesign, or prepare your Adobe Illustrator 8.0 graphics for remote printing.

For example, you may want to use the postcard artwork in a multipage brochure that you are designing in Adobe InDesign. To continue to color-manage the artwork so that the specified colors match other art in InDesign, you must save the Illustrator file in the PDF format. Saving in PDF format embeds profiles and ensures that InDesign will color-manage the display and printing of the Illustrator artwork. Illustrator 8.0 does not embed profiles into Illustrator format files or EPS files.

Preparing Illustrator graphics for remote printing

To facilitate color management when printing to a remote location, such as an off-site print provider, you can save your Illustrator 8.0 file as a PDF file. You can later open the file as an Illustrator file, without losing many file features such as fonts, color characteristics, patterns, and so on.

As an option, you can prepare your Illustrator graphics for remote printing. To skip this procedure and create the Web-based art for the postcard, save and close your file. Then continue to "Creating Web-based art" on page 203.

1 Choose File > Save As. For Format, choose Acrobat PDF, and save the file as **Postcard_final.pdf**.

2 Click Save to display options for Adobe PressReady, for Printing, and for Web display.

3 In the PDF Format dialog box, for PDF Options Set, choose Print Quality to print the postcard.

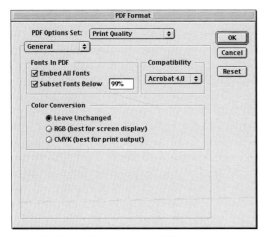

General print quality options for PDF format   *Choosing Print Quality*

The General options let you choose to embed fonts and specify compatibility with a version of Adobe Acrobat.

4 For Fonts in PDF, deselect Embed All Fonts. The postcard file contains no fonts (only type outlines), so no fonts will be embedded in the file.

5 For Compatibility, specify the version of Acrobat you own and plan to use to open the PDF file.

6 Choose Compression from the General pop-up menu to specify compression for the postcard.

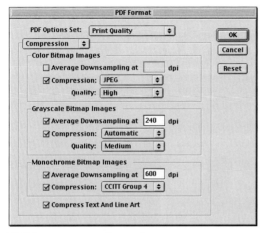

PDF Format compression settings

Be very careful when specifying compression settings for artwork to be printed. Specifying higher compression can cause compression artifacts to appear in printed images. Judiciously chosen, compression settings can help reduce file size, which can be particularly helpful in transporting the files for remote printing.

7 Set the following compression options for the best printed results for the postcard:

• Deselect Average Downsampling.

• Select Compression, and choose JPEG.

• For Quality, choose High.

• Deselect Compress Text or Line Art if you are concerned about compression artifacts ("jaggies") in your printed line art.

8 Click OK. The PDF file is now ready for printing to a remote location.

9 Save and close the file.

10 Quit Illustrator.

Producing color-managed digital color proofs

One of the main aims of digital color-proofing is to simulate the final CMYK on a composite color printer. You can proof images individually from applications such as Adobe Photoshop; or from a layout with multiple images, color-separated with different intents, from an application such as Adobe InDesign.

To produce a color-managed color proof from Photoshop, do the following:

1. Choose Image > Duplicate. Rename the duplicate file, and click OK. You will perform the profile-to-profile conversion on the duplicate file.

2. Choose Image > Mode > Profile-to-Profile.

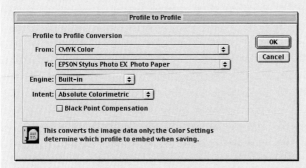

3. In the Profile-to-Profile conversion dialog box, set these options:

• For From (the source), choose CMYK Color, indicating the current settings in CMYK Setup.

• For To (the target), choose the composite color printer you wish to use as a digital proofing device.

• For Intent, choose Absolute Colorimetric.

• Deselect Black Point Compensation.

Note: Absolute Colorimetric tries to reproduce the colors in the source color space as accurately as possible; hence it is a better choice for proofing. Black Point Compensation tries to match the black point of the source color space to the black point of the target color space. But for proofing purposes, it's better to see the shadows that you are likely to get on the final CMYK device, rather than the potentially richer blacks you will get from a composite color printer.

4. Click OK.

The resulting image may look quite different on your monitor, but when printed to the composite printer, the image is likely to match the final CMYK print.

Creating Web-based art

Now you will learn about issues with Web-based color and how to optimize images for Web art. The main objective in this workflow is to re-use and optimize source images for screen display. Using a color-managed workflow gives you the flexibility to make many uses of the original scans.

Color-managing Web-based art

In an ideal workflow, you would be able to re-use source images with embedded ICC profiles. Web browsers would then use color management technology to consistently display the colors across calibrated and characterized monitors all across the Web. Unfortunately this scenario is premature. Currently, only a handful of browsers, such as Internet Explorer 4.0 or later, are able to read embedded ICC profiles and manage them.

Even if browser support for ICC profiles becomes more widespread in the near future, as more browsers become ICC-compliant, another hurdle lies in the ability of every monitor to display these tagged images accurately. Every display system would have to be accurately profiled for the CMS to know which monitor color space to use when displaying the tagged images accurately.

Determining a Web color strategy

The first step in re-using the original RGB image is to determine the strategy to display colors consistently on all monitors. It is estimated that currently only 8% of all Web users have low resolution 8-bit color displays. For these users' benefit, you may choose to specify the colors for any logos, type, and illustrations from the Web-safe color palette. For more information on the Web-safe color palette, see "Editing colors to be Web-safe" on page 204.

Because you do not expect browsers to color-manage your file, you don't need to embed an ICC profile. The splash page you will work on is an untagged file, that is, one without embedded profiles. This can result in a reduced file size, as embedded profiles can add to file size overhead.

> ### Saving an untagged file in Adobe Photoshop
>
> *You can remove embedded profiles from a file intended for the Web to reduce the file size. When you strip embedded profiles, you can remove all nonimage elements that are normally saved with the file—including the embedded profiles, and paths, channels, guides, captions, and thumbnail previews—or you can strip only embedded profiles.*
>
> *1. Choose File > Open, and open the Photoshop image that you will strip of its embedded profiles.*
>
> *2. Strip all nonimage elements or only embedded profiles from the file:*
>
> • *To strip all elements normally saved with the file, choose File > Save A Copy, and rename the file. Select Exclude Non-Image Data. Click Save to save a copy of the file in the chosen location on your hard drive.*
>
> • *To strip only embedded profiles and keep nonimage elements, choose File > Color Settings > Profile Setup. At the top of the dialog, deselect Embed Profiles for all modes listed. Click OK. Save the file and close it. You can then reset the Profile Setup dialog if needed.*

With any art destined for the Web or on-screen display, it is recommended that you perform most tonal and color correction in the application in which the artwork originated, such as in Illustrator or Photoshop. You can then export the corrected artwork to an application that fine-tunes it for Web-based publishing.

In this lesson, the Web splash page for Lotus Garden Tea was designed for you. You will open the splash image in Adobe ImageReady to perform a couple of color-editing tasks. Then you will optimize the colors and save the file for Web publishing.

For more details on Web-based color issues, see the PDF document "Color Management Basics" in the Lesson06 folder on the Advanced Classroom in a Book CD.

Editing colors to be Web-safe

The splash page was designed in Adobe Photoshop using elements from the postcard design. The colors in the image were specified with no heed to Web-safe colors. You will use the colors as-is in the final splash page design, with the exception of some elements such as the type, illustration, and so on. If you do not edit the type and illustration colors, they could appear dithered in a Web browser on an 8-bit display. While a dithered illustration may degrade gracefully, type on-screen suffers greatly from dithering and can appear unreadable at small sizes.

1 Start Adobe ImageReady.

2 Choose File > Open, and open the Splash.psd file, located in the Lessons/Lesson06/06PSD folder on your hard drive.

Splash image

3 Choose File> Save As, rename the file **Splash1.psd**, and click OK.

Note: If the image opens with slices displayed, you must hide them temporarily. Choose Slices > Hide Slices.

The image opens with all layers intact. You will work on the individual layers to edit the colors to be Web safe, using either the Color palette or color picker.

4 In the Layers palette, make the Type 2 (tangerine type) layer active; in the image, use the eyedropper tool to sample the color you want to change.

5 Select a Web-safe color that matches the original color closely using either the Color palette or color picker.

6 To use the Color palette, choose Window > Show Color and use one of these methods to select Web colors:

• With the sliders set to any mode, click the alert cube to select the closest Web-safe color. The alert cube icon indicates the color you sampled is a non-Web color.

• Choose Web Color Sliders from the Color palette menu. This shows tick marks on the sliders indicating Web-safe colors. Use the sliders to choose an alternative Web color.

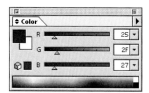

Web color sliders and alert cube

Although you're working with RGB sliders in this palette, you are actually selecting colors by their hexadecimal values. Unlike illustration and painting programs that let you specify colors intuitively in RGB, CMYK, HSB, and other color models, Web page design of HTML uses only the hexadecimal color model. Hexadecimal numbers are used to convert RGB values, so that HTML can interpret which colors you've chosen.

For example, a salmon pink RGB color may record RGB values of R=204, G=51, B=51. The same color would be represented in hexadecimal values as CC3333. As of HTML version 3.2, you can select several colors by name such as aqua, black, blue, fuchsia, gray, green, lime, maroon, navy, olive, purple, and so on.

7 To select Web-safe colors using the color picker, click the foreground color swatch to display the color picker. Then use one of these methods to select the Web-equivalent of the sampled color:

• Click the alert cube icon at the top right corner to select the closest Web-safe color.

• Select Only Web Colors to limit the display of colors to the Web color palette and select the closest color match. Select a color and click OK.

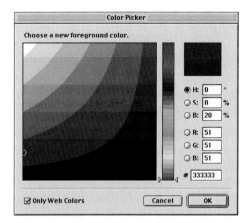

Choosing a Web Color in the Color Picker

8 When you have selected the Web-safe color, press Shift+Alt+Delete (Windows) or Shift+Option+Delete (Mac OS) to fill the layer with the foreground color while preserving the layer's transparency.

9 Repeat steps 1 through 5 for the Teapot and Background layers.

Now that you have finished editing the Web-safe colors, you are ready to optimize the image to make it ready for Web publishing.

In Web pages, designers sometimes avoid using gradients because they do not render as smoothly as an undithered GIF file, and the limited number (256) of colors available gives a stair-stepped look. A dithered GIF image may simulate the original colors in the gradient, but will show the dither pattern on-screen, which can be distracting. (Dithering mixes different color pixels to give the illusion of another color.) A dithered GIF image also can be signifi-cantly larger in size than the undithered GIF version. For gradients in Web page-designs, the JPEG format offers the best options for compression and smooth appearance on-screen.

> ### *Web-safe colors*
>
> *Every operating system has a set of 256 colors that are known as its system palette. These colors are available to applications to display an image. Of these, Windows and Mac OS share 216 colors in their respective system palettes. Web browser applications, which have to run on all computer platforms, have synchronized these 216 colors in a color palette termed "Web-safe."*
>
> *When a color in an image is not available for display by an 8-bit color or grayscale monitor, the browser dithers the colors, or breaks them up into a pattern of small colored dots, using compatible colors from its system palette. Dithering can produce objectionable and distracting moiré-like patterns on-screen.*
>
> *Web designers strive hard to keep color-critical graphics such as logos, corporate colors, catalog items, and so on, from dithering, because it affects the color fidelity of these graphics. On the other hand, using a color from the Web-safe color palette ensures that the color will not dither on any color display (even on 8-bit monitors!) because the color belongs to the lowest-common-denominator set of colors available to all platforms and displays. Whenever possible, limit the color of flat-art, illustrations, and type, to colors from the Web-safe palette.*

Optimizing Web-based art

Adobe ImageReady 2.0 features slicing to let you divide a file into smaller files that can be optimized independently. A *slice* is a rectangular area of the image that becomes a cell within a table in the HTML file for the image. Each slice can contain its own color palettes and references, URLs, rollover, and animation effects! Slices thus speed download time and increase image quality in images that contain many styles of artwork.

Optimizing JPEG slices

The Splash1.psd image has been saved with slices, which will let you optimize individually the different colored elements in the image. The lotus art and the gradient must be optimized as JPEG slices to preserve the subtle tones and color variation.

1 In ImageReady, choose Slices > Show Slices.

2 With the slice-selection tool, click the gradient slice and Shift-click the lotus slice. This selects slices 02 and 04. You will optimize them together as JPEG files.

3 In the Optimize palette, select the JPEG Medium setting. This is a preset, with its options displayed below.

4 Click the 4-Up view tab.

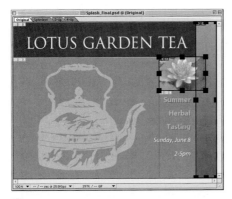

Slices

5 View the previews at 100%. Use the hand tool to scroll in any of the image previews to display the lotus art and gradient clearly. Image quality is set to 30, which is reflected in the view to the right of the original view. Two lower-quality variations are displayed in the following illustration.

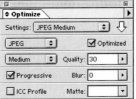

JPEG Medium setting

6 Experiment with the Quality value or slider in the Optimize palette. I chose the following options for the JPEG slices:

• Optimized, to produce a slightly smaller file size.

• Blur of 0.15. This functions like the Gaussian Blur filter, and slightly blurs the selected slices to make a smaller file size.

• ICC option deselected. The ICC option embeds the RGB color space profile in the sliced images. This option is only relevant in a workflow that relies on the browser to manage color on the Web.

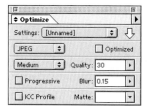

Optimize palette settings

Optimizing GIF slices

The teapot illustration, type, and flat background color will be optimized as GIF slices, because it is important to preserve their exact shape and color when viewed on-screen. The GIF format handles illustration-style art, type, and flat color better than the JPEG format.

1 Return to the Original view tab.

2 Select the remainder of the slices using the slice-selection tool.

3 Click the Optimize tab.

The Optimize palette includes several GIF settings.

4 Set options for the GIF slices. I chose the following options:

• GIF format.

• Web Palette, because all of the art elements in the slices feature Web-safe colors.

• 22 colors, which appeared to maintain the image quality nicely.

• No Dither option. You carefully chose Web-safe colors in all the art elements in the selected slices, so dither is unnecessary. If the artwork contained non-Web-safe colors, you would have to dither the image using compatible colors from the Web-safe palette.

• Matte color of None.

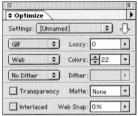

Optimized GIF slices   *Optimize palette settings for GIF slices*

You have now optimized the image and are ready to save the files for Web publishing.

Saving optimized images

As a final step, you'll save the optimized file.

1 Choose File > Save Optimized. Name the file **Splash_final.html**.

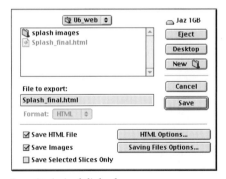

Save Optimized dialog box

2 Select the Save HTML File and Save Images options.

3 To save the sliced, optimized images in a folder, click Saving Files Options. Select Put Images in a Sub Folder, and specify the folder name. Click OK.

4 Select a location to save the resulting HTML file and folder with the sliced images, and click Save.

As a final step, you will verify that a browser can read the file.

5 Launch your Web browser, and open the Splash_final.html file. All of the optimized elements should download and appear on-screen.

You have successfully color-managed the creation and production of two projects involving print and Web publishing.

Lesson 1 — Preparing Images for Print

evelyn schichtl

Gallery 617 • June 6-30

*Final Lesson 1 artwork
for print*

Original scan

Adjusted color balance

Before adjusting levels

After adjusting levels

After glaze

After increased shadows

Lesson 1 — Preparing Images for Web

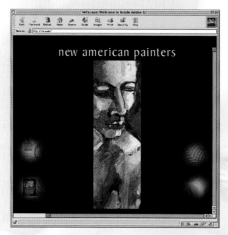

Final Lesson 1 artwork for Web

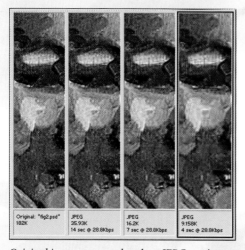

Original image compared to three JEPG versions

Lesson 2 — Shading and Blending

Final Lesson 2 Photoshop image

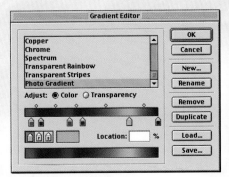

Final gradient setup

Six-color gradient applied

Multiply layer mode, 30% opacity

Contracting selection

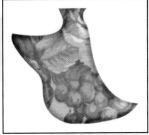

Lightening area using Levels

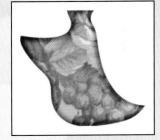

Saturate sponge applied to edges

Lesson 2 — Shading and Blending

Final Lesson 2 Illustrator artwork

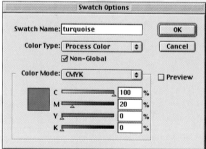

Color in artwork changed automatically

Lesson 2 — Shading and Blending

Shapes filled with gradient 1

Shapes filled with gradient 2

Adjusting direction of gradient

New gradient applied and updated

Final scanned and cropped image

Dirt revealed

Subject selected

Blue streak selected

Background selected

Final image

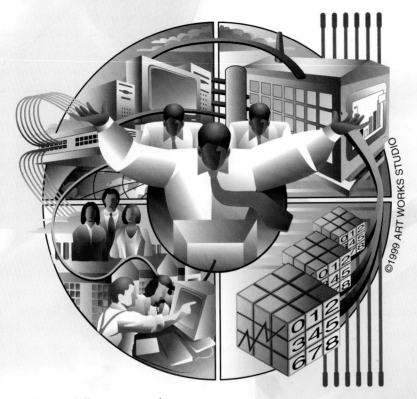

Final Lesson 4 Illustrator artwork

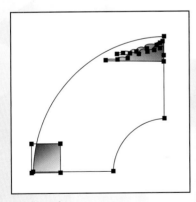

Masking object

Result

Lesson 4 — Advanced Masking (Photoshop 5.5)

Final Lesson 4 Photoshop artwork

Edges highlighted

Selecting with Color Range eyedropper

Edge artifacts

After Defringe

Quick Mask mode

Editing with paintbrush tool

Final Lesson 5 artwork

Color Dodge mode

Painting out duplicate lip and nose

Clipped adjustment layer

Type layer

Lesson 6 — Color Management and Distribution

Final Lesson 6 artwork for printed postcard

Splash page art

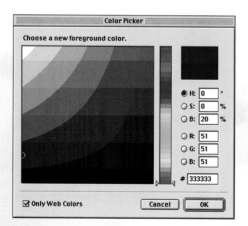

Web color

Web color sliders

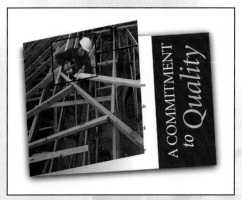

Printed sample of final Lesson 7 artwork

Project	Style	Duration	Price
House	Colonial	6 months	$220,000.00
House	Tudor	6 months	$250,000.00
House	Split-level	5 months	$185,000.00
Kitchen	Contemporary	3 weeks	$20,000.00
Kitchen	Old Style	3 weeks	$20,000.00
Bathroom	Contemporary	2 weeks	$12,000.00

Thumbs Up Construction

395 Madison Avenue, Suite 201
Chelsea Gardens, FL 35732
(305) 782-1100 • Fax (305) 782-1101

www.thumbsupconstruction.com

Make your dream come true.

We know what it means to dream. After all, making dreams come true is what we do best. At first, it might seem like it's too expensive to build that dream house, or to remodel that aging kitchen or bathroom. But at Thumbs Up Construction, we can do the perfect job for you, and you'd be surprised how affordable it can really be. Our work is top-rate and we take pride in the things we do. Unlike other construction companies, we offer up-front pricing, so you never get unexpected surprises when you get your bill. And that's just the beginning. Our friendly workers are well-trained and will make sure everything is exactly the way you want it. So call us today! We'll send down a contractor for a free estimate, and let us make your dream come true!

"I never believed I could afford my dream house. Thumbs Up made it happen — at a price I could afford."

We finish our work on time

We use the finest materials

We take pride in our work

Our prices are reasonable

A COMMITMENT to *Quality*

Final Lesson 8 artwork

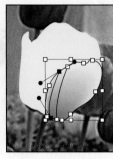

Red added—gradient mesh

Additional gradient mesh patch

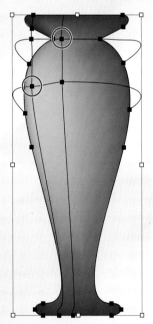

Gradient mesh

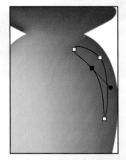

Drawing highlight

Shadow

Lesson 9 — Two-Color Print Projects

Final Lesson 9 artwork

Positioning the Duo.eps file

Reducing black in saxophone

Curvy type aligned with saxophone

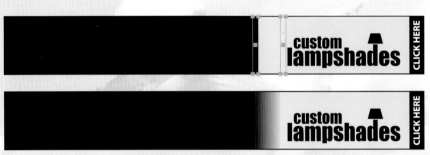

Artwork for panel of animated ad banner

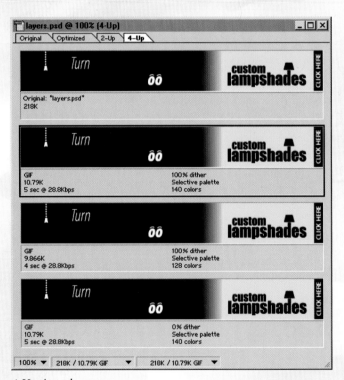

Selected rectangles indicating blend (top); result (bottom)

4-Up view tab

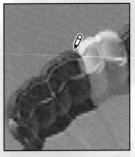  

Tracing parachute; filling with white, stroked 2-point lines

Before Gaussian Blur   *After Gaussian Blur*

Resolution at 75% magnification   *Pixelation apparent at 400% magnification*

Lesson 7

7 | Advanced Typography and Layout

By Mordy Golding

Adobe Illustrator has all the tools necessary to compose complete layouts for brochures—from setting professional-looking type with ligatures, to specifying spot varnish inks, and setting folds, trim, and bleeds. You can also output film separations directly from Illustrator.

In this lesson, you'll learn how to do the following:

- Set crop and trim marks.
- Apply a registration color.
- Use the Smart Punctuation feature.
- Apply a spot color and a spot varnish.
- Create a table using tabs.
- Create text wraps.
- Print tiled portions of the document.

This lesson will take about 1 hour to complete.

If needed, remove the previous lesson folder from your hard drive, and copy the Lesson07 folder onto it.

Getting started

In this lesson, you will create a six-color short-fold brochure in Adobe Illustrator for a construction company, and prepare it to send to a printer or a service bureau for color separations. Before beginning this lesson, restore the default application settings for Adobe Illustrator. For instructions, see "Restoring default preferences" on page 3.

You'll start the lesson by viewing the final Lesson file to see the brochure that you'll create.

1 Restart Adobe Illustrator.

2 Choose File > Open, and open the 07End.ai file, located in the Lessons/Lesson07 folder.

3 When you have finished viewing the file, either leave the End file open on your desktop for reference, or close it without saving changes.

For an illustration of the finished artwork for this lesson, see the color section.

Now you'll open the start file and set up your brochure document.

4 Choose File > Open, and open the 07Start.ai file, located in the Lessons/Lesson07 folder on your hard drive.

5 Choose File > Save As, name the file **Brochure.ai**, and click Save. In the Illustrator Format dialog box, select version 8.0 of Illustrator, and click OK.

Setting up your document

The brochure you will create is larger than letter size, so you'll need to enlarge your Artboard to accommodate both the front and the back of the brochure. Although you can place objects both on and off the Artboard, only objects that lie on the Artboard will print. You will also adjust the view of your document to make it easier to work with.

Artwork larger than the Artboard

1 Choose File > Document Setup.

2 For Width, enter **19** inches, and for Height, enter **17** inches. Click OK to set the new Artboard size.

*Note: When entering values into dialog boxes, you can specify a particular measurement system by typing **in** for inches, **pt** for points, and so on. You can also set the default in preferences, or press Ctrl/Command+U to cycle through the measurement systems.*

Page tiling places an outline in your document window to indicate the physical print area of your selected printer. For now, you will hide page tiling so that it doesn't distract your view.

3 Choose View > Hide Page Tiling.

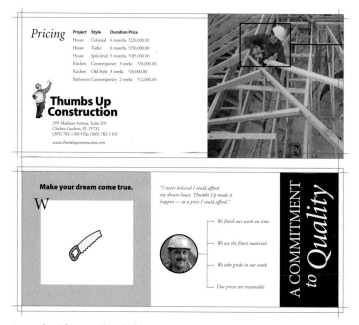

Artwork with page tiling hidden

Now you'll turn on the grid, to make it easier to position objects as you create the brochure. You can turn the grid on and off as needed by pressing Ctrl/Command+Quotation Mark (").

4 Choose View > Show Grid.

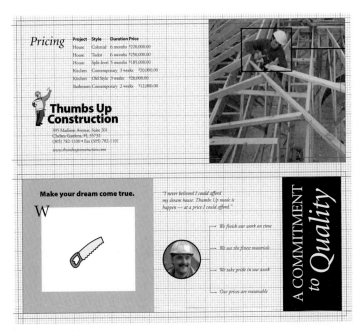

The layout grid

Aligning in Photoshop and Illustrator

Aligning in Photoshop is quite different from aligning in Illustrator. Photoshop uses a stationary object (a selection or layer object) to align to, while Illustrator averages among all selected objects.

In Photoshop, you can align any layer to either a selection or all linked layers. To align to a selection, create the selection, and then select the layer in the Layers palette that you'd like to align with the selection. Choosing Layer > Align to Selection (and the corresponding horizontal or vertical position) moves the object on the active layer so that it aligns with the selection. To align two layers quickly, Ctrl/Command-click the stationary layer, make active the layer that will move, and then apply Align to Selection.

To align a series of layers, you must link several layers together in the Layers palette. The active layer will be the stationary layer that the other layers will align to. Choose Layer > Align Linked (and the corresponding horizontal or vertical position), and the layers will be aligned.

Both products let you set up a grid for manual alignment and create guides to align objects (and layers) to horizontal and vertical planes.

Illustrator moves many of the selected objects when you align. The objects that don't move can be treated as stationary objects. When aligning Left, Right, Top, or Bottom (using the appropriate Align palette buttons), the leftmost, rightmost, topmost, or bottommost object will not move, respectively. If you want to align to another object, make that object the furthest (move the other objects with the Shift key to achieve this).

When aligning to vertical or horizontal center in Illustrator, all objects move to find the center based on the original position of all selected objects. To align to the center of a specific object, create a guide at the center of that object, align the objects, and then move them so that their combined center is on the guide. You can also turn on Smart Guides, which lets you drag items around the screen, touching items you wish to align to, which will instantly snap objects to those you've touched.

—Ted Alspach

Creating trim and fold marks

For a print shop to print a job successfully, it requires certain information, such as where to cut the paper and make the folds. When you specify trim and fold marks, the print shop knows exactly how the final brochure should appear. Fold marks are particularly important for this short-fold brochure, as the front panel is supposed to be 3 inches shorter than the back panel.

Final brochure's appearance when folded

First, you will create a new layer for the printer's marks so that you can quickly lock and hide them at will.

1 In the Layers palette, create a new layer and name it **Registration**.

With the Registration layer selected, anything you now create will appear on the that layer. Next, you will create the trim marks.

2 Create a rectangle the size of the brochure's flat size (the size of the piece when it lies open flat), 17 inches by 7 inches. Create a rectangle of that size. Then position the rectangle to align with the inner guide on the top panel.

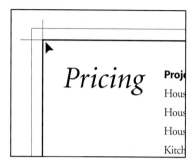

Aligning the rectangle to the inner guide

3 Choose Filter > Create > Trim Marks.

4 Select the rectangle again, and move it to align with the inner guide on the bottom panel.

5 Press Ctrl/Command+E to reapply the Trim Marks filter.

6 Delete the rectangle.

Next, you will create the fold marks.

7 Using the pen tool, draw a straight vertical line. Any length will do for now.

8 Give the line a fill of None and a stroke of 0.3 points.

9 In the Stroke palette menu in the Dashed Line area, enter a Dash of **2** points and a Gap of **1** point.

10 With the Stroke box selected in the toolbox, in the Swatches palette select the registration color swatch.

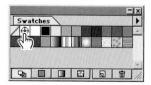

Selecting the registration swatch

11 Show Window > Transform to display the Transform palette.

12 For Height (H), enter **0.25** inches, and press Enter. This will set the length of the line.

13 For the X value, enter **11** inches; for the Y value, enter **16.375** inches.

Positioning the fold marks

14 Duplicate the fold mark. Repeat step 13, setting the X and Y values to 11 inches and 8.625 inches, respectively. The fold marks for the top panel are now complete.

15 Make another copy of the fold mark, and set its X and Y values to 8 inches and 8.375 inches, respectively.

16 Make a final copy of the fold mark, and set its X and Y values to 8 inches and 0.625 inches, respectively.

17 In the Layers palette, lock the Registration layer and click the Artwork layer once to make it the active layer.

Fold marks added

Defining bleeds

Many designs call for items to print up to the edge of the piece. To ensure that the color goes right to the edge, you make the color extend beyond the trim of the piece. In this way, even if the printer's trim is off just a little bit, the color will still print right to the edge. Bleeds usually extend between 0.125 and 0.25 inch (1/8- and 1/4-inch) beyond the trim.

1 Choose File > Preferences > General.

2 For Keyboard Increment, set the Cursor Key amount to 0.25 inches, and click OK.

3 Notice on the bottom panel the two areas where the object comes right to the edge. Start with the panel that says "Make your dream come true." Using the direct-selection tool, click once on the top edge of the gray box that is the background. Then press the Up Arrow on your keyboard once.

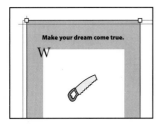

Defining the bleed on top

4 Do the same for the left side and the bottom of the background using the Left and Down arrow keys, respectively. The right side doesn't need bleed, as the brochure folds where the color ends.

Now you'll work with the right side of the bottom panel.

5 Using the same technique as in steps 3 and 4, add bleed to the top, bottom, and right side of the background behind the words "A Commitment to Quality."

Bleed applied to the top, bottom, and right

Because this area background will be visible when the brochure is folded, you want to make sure that the color extends beneath the front flap as well. To ensure this, you will extend the background on the left side as well, but 0.25 inch is a bit excessive. You will reset the Cursor Key increment.

6 Press Ctrl/Command+K to display your General Preferences dialog box, and set the Cursor Key value to 0.125 inch. Click OK.

7 Now select the left side of the background, and press the Left arrow on your keyboard once.

Using Rich Blacks in Photoshop and Illustrator

Trapping is needed when two areas of solid color run right up against each other. While everything will look just fine on screen, slight variations or shifts in color plates during the printing process can result in white lines between objects, where there should be none. Trapping is needed most when black areas are butted up against other colors.

Typically, trapping is needed much more often with Illustrator documents than with Photoshop, but if you're creating areas with solid colors in Photoshop (such as text or borders), or if you're using Photoshop's spot color function, you might need to trap those areas. If you're printing process colors only in Photoshop or Illustrator, avoiding solid cyan, magenta, and yellow can reduce the need for the most dramatic of trapping.

Rich blacks and other rich colors can eliminate the need for creating trapping manually. A rich black is black with a certain amount of another color added to it, typically the same or a reduction of the colors in neighboring objects. For instance, if bright red type (100% Magenta, 50% Yellow) were in a black background, and the black plate shifted a bit, white lines would appear around the edges of the type. However, if the black background was defined as 0% Cyan, 100% Magenta, 50% Yellow, and 100% Black, the black plate could shift around all it wanted, and the type would still look good and crisp. That would the most typical of rich black usage.

A rich color can be a bit more difficult to determine, but is much less likely to be needed, if good design sense is used when creating artwork. Most colors that are complementary to the red type we defined will tend to have a bit of magenta and yellow in them already. However, if the background was 50% cyan (not the most pleasant of combinations, but let's say a client wishes it so), a shift in the cyan plate would again result in a bit of white around the edges. To prevent it from happening, you can either add Magenta (possibly a bit of yellow as well) to the background, although this will give it a purplish hue, or add cyan to the type, which will darken the type a bit but prevent trapping issues from rearing their ugly head. If it is acceptable to change the color of either object, this is typically a better alternative than creating trapping along the edges of the cyan background (resulting in a "shadowing" around the type, even if there's no shift at all in the plates when printing).

—Ted Alspach

Applying a PANTONE color

Even though four-color process printing (CMYK) is referred to as full color, the gamut (range of colors) of CMYK does not include many colors. Bright oranges and blues are examples. A *spot color* is an additional ink added to the job that can be formulated to an exact color match. Where large blocks of color occur or an exact color match is required (a logo, for example), it might be a good idea to print an additional spot color.

For this brochure, you will create a spot color and apply it to the solid background behind the words "A Commitment to Quality." You will also apply it to the company name in the logo.

1 Choose Window > Swatch Libraries > PANTONE Coated. The PANTONE Coated Swatch palette will appear on-screen.

2 Press Ctrl+Alt (Windows) or Command+Option (Mac OS), and click once in the palette. Notice the black outline that appears within the palette border to indicate that the focus is in the PANTONE Coated swatch palette.

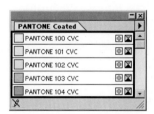

Black outline indicating focus in the palette

3 Enter the number **188.** PANTONE 188 CVC will appear highlighted in the palette. Press Enter or Return to add the color automatically to the document swatch palette.

4 Apply PANTONE 188 CVC as the fill for the background behind the words "A Commitment to Quality," which appears on the lower panel.

5 Using the group-selection tool, select the words "Thumbs Up Construction" on the left side of the upper panel. Also fill this with PANTONE 188 CVC.

Illustrator lets you sample colors from placed photographs. In this way, you can match colors or add complementary colors to your documents. For this project, you will sample a yellow color from the worker's hard hat that appears in the photo on the cover, and you will apply that color to objects in the brochure.

Note: When working with placed images, make sure that they are in CMYK and not RGB mode. Otherwise, colors you sample from them with the eyedropper tool will be RGB. RGB files may not separate correctly on an imagesetter, causing color shifts.

6 Make sure that the Fill box (not the Stroke box) is selected in the toolbox.

7 Deselect All by pressing Shift+Ctrl/Command+A, or by clicking an empty area on your screen.

8 Select the eyedropper tool (press the I key).

9 Press Ctrl/Command+spacebar, and zoom into the area of the yellow hard hat in the CMYK image. When you release the keys, your cursor returns to the eyedropper tool.

10 Hold down the mouse button as you drag through the hard hat to sample a color. As you drag, notice that the colors change in the Color palette. Release the mouse button when you see a color you like. This example used the color C=10, M=16, Y=78, K=0.

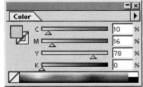

Sampling a color

11 Click the New Swatch button in the Swatches palette. Double-click the new swatch, and name it **Hard Hat Yellow**.

12 Zoom out and apply the new color in the lower panel to the word "Quality" and to the background that appears behind the words "Make your dream come true." (Access the paint bucket quickly by pressing Alt/Option.)

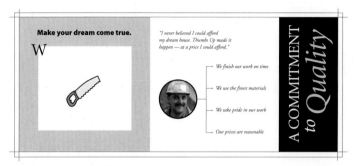

Sampled color applied to type and background

Creating a tabbed price chart

With tabs, you can create easy-to-read charts that present information clearly. Tabs let you align text in several ways. Especially useful is the decimal tab, which aligns prices perfectly. Tabs sometimes are difficult to work with because you can't see where they are inserted in text. You can use the Show Hidden Character feature to display them, as well as hard and soft returns and spaces. These symbols do not actually print—they only appear on-screen to help you when you edit type.

1 Choose Type > Show Hidden Characters. Blue symbols indicate hidden characters.

Showing hidden characters

2 Using the type tool, in the upper left of the top panel, select all of the text in the Pricing section.

3 Choose Type > Tab Ruler.

4 In the Tab palette, select the Snap box. This option makes it easy to align tabs to the ruler.

5 Place a tab at 1.625 inches.

💡 *If the tab ruler is not set to inches, you can click in the area to the right of the X to cycle through the measurements. You can also zoom in to see more tick marks, like eighth- and sixteenth-inch marks.*

6 Place another tab at 4.125 inches, and then click the Center-Justified Tab icon.

7 Place another tab at 6 inches, and click the Decimal-Justified Tab icon.

Project	Style	Duration	Price
House	Colonial	6 months	$220,000.00
House	Tudor	6 months	$250,000.00
House	Split-level	5 months	$185,000.00
Kitchen	Contemporary	3 weeks	$20,000.00
Kitchen	Old Style	3 weeks	$20,000.00
Bathroom	Contemporary	2 weeks	$12,000.00

Setting tabs to align text perfectly

8 Close the Tab palette.

To make the chart even easier to read, you will add rules between each line.

9 Using the pen tool, draw a straight horizontal rule as wide as the text block. To make this easy, turn on Smart Guides.

10 Apply a fill of None. Apply a stroke of black, set to 0.5 point. To create a dashed line, in the Stroke palette options, set the dash to 0 point and the gap to 1 point. Click the Round Caps icon to make the rule appear as a dotted line (zoom in close to get a better look at it).

11 Position the rule under the first line of type.

Project	Style	Duration	Price
House →	Colonial →	6·months →	$220,000.00¶
House →	Tudor →	6·months →	$250,000.00¶
House →	Split-level →	5·months →	$185,000.00¶
Kitchen →	Contemporary →	3·weeks →	$20,000.00¶
Kitchen →	Old Style →	3·weeks →	$20,000.00¶
Bathroom →	Contemporary →	2·weeks →	$12,000.00∞

Positioning the first rule

12 With the rule selected, double-click the selection tool to display the Move dialog box.

13 Enter –29.5 points in the Vertical box, and click Copy.

14 Press Ctrl/Command+D to replicate step 13. Repeat this step until the last line of text has a rule below it.

Project	Style	Duration	Price
House →	Colonial →	6·months →	$220,000.00¶
House →	Tudor →	6·months →	$250,000.00¶
House →	Split-level →	5·months →	$185,000.00¶
Kitchen →	Contemporary →	3·weeks →	$20,000.00¶
Kitchen →	Old Style →	3·weeks →	$20,000.00¶
Bathroom →	Contemporary →	2·weeks →	$12,000.00∞

Completed price chart

15 Turn off the hidden characters by choosing Type > Show Hidden Characters.

Importing and styling text

You can easily tell a professionally designed piece from one done by a novice simply by looking at the typography. Do apostrophes and quotation marks appear as inch and foot marks, or as the correct curly quotes? Are ligatures used? Do large gaps appear in the word spacing of justified text? Is hanging punctuation used? Illustrator lets you address all of these issues and more—including specifying type to wrap around images for eye-catching typography.

In this step, you'll work on the body copy of the brochure, creating an initial drop cap and wrapping the copy around the drop cap and an image.

1 First, select the white box that appears below the words "Make your dream come true."

The copy will read better if it appears in two columns. You'll create those first.

2 Choose Type > Rows & Columns.

3 Enter **2** for the number of columns, and set the gutter to 0.5 inches. Click OK. The box is split into two equally sized boxes.

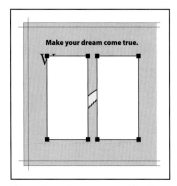

Two-column layout created by Rows & Columns command

4 With both boxes still selected, choose Type > Blocks > Link.

5 Switch to the type tool by pressing the T key on your keyboard, and click on the top line of the first box. A blinking text cursor appears in the first box.

6 Choose File > Place. Locate the 07Place.txt file in the Lessons/Lesson07 folder, and click Open. The text appears in your text block, flowing from the first block into the second one.

Text flowing from one column to the next

Next, you'll style the text and add the proper quotation marks and ligatures. *Ligatures* are special letter combinations, such as *fi* and *fl*, that are combined into one character for a more aesthetic look.

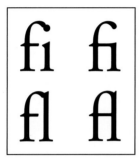

Regular letters (left) and ligatures (right)

7 Using the type tool, select all of the text. Set the Font to Minion, 14 points over 20 points Leading, and set the type to be Justified.

8 Choose Type > Smart Punctuation.

9 Select all options in the Replace Punctuation section, and click OK. Selecting Report Results displays how many items were replaced.

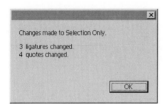

Report Results display

Next, you'll create a type wrap around the initial drop cap and the illustration of the saw that appears between the two columns. To specify an offset amount for the distance at which the text wraps around the image, you will first edit the drop cap and the illustration so that the text does not flow right to the edge of them. You do this using the Offset Path function.

Note: *Remember that a drop cap must be converted to outlines before you can wrap type. You can also draw a box—or any other shape for that matter—behind your drop cap and use that shape to create a wrap.*

10 Using the selection tool, select the initial cap.

11 Choose Object > Path > Offset Path. For Offset, enter 0.125 inch, and click OK.

12 Give the new outline a fill and stroke of None.

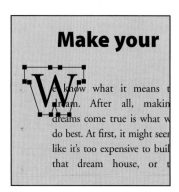

Offset path for the initial drop cap

Now you'll apply an offset to the illustration.

13 Using the direct-selection tool, select the outer edge of the saw.

14 Choose Object > Path > Offset Path. For Offset, enter **0.125** inches, and click OK.

15 Apply a fill and stroke of None.

16 Using the selection tool, select both the saw and the path you offset from the drop cap (if you cannot see the outline, switch to Artwork mode). Choose Object > Arrange > Bring to Front.

17 With the saw and drop cap still selected, add the text blocks to the selection using the selection tool.

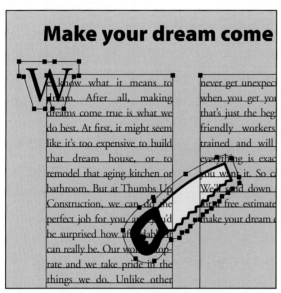

Drop cap offset path, saw offset path, and text blocks selected

You can wrap type around multiple objects by selecting all of the objects and then applying the Wrap command.

18 Choose Type > Wrap > Make.

Wrapped type

Because the type is justified, the wrap can cause some undesirable line breaks, which can make the copy difficult to read. Copy can be made to fit better and read easier by adjusting the word spacing or letterspacing. Unlike kerning, which adjusts the spacing between specific characters, letterspacing and word spacing specify how characters and words are spaced over a range of text. A professional typesetter knows that copy has to be more than just pretty—it has to be readable as well.

19 Using the type tool, select the copy within the text block.

20 Choose Type > Paragraph to open the Paragraph palette.

21 For Word Spacing, change the Minimum to **85**. Position the palette so that you can see the effect of adjustments.

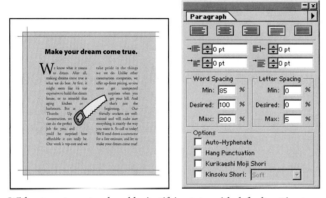

Wide-open spaces produced by justifying type with default settings

22 For Letter Spacing, change the Maximum setting to **50**. This setting spaces out the words on lines where wide gaps appear between words.

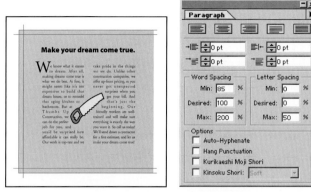

Paragraph spacing adjusted for better type appearance

23 Continue to make adjustments as needed.

As a final touch, you'll adjust the quotation mark that appears to the right of the panel you were just working on. The quotation mark at the beginning of the quote makes the text on the next line look uneven. Moving the punctuation to the left will make the text align perfectly at the beginning of each line and make it more pleasing to the eye.

24 Using the selection tool, select the quote that begins, "I never believed…".

25 In the Paragraph palette, select Hang Punctuation. The text now aligns perfectly.

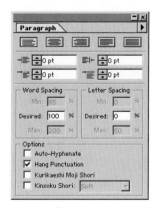

> *"I never believed I could afford*
> *my dream house. Thumbs Up made it*
> *happen—at a price I could afford."*

Improved text alignment with hanging quotation mark

Creating and applying a spot varnish

As an optional design technique for this brochure, you can add a spot gloss varnish to parts of photographs to make the parts seem to pop off the page. *Spot varnishing* is often used to emphasize or enhance certain parts of a printed piece. You will define a spot color that will separate onto its own plate when you print separations.

1 Deselect all artwork. In the Swatches palette, click the New Swatch button.

You cannot preview a spot varnish on-screen, so you will select a color for it that you can see easily.

2 Double-click the swatch, and set the color to 100% Cyan. This way, you can easily see where your varnish is on-screen.

3 For Color Type, choose Spot Color. Name the color **Gloss Varnish**, and click OK.

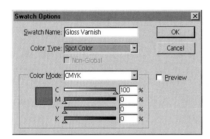

Defining the Gloss Varnish color swatch

Now you'll create a layer for your spot varnish elements. Because the varnish will cover objects on your screen, putting the varnish on its own layer will make it easy to quickly hide and show the varnish plate. Just remember that before you send your job to print, make sure the varnish plate is not hidden, or else it won't print. (Illustrator does not print hidden layers.)

4 Alt/Option-click the New Layer button in the Layers palette. Name the layer **Spot Varnish**.

To make the construction worker on the cover stand out, you will create a spot varnish inside the rectangle that surrounds that part of the photo.

5 Select the rectangle that outlines the construction worker on the cover of the brochure (the upper right side of the upper panel).

6 Copy it and then paste it in front by pressing Ctrl/Command+F.

7 With the copy of the rectangle still selected, in the Layers palette drag the current selection dot from the Artwork layer up to the Spot Varnish layer.

8 With the rectangle still selected, choose Object > Path > Outline Path.

9 Using the direct-selection tool, select the outer path and delete it. The shape now covers only the part of the photograph that falls on the inside of the rectangle and does not cover the black rule.

10 Fill the new shape with the Gloss Varnish color.

11 Choose Window > Show Attributes. In the Attributes palette, select Overprint Fill. This will allow the objects that appear below the varnish to print when separations are made.

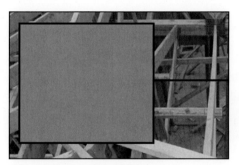

Selecting the Overprint Fill option

Printing tiled sections

When your artwork is larger than what your printer can handle, you can print your artwork in sections, letting you proof the entire piece. The construction brochure you are working on has an Artboard size of 19 inches by 17 inches—a size that even a tabloid printer couldn't handle. Print *tiles* let you print the entire brochure on several sheets, so that you can paste them together to proof the entire piece at once or show the complete piece to your client. Printing tiles manually lets you control exactly how each tile is positioned, and ensures that copy or artwork does not get cut off at the edge of a tiled sheet.

1 First, choose View > Show Page Tiling (you turned it off earlier in the lesson). A gray outline appears, identifying the part of the page that will be sent to your printer. The size of the outline depends on the settings in your Page Setup.

2 Select the page tool. Drag the outline over the part of the brochure you want to print.

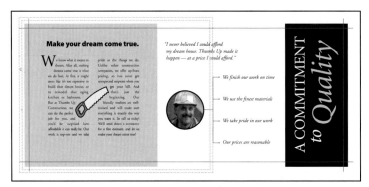

Positioning the Page Tiling outline

3 Print as you normally would. Whatever is inside the outline will print.

4 Repeat steps 2 and 3 until you have printed your entire artwork.

Another way to print large artwork on multiple tiled pages is to use the Tile Imageable Areas option in the Document Setup dialog box. This option divides the imageable area of the document into pseudo pages and prints them all at once, so that you don't have to move the gray outline to print each section.

5 Close your file, and quit Illustrator.

Exploring on your own

Try exploring these techniques to enhance the look and feel of the brochure.

• Use more spot colors. Create your own or use more PANTONE colors. Press Ctrl/Command+Tilde (~) to quickly re-enter the focus of the last-used palette. (This is great when adding multiple PANTONE colors to your Swatches palette.)

• Create a spot varnish for other objects throughout the brochure, such as the round photo on the brochure's bottom panel, the word "Quality," the drop cap, and the saw illustration.

• Using several different text blocks, experiment with word spacing and letterspacing. Make printouts as you go to better see how the spacing is affected.

• Experiment using tabs to align text and to set up tables.

• How about creating a custom die cut for a unique look? Draw the outline for the die cut, put it on its own layer, and set the stroke to overprint.

Lesson 8

8 | Mastering the Pen Tool

By Andrew Faulkner

This lesson teaches the finer details of editing with the pen tool, making detailed shapes and gaining fine control over the shapes of paths for selection and drawing. It covers the use of paths in Adobe Illustrator versus Adobe Photoshop as well as similar functions in each application.

In this lesson, you'll create a still life of a tulip and vase. You'll explore three different methods of drawing in Adobe Illustrator and learn to do the following:

- Draw precision shapes using the pen tool.

- Use a grid and Smart Guides.

- Draw Bézier curves.

- Adjust curved and straight lines.

- Create 3-D effects using the gradient mesh tool.

- Edit curves from smooth to pointed.

- Draw and edit shapes with the pencil tool.

- Edit with the smooth tool.

And you'll learn how to do the following in Adobe Photoshop:

- Drag and drop art from Illustrator into Photoshop.

- Use the pen tool.

- Create shadows and highlights.

This lesson will take about 40 minutes to complete.

If needed, remove the previous lesson folder from your hard drive, and copy the Lesson08 folder onto it.

The first method of drawing that I'll show you involves precision drawing of shapes. I'll walk you through the steps of using the pen tool to draw precise curves and angles, which you can then combine to form distinct shapes and objects. The second method uses the gradient mesh tool to add color and dimension to your artwork. You'll experiment with the world of organic shapes using pen tool outlines and gradient mesh colors.

Finally, you'll see how to bring it all together with Photoshop's superb ability to create subtle highlights and details.

About Bézier curves

Sooner or later, the topic of Bézier curves comes up when talking about Illustrator. That's because they're a very important and versatile feature of the program. They offer almost infinite possibilities with vector (line) art by letting you go beyond straight point-to-point lines.

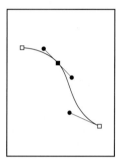

Bézier curve with anchors and handles

There are two central concepts to Bézier curves. *Anchors* are points at which a line is fixed. Selecting and moving an anchor stretches, shrinks, or otherwise adjusts the line that it's on. The other part of a Bézier curve is the *handle*. Handles are visible only when the anchor they're attached to is selected. Selecting and moving a handle stretches, shrinks, or otherwise changes the *curve* between that handle's anchor and the adjacent anchor.

Bézier curves are an intuitive function of Illustrator, so the best way to become skilled with them is to practice. Try drawing the curved line in the example above using the pen tool by clicking and dragging. For each anchor you see without a handle, just click to create an anchor. For each anchor with handles, click the desired location of the anchor and drag in the direction that you want the handle to extend.

Once you've created a Bézier curve, you can use the direct-selection tool to adjust it. First select the anchor, and then select and drag the handles that appear.

You can also convert existing anchors (or *direction points*) to and from Bézier curves. Use the convert-direction-point tool to do this. Clicking a corner point and dragging will turn the corner into a curve; clicking again will change it into a corner again.

Getting started

Before beginning this lesson, restore the default application settings. For instructions, see "Restoring default preferences" on page 3.

In addition, make sure that you have enough memory allocated to complete this lesson. Ideally, Windows computers should have at least 64 MB of RAM. Macintosh computers should have a Preferred Size setting for Photoshop and Illustrator of 40 MB or more, but for this lesson, Photoshop can be set as low as 15 MB. For more information, see "Memory requirements" on page 2.

You'll start the lesson by viewing the final Lesson file to see the tulip artwork that you will create.

1 Restart Adobe Photoshop. Click Cancel to exit the color management dialog box that appears.

2 Choose File > Open, and open the 08End.psd file, located in the Lessons/Lessons08 folder on your hard drive. Click Don't Convert in the Profile Mismatch dialog box. (For information on setting up a color profile, see "Setting up a color profile" on page 182.)

3 When you have finished viewing the file, either leave the End file open on your desktop for reference, or close it without saving changes.

For an illustration of the finished artwork in this lesson, see the color section.

Now you'll open the start file and begin drawing with a template.

4 Restart Adobe Illustrator.

5 Choose File > Open, and open the 08Start.ai file, located in the Lessons/Lessons08 folder on your hard drive.

The file includes four separate layers: a Working layer, where you'll do most of your work; a Stem layer with the basic shape for the tulip stem; a Photo layer with the photograph you'll start from; and a Profile Template layer that contains a template for the basic vase shape. You can show and hide each layer by clicking the eye icons on the left side of the Layers palette.

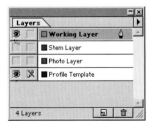

08Start.ai file layers

6 Choose File > Save As, name the file **Tulips.ai**, and click Save. In the Illustrator Format dialog box, for Compatibility, select Illustrator 8.0, and click OK.

7 Press Shift+Tab to hide all palettes but the toolbox; this key combination toggles between hiding and showing. Pressing just Tab also hides or shows the toolbox.

Drawing precise shapes

The first part of this lesson involves tracing the profile of a vase, editing its curves, and reflecting the half shape to create a whole.

I've created a template layer in this file so you can practice using the pen tool, edit your shape, and reflect it to form a silhouette of a vase.

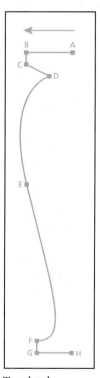

Template layer

Using Smart Guides to draw a vase profile

The Smart Guides feature helps you align objects as you draw them. Rather than zoom in and align lines and points visually, you can refer to the Smart Guides that appear on screen. In the first step of this lesson, you'll use Smart Guides to align the anchor points you make with the anchor points created for you in the template file.

1 Choose View > Smart Guides.

2 Choose View > Zoom In to zoom in on the profile.

3 Select the pen tool in the toolbox (or press the P key on the keyboard), and move the pointer to the starting point of the drawing (point A).

As you use the pen tool to draw the vase profile, the word "anchor" will appear when you move the pen tool over an anchor point. When this guide appears, you know that the pen tool is on top of an anchor point in the template layer I've provided for you.

4 Click point A at the upper right end of the profile to create a starting anchor point for the vase profile.

5 Click points B and C at the top edge of the shape. The Smart Guides align along the horizontal and vertical axis, allowing precise placement of anchor points.

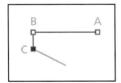

6 Click point D to set an anchor there.

7 Next, Alt/Option-click point D —don't release the mouse button—and drag the pen tool down and to the left. This creates a starting handle for the curved vase body. Release the mouse button.

8 Drag point E down and slightly to the right to create the curve of the vase body, releasing the mouse button when you've positioned the handle so that the curve is close to the template.

To zoom out without changing tools press Alt+Ctrl+spacebar (Windows) or Option+Command+spacebar (Mac OS). To zoom in, press Ctrl/Command+spacebar.

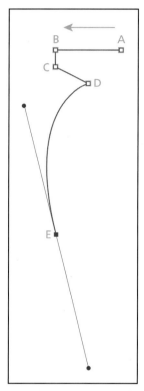

Dragging to create vase curve

9 Click point F, and drag left and up to complete the curve of the main body. Don't worry if the curve doesn't match the template exactly; you'll have a chance to adjust it in a bit.

10 Click point F once with the pen tool to change it to a corner point.

11 Click points G and H to finish the shape. Watch your Smart Guides or hold down the Shift key to ensure that your lines are straight.

12 Ctrl/Command-click away from the path to deselect it, and choose File > Save.

13 If the curve does not match the template precisely, deselect the shape. Then use the direct-selection tool to select point D, E, or F. Selecting a point displays its handle or handles; you can then drag a handle to adjust the point. Continue using the direct-selection tool to adjust the handles until the curve closely resembles the template.

Redirecting points and editing curves

To ensure accurate proportions and symmetry, I drew this profile on a grid. Now you'll change some corner points to smooth points and edit your curves.

1 Zoom in by using the zoom tool to draw a marquee across the upper third of your drawing.

💡 *Use the Navigator palette to zoom and pan your artwork. Dragging the red box pans around in the artwork, and dragging the slider at the bottom zooms in and out.*

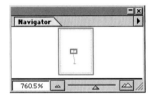

Navigator palette

2 If the anchor points don't appear as hollow red squares, use the direct-selection tool: click away from the line to deselect it, and then click any part of the line (not an anchor) to display the anchor points.

3 Make sure that the pen tool is selected. Then hold down the Alt/Option key to get the convert-direction-point tool. Drag point B straight to the left. This will create a handle and begin a curve between points B and C.

💡 *Pressing Shift as you Alt/Option-drag constrains the handle to 90-degree angles.*

4 Alt/Option-click and drag point C down and slightly to the right until the curve. (See the following illustration.)

5 Fine-tune the curve by Ctrl/Command-clicking it and dragging. To adjust a handle individually, Ctrl/Command-click the handle and drag it. If the handles are no longer selected, use the direct-selection tool, click point B or C, and adjust the handles with that tool.

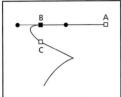

Converting B to a curved corner point　　*Alt/Option-dragging C to adjust curve*　　*Ctrl/Command-dragging to fine-tune curve*

6 Hold down the spacebar to temporarily switch to the hand tool. Drag upward to reposition your artwork so that you can see the base of the vase profile.

7 Alt/Option-click, and drag point F directly to the left to start a curve at the bottom of the vase.

8 Alt/Option-click, and drag point G to the right to finish the other end of the curve.

You now probably have a large curve between points F and G.

9 To tame this curve, hold down the Ctrl/Command key for the direct-selection tool. Drag the left end of each anchor point's direction handles to the right to match the curve shown below. You can also Ctrl/Command-click the middle of the curve and drag to adjust both handles simultaneously.

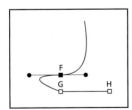
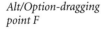
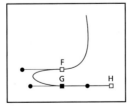
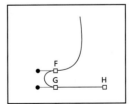

Alt/Option-dragging point F　　*Dragging point G to right*　　*Dragging handles to tame curve*

10 Save your work.

Reflecting and joining your profile using Smart Guides

You should now have half of your vase outline. To complete your vase outline, you'll need to make the other side. You'll do this by *reflecting* a copy of your vase profile and joining the two.

1 Select your profile with the selection tool. Select the reflect tool (press the O key on the keyboard).

2 Position the cursor over point A. Smart Guides highlight your profile and add the word "anchor" to indicate that your cursor is directly over the point.

3 Alt/Option-click point A to display the Reflect dialog box.

4 Select Vertical to reflect the profile along a vertical axis. Click Copy to keep the original profile and create a reflected copy, resulting in both sides of your vase.

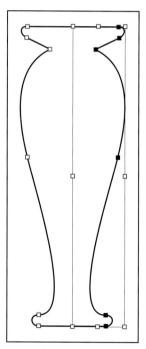

Reflected vase profile

5 Turn off the Smart Guides (Ctrl/Command+U).

6 Use the direct-selection tool to marquee-select the two points at point A. Join the points you selected with the Join command (Object > Path > Join, or Ctrl/Command+J). In the dialog box, select Corner and click OK.

7 Repeat step 6 for point H.

Now that you joined these segments, you'll remove the points where they're connected to ensure a straight line at top and bottom.

8 Press the P key to get the pen tool. Move the cursor over point H until it changes to the delete-anchor-point tool.

9 Click the anchor point on the vase profile at point H to remove it. Repeat for point A.

10 Press Shift+Tab to display the palettes. In the Layers palette, click the eye icon next to the Profile Template layer to hide it.

Adding color with the gradient mesh tool

A good working knowledge of the pen tool is important to make the best use of the gradient mesh tool, which is used in much the same way to give color and dimension to closed shapes.

1 Select your vase outline with the selection tool. In the Color palette, select a CMYK purple swatch to fill the vase profile. Set the Stroke color to None.

2 Deselect the vase (Shift+Ctrl/Command+A).

3 Select the gradient mesh tool (press the U key on the keyboard).

4 In the Colors palette, make sure that the Fill box is selected. Create a light tint of your purple by Shift-dragging the cyan slider to the left to a very light tint of the purple.

The Shift key locks the color's hue. The color you choose here will be the lightest color in the gradient, or the color of the vase's highlight.

5 Click the filled vase with the gradient mesh tool to convert the vase to a gradient mesh object with mesh lines. Click a quarter inside the upper left edge of the vase to add a mesh point—a diamond-shaped anchor point. You'll continue to add highlight points.

(To delete a mesh point and start over, hold down the Alt/Option key and click again on the mesh point you want to remove. Then repeat step 4 to reselect your tint.)

Notice the path-like controls of the gradient mesh.

6 Take some time to experiment with them. Select an anchor point with the gradient mesh tool and adjust its handles to manipulate the shape of the mesh.

7 When you're comfortable with the gradient mesh tool, add more dimension to the vase. Deselect the first mesh, choose a darker tint of purple in the Colors palette, and then click up and to the right of your first highlight point.

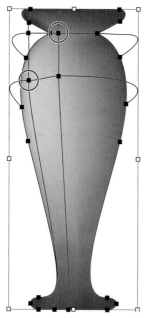

Creating highlight points on the gradient mesh

Now that you have completed the first part of the lesson, you'll lock and hide the artwork, and then create some flowers in the same file.

8 In the Layers palette, double-click the Working layer, and rename it **Vase**.

9 Click the eye icon next to the Vase layer to hide it.

10 Save your file.

Drawing natural shapes with the pen and pencil tools

In this part of the lesson, you'll trace the contour of a tulip from a photo saved on a layer in your file. You can also sample colors from the photo to make your own stylized version of the tulip.

1 In the Layers palette, click the leftmost column next to the Photo layer to show the layer containing the tulip photograph. Click the Lock column (to the right of the eye icon) to lock the layer.

2 Alt/Option-click the New Layer button at the bottom of the Layers palette to create a new layer, and name it **Working**.

3 Using the zoom tool, drag a marquee to zoom in on the red tulip blossom in the center of the photograph.

4 Press D on the keyboard to reset the colors to their defaults (white fill, black stroke). To better see the outlines you'll draw, you can also set your fill to None.

5 With the pen tool, trace the outline of the right front tulip petal with your pen tool. Then lock your shape (Ctrl/Command+2). You'll color the tulip leaves later, but you may want to set your fill to none to see the outlines better.

Photo layer *Detail* *Tracing the front tulip petal*

6 Select the pencil tool and loosely trace the outline of the centermost petal.

Drawing with the pencil tool tends to make less smooth lines than those drawn with the pen tool. You can make the edge of your shape smoother by deleting points or using the smooth tool. You'll try both techniques.

7 Use the selection tool to select the petal you just drew.

8 Position the pointer on the pen tool and drag to select the delete-anchor-tool from the hidden tools.

9 In the image, use the delete-anchor-point tool to click some points on the right side of the shape to remove them. Try removing points in areas where many are grouped together; removing points in these areas helps smooth the line.

Deleting anchor points

Now you'll try using the smooth tool.

10 Position the pointer on the pencil tool in the toolbox, and drag to select the smooth tool from the hidden tools. With the petal still selected, drag over the left edge of your shape using the smooth tool. When you've smoothed the shape enough, use your direct-selection tool to adjust the shape so that it closely matches the photograph.

Using the smooth tool

11 Lock your shape (Ctrl/Command+2).

12 Continue tracing and arranging the remaining petals:

• Draw each petal as if no petals were around it using either the pen or pencil tool.

- When you've finished drawing a petal, arrange it in the front-to-back look that you see in the original flower. Use the Bring Forward command (Object > Arrange > Bring Forward) and the Send Backward command (Object > Arrange > Send Backward) command.

- To avoid confusion, lock your petals (Ctrl/Command+2) as you finish them.

13 Save your file.

Coloring the tulip with the pen tool and gradient mesh tool

You'll work with the tulip shapes you just drew, first unlocking them.

1 Choose Object > Unlock All or press Alt/Ctrl+2 (Windows) or Option+Command+2 (Mac OS).

2 Select all of the petals you just drew.

3 Select the eyedropper tool (press the I key on the keyboard). Click a bright yellow area of the yellow tulip below and to the right of your red tulip. The petal color changes as you sample different shades of yellow in the photograph. Stop when the petals are a bright shade of yellow.

Now that all the petals are the same color, it's hard to discern the individual shapes. Smart Guides can help you with this.

4 Choose View > Smart Guides to display the guides. Move the pointer over the petal shapes and notice that Smart Guides shows you the outline of the petal under the pointer.

5 Deselect the tulip (Shift+Ctrl/Command+A).

6 With the eyedropper tool, select a rich, vibrant red from the tulip photo.

7 Then select the gradient mesh tool, and click the bottom center edge of the first petal you drew. Click again at the bottom edge on either side of your original points to add mesh points. Practice clicking other points on the petal and then removing the mesh point by Alt/Option-clicking it. You can also experiment using multiple colors within the same mesh path (the area between any four mesh points).

8 Try to add several gradient mesh points on each petal, using the right illustration as a guide. This will help fill the petal with the red color you selected, but should leave an organic yellow edge to each petal.

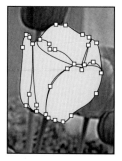 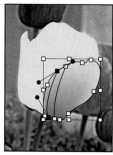 

Petals painted yellow   *Adding sampled color to gradient mesh*   *Selected petal with mesh lines and points*

Gradient meshes work in a similar fashion to the pen tool: each point in a gradient mesh has Bézier curves and handles that let you infinitely adjust the size, shape, and contours of the mesh. You can use the gradient mesh tool to select and move points in the mesh. You can also adjust handles on each point to control the gradients that start from that point. The more meshes you add to an object, the more the possibilities grow.

   For more information on gradient meshes, see Chapter 8 of the Illustrator 8.0 User Guide or "Creating multicolored objects with the gradient mesh tool" in Illustrator 8.0 online Help.

9 When you have finished adding the gradient meshes, select the petals of the tulip and group them (Object > Group).

Arranging your art in the Layers palette

In this part of the lesson, you'll learn about using layers to organize and arrange your artwork.

1 In the Layers palette, rename the Working layer by double-clicking it and naming it **Tulip layer**.

2 Click the eye icon next to the Photo Layer to turn off the layer.

Stem art has already been provided for you. You'll add the tulip petals to it.

3 Click the eye icon next to the Stem layer in your Layers palette. Then Alt/Option-click the Stem layer to select everything on it.

4 In the image, select the stem, and drag it to align the top of stem with the petals you drew earlier.

5 Zoom out so that you can see the stem and tulip.

6 Use the Select All command (Ctrl/Command+A) to select the stem and petals.

7 Select the reflect tool, position the pointer slightly to the left of the selected tulip, and Alt/Option-click. In the dialog box that appears, select Vertical, and click Copy to create a new, reflected tulip.

8 Move the second tulip so that it overlaps the first.

Stem added to tulip   *Reflected and repositioned tulip*

9 In the Layers palette, click the eye icon next to the Vase layer to reveal it. Drag the Vase layer above the Tulip layer to position it there.

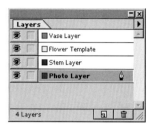

10 In the image, adjust the position of the vase, if necessary.

11 In the Layers palette, delete the Profile Template and Photo layers by dragging them to the Trash button at the bottom of the palette.

12 Save your changes.

Moving paths between Photoshop and Illustrator

To move paths between Illustrator and Photoshop, you can use a number of different methods.

The most basic method is to copy and paste the paths. Copying paths in Illustrator and pasting them in Photoshop displays a dialog box prompting you to paste pixels or paths. Choosing paths adds a new path to Photoshop's Path palette. To copy paths from Photoshop to Illustrator, you must select the paths with the direct-selection tool in Photoshop. A quick way to select all paths using a single path in the Paths palette is to Alt/Option-click the path in the Paths palette. Alt/Option-clicking can save time because the direct-selection tool in Photoshop is hidden beneath the pen tool.

You can drag paths from Illustrator to Photoshop, but not from Photoshop to Illustrator. In Illustrator, press Ctrl/Command while dragging selected paths to Photoshop, to have them appear as paths. If you don't press Ctrl/Command, paths will be rasterized in Photoshop.

To use a mask you've created in Photoshop as a clipping path, for best results, make a path from that mask via the Make Work Path command in the Paths palette. Then copy the path and paste it in Illustrator. The path will retain its smooth, curved corner and combination corner-anchor points.

If you save a Photoshop file with a clipping path as an EPS file, and then open (not place) that file in Illustrator, the clipping path becomes an editable path in Illustrator. However, the path's points will all be straight corner anchor points. (This happens on export from Photoshop.) The detail of these points (how many exist) depends on the flatness setting in the Clipping Path dialog box in Photoshop. A low flatness setting results in more points (and detail); a high number results in fewer points and a polygon-looking mask.

—Ted Alspach

Using the pen tool in Photoshop to create highlights

Now you'll export your Illustrator art to Photoshop—preserving your layers—and create a highlight on the upper right edge of the vase. You'll also add shadows to the flowers and texture to various parts of the image.

1 Choose File > Export, and name your file **Tulips2.psd**, and navigate to the Lessons/Lesson08 folder. For Format, choose Photoshop 5. In the Photoshop Options dialog box, choose RGB for Color Model, select the Screen (72 dpi) resolution, and make sure that Anti-Alias and Write Layers are selected. Click OK.

2 Quit Illustrator.

3 Start Photoshop. Open the Tulips2.psd file that you just created. Notice that all of your Illustrator layers have been preserved.

4 Enlarge the image's canvas by choosing Image > Canvas Size. Specify canvas dimensions of 6 inches wide and 8 inches high. Click OK. You may need to fill the new areas of the canvas with white on the Background layer.

5 In the Layers palette, select the Vase layer. Alt/Option-click the New Layer button at the bottom of the Layers palette to create a new layer, and name it **Vase highlight**. The new layer appears in the palette above the Vase layer.

6 Select the pen tool, and draw a teardrop-shaped highlight on the upper right side of the vase. Adjust the direction points to make a simple teardrop shape.

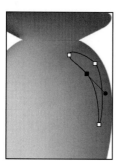

Teardrop shape drawn with pen tool

7 Ctrl/Command-click the path's thumbnail in the Paths palette to make a selection from the path.

8 In the image, fill the shape with white.

9 Deselect the highlight (Ctrl/Command+D). Apply a Gaussian Blur (Filter > Blur > Gaussian Blur) with a radius of 3.3 pixels.

10 In the Layers palette, set the layer opacity to 90% to blend the highlight with the vase behind it.

Transforming paths to add a shadow to the vase

In the final part of the lesson, you'll add a shadow to the vase by creating and transforming a path.

1 In the Layers palette, Alt/Option-click the New Layer button at the bottom of the palette to create a new layer, and name it **Shadow**. Drag the new layer beneath the Vase layer in the palette.

2 Make a selection of the vase by Ctrl/Command-clicking the Vase layer in the Layers palette.

3 Click the Paths palette tab, and select Make Work Path from the palette menu. In the dialog box that appears, enter a tolerance of 0.5. Click OK. This creates a path based on the selection you just made.

4 In the Paths palette, double-click the Work Path and name it **Shadow Path**.

5 Position the pointer on the pen tool in the toolbox, and drag to select the direct-selection tool from the hidden tools. (Or press the A key on the keyboard.) In the image, drag across the entire path to select all the points on that path.

Shadow Path selected

You can now transform the path in the same way that you can transform a layer or part of a layer.

6 Choose Edit > Transform Path > Distort. In the bounding box that appears around the selection, drag the top center point down and to the left as shown in the illustration. Press Enter or Return to apply the transformation.

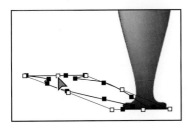

Shadow Path distorted

Now you'll fill the selection with a shadow.

7 In the Paths palette, Ctrl/Command-click the Shadow Path thumbnail to create a selection of that path.

8 Press D on the keyboard to restore the default colors. In the image, drag the linear gradient tool to fill the selection with a black-to-white gradient.

9 Deselect.

Distorted shadow path filled with linear gradient

10 Choose Layer > Flatten Image.

11 Save your file.

12 Close your file, and quit Photoshop.

For greater impact and a more realistic effect, in Photoshop you can fill the shadow's gradient with a color sampled from the vase, and then adjust the color's opacity.

Lesson 9

9 | Two-Color Print Projects

By Andrew Faulkner

Advanced Adobe Photoshop users know that duotones are a powerful way to get a high impact and a sophisticated look from any two-color project. They also know that it can be very tricky to predict how their duotone will print from looking at a black-and-spot color swatch. In this lesson, you transform a color photograph into a complete two-color poster by combining the complementary strengths of Photoshop and Illustrator.

Adobe Photoshop and Adobe Illustrator have different strengths. Both applications do many things well, but usually one application can handle a particular job better than the other. In this lesson you'll use each application where it's best suited.

Photoshop, for example, has powerful features to edit and adjust tones directly in a raster image—so the application is perfect for creating a duotone of the color photograph. Although Photoshop has type tools, Illustrator excels at typography with kerning, size, and scaling adjustments, as well as its ability to set type on a curve.

In this lesson, you'll learn how to do the following in Photoshop:

• Improve the image quality of a color image by converting it to a grayscale and then to a duotone.

• Use layers and curves to selectively improve the image contrast.

• Use spot color channels and clipping paths to apply a PANTONE® spot color to a portion of an image.

• Add a film grain effect.

In Illustrator, you'll learn how to:

• Create type to use as a text highlight in Photoshop.

• Use the Links palette when working in Illustrator and Photoshop side-by-side.

• Learn how to prepare final files for two-color printing.

This lesson will take about 1 hour to complete.

If needed, remove the previous lesson folder from your hard drive, and copy the Lesson09 folder onto it.

About channels

In this lesson, you'll use three types of *channels*. You'll learn to mix color channels to improve the quality of an image. You'll select areas of the image by loading a selection from an alpha channel. And you'll use a spot color channel to add a second color to the image.

A *color channel* in Photoshop stores information for a particular color used in an image; all channels combined form the hues and tones of a complete image. For example, a CMYK image has four color channels: cyan, magenta, yellow, and black. In this lesson, you'll work with the three channels of an RGB image, as well as *spot color channels*, which let you specify additional color separations for printing an image with spot color inks. A third type of channel, an *alpha channel*, stores masks or selections of an image for later use; alpha channels do not print.

You use the Channels palette to view and work with channels.

Getting started

Before beginning this lesson, restore the default application settings for Adobe Photoshop and Adobe Illustrator. For instructions, see "Restoring default preferences" on page 3.

In addition, make sure that you have enough memory allocated to complete this lesson. Ideally, Windows computers should have at least 64 MB of RAM. Macintosh computers should have a Preferred Size setting for Photoshop and Illustrator of 40 MB or more, but for this lesson, Photoshop can be set as low as 15 MB. For more information, see "Memory requirements" on page 2.

You'll start the lesson by viewing the final Lesson file to see the duotone image that you will create.

1 Restart Adobe Illustrator.

2 Choose File > Open, and open the 09End.ai file, located in the Lessons/Lesson09 folder.

3 When you have finished viewing the file, either leave the End file open on your desktop for reference, or close it without saving changes.

Now you'll open the start file for the lesson.

4 Restart Adobe Photoshop. Click Cancel to exit the color management dialog box that appears.

5 Choose File > Open, and open the 09Start.psd file, located in the Lessons/Lesson09 folder on your hard drive. Click Don't Convert in the Profile Mismatch dialog box. (For information on setting up a color profile, see "Setting up a color profile" on page 182.)

6 Save the file as **Poster.psd**.

Improving the image quality

Because this photograph was made using the available fluorescent Metro lights, the subjects are not well lit. The photo has an overall greenish cast, which makes it a good candidate for this duotone project. You'll get rid of the greenish tones in the photograph and replace them with the duotone color.

The background is a bit too busy as well. The eye is distracted by the lights, which are the whitest point in the image. There's also a distracting pole bisecting the image. As a result, the subjects are de-emphasized and the photograph loses some of its impact. You'll adjust the tonality of the image using Curves to lessen the distracting elements.

Adjusting the foreground of your image

Your image currently has one layer. You'll duplicate that so that you can tune the background on one layer and the foreground on the other.

1 Choose Image > Mode > Grayscale to convert your image to grayscale.

2 In the Layers palette, select the Background layer. Choose Duplicate Layer from the Layers palette menu, and name the new layer **Foreground**.

3 Choose Image > Adjust > Curves to open the Curves dialog box. Adjust the foreground layer so that the subjects' faces appear lighter and more even. Start with the sample Curves settings in the following illustration, and experiment until the faces have better tone and contrast. Don't worry about how the background looks; you'll work on that next. Click OK.

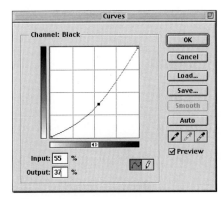

Adjusting the foreground layer

4 Hide the Foreground layer by clicking the eye icon next to it in the Layers palette.

Adjusting the background image

One effective way to reduce a busy background is by reducing the contrast and toning down the white points.

1 In the Layers palette, select the Background.

2 Choose Image > Adjust > Curves. Use the following illustration as a starting point for your adjustments:

• To reduce the background's busy appearance, select the white point (lower left point) and drag it upward.

• To lighten the blacks, select the black point on the curve (in the upper right corner) and drag it down.

- To lighten the gray values, click the center of the curve and drag it down.

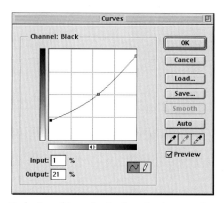

Reducing white point by dragging it upward

In the sample Curves settings, I've reduced the white point of this layer so that the overhead lights in the photo appear as a light gray rather than a bright white. I've also lightened the blacks so that they appear as a dark gray. This effectively reduces the contrast of the layer.

Because the eye is drawn to edges of color fields, reducing the contrast makes the background less distracting. Remember that you're only concerned about the background in this layer.

3 Click OK.

Combining the layers

Your next task is to combine the subjects in the Foreground layer with the toned-down background in the Background layer. To make this easier, the image provided for this lesson contains an alpha channel that you can load to select the subjects.

1 In the Layers palette, select the Foreground layer. Click the eye icon to show it.

2 Choose Select > Load Selection. In the dialog box, choose Foreground from the Channel menu to load a selection that outlines the figures in the foreground. Click OK.

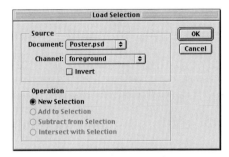

A thumbnail preview of this alpha channel, named Foreground, appears in the Channels palette. Command/Ctrl-click the alpha channel thumbnail to load that selection.

Foreground selection loaded

Next, you'll mask the background part of the Foreground layer so that the Background layer will show through.

3 Choose Layer > Add Layer Mask > Reveal Selection. The foreground and background now appear combined. If desired, use the Curves dialog box (Ctrl/Command+M) again to fine-tune the appearance of each part of the image.

4 When you are satisfied with the results, choose Layer > Flatten to flatten your image.

5 Save your file as **Duo2.psd**.

Adding grain texture to your image

Now that the levels and contrast have improved, you'll add a grainy texture to give the image a traditional black-and-white photo look.

1 Choose Filter > Texture > Grain.

2 Set the Intensity to 20 and Contrast to 50. For Grain Type, choose Regular. Click OK.

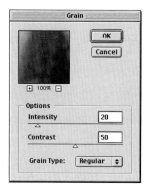

Creating a duotone

Next, you'll create the duotone image you will use in the poster. In this case, you'll make a duotone of black and PANTONE® 485.

1 Choose Image > Mode > Grayscale. Click OK to discard the color information. Before you can convert your image to a duotone, you must first covert it to a grayscale.

2 Choose Image > Mode > Duotone.

3 In the Duotone Options dialog box, for Type, choose Duotone. Click Load, and locate the PANTONE® Duotones folder at the following path: Adobe Photoshop 5.5/Goodies/Adobe Photoshop Only/Duotone Presets/Duotone. Click Open.

4 Select Red 485 bl 2 to create a red-toned duotone. Try other preset options, such as 327 aqua (50%) bl1. Photoshop previews the photograph with the color combination of each preset you load. Click OK.

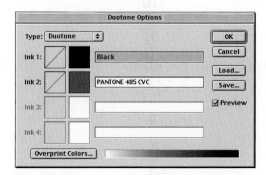

Red 485b12 duotone curves loaded

Now you need to save your work as an EPS file so that you can place it in Illustrator when you're ready to assemble the poster.

5 Choose File > Save a Copy. For Format, choose Photoshop EPS. Name the file **Duo2.eps**. Click OK. In the EPS Options dialog box, accept the default options.

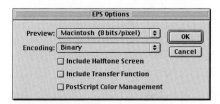

Default EPS options

6 Save the file.

Preparing to add a spot color

Spot colors, also called *custom colors,* are premixed inks that are used instead of, or in addition to, the cyan, magenta, yellow, and black process color inks. Each spot color requires its own color separation or printing plate. Graphic designers use spot colors to specify colors that would be difficult or impossible to achieve by combining the four process inks.

For added impact, you'll use a spot color to highlight the saxophone in the image. This task presents a unique challenge. The spot color and the duotone can't be saved in the same file. The EPS file format supports duotones, but not spot colors. The DCS (Desktop Color Separations) supports spot colors—the only format that does other than native Photoshop files—but does not support duotones. A CMYK image is not a viable option because this is a two-color project.

The solution is to create and save the saxophone in a separate DCS file, and then combine the spot color and duotone in Illustrator. The combination will highlight the saxophone as a bright red element in the composition.

This time, you'll use a preset path to select part of the image to which you'll add the spot color.

1 Reopen the Duo2.psd file, located in the Lessons/Lesson09 folder. Save the Duo2.psd file you've been working on as **Sax.psd**.

You'll want to be working with a grayscale image this time.

2 Choose Image > Mode > Grayscale to convert the image to grayscale. Click OK to discard the color information.

3 In the Channels palette, choose New Spot Channel from the palette menu.

4 In the New Spot Channel dialog box, click the color box; then click Custom, and choose PANTONE 485.

*Type **485** quickly to move the selection to PANTONE 485.*

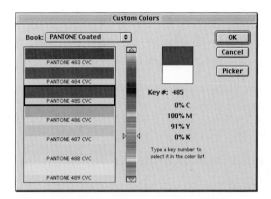

5 In the New Spot Channel dialog box, enter 100% for Solidity. The Solidity setting simulates on-screen the ink solidity of the printed spot color, but has no effect on the printed output. Inks range from transparent (0% solidity) to opaque (100% solidity).

6 Click OK to create the spot color channel. A new spot color channel named PANTONE 485 CVC is added to the Channels palette.

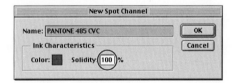

7 Save your changes.

Adding a spot color

You can add a spot color to selected areas of an image in different ways with varying effects. For example, you can apply a spot color to part of a grayscale image so that the selection prints in the spot color rather than in the base ink. Because spot colors in Photoshop print on top of a fully composited image, you also may want to lighten or remove the base color in an image (in this case, black) when adding spot color to it.

In this part of the lesson, you'll set up the saxophone to print as a spot color. Then you'll mix the spot color and black using Curves.

You can also use spot color to add solid and screened blocks of color to an image. By screening the spot color, you can create the effect of adding a brighter, more saturated color to the printed piece.

1 Make sure that white is set as the background color. (Press the D key to switch the foreground and background colors to black and white, respectively.)

2 Select the saxophone by dragging the saxophone path to the Load Path as Selection button at the bottom of the Paths palette.

The lesson file included this premade selection, saved as an alpha channel.

3 In the Channels palette, make sure that the Black channel is selected. Choose Edit > Copy to copy the selection from the image.

4 In the Channels palette, select the PANTONE 485 CVC channel. Because this is a spot color channel, anything put in this channel will appear in the PANTONE 485 CVC color.

5 Choose Edit > Paste to paste the saxophone selection into the spot color channel. Don't deselect yet!

6 Save your changes.

Adding definition to your colored object

Now you have a flat area of color in your saxophone selection. You'll take it one step further by adding back some definition and dimension into the area.

To do this, you'll mix the spot and black color behind the saxophone using the Curves tool, so that the saxophone not only blends well with the image, but has greater dimension.

1 With the Black channel selected, choose Image > Adjust > Curves.

2 Use the following Curves settings as a guide to lighten the saxophone. You want to lighten the channel, reducing the amount of black ink that will print in the area of the saxophone. (If you lose your selection, drag the saxophone path to the Load Path as Selection button at the bottom of the Paths palette.)

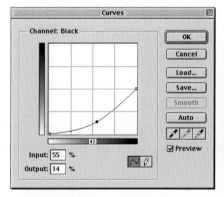

Reducing the black ink in the saxophone

To isolate the saxophone, you'll create a clipping path. That is, you'll mask the rest of the image so that the duotone you created earlier will be visible. (You'll place the duotone and spot color files on top of each other.) Certain file formats support *clipping paths*, which function as masks for applications such as Illustrator.

3 Create a clipping path around the saxophone by selecting the Paths palette, and choose Clipping Path from the palette menu. In the Clipping Path dialog box, choose Saxophone for Path. Leave the Flatness field blank; a value won't be obvious in Photoshop. Click OK.

Creating a clipping path

4 Choose File > Save As, rename the file **Sax**, and for Format, choose Photoshop DCS 2.0 file. Photoshop automatically appends *asc.eps* (Windows) or *.eps* (Mac OS) to the file name. In the dialog box that appears, leave the options set to their defaults, and click OK.

5 Keep Photoshop open as you switch to Illustrator. You'll work more in Photoshop later in the lesson.

> ### File size in Photoshop and Illustrator
>
> *When you bring a high-resolution Photoshop file into Illustrator, it's important to be aware of the size of your resulting Illustrator file.*
>
> *The size of your artwork can affect the speed in which you work with it. The smaller the file, the faster your computer can deal with it. There are two types of size to be concerned about: file size (the size of the document in bytes) and physical size (the dimensions of the document). File size directly affects the speed at which you can work with a document; physical size may or may not affect saving the file as well as using it within other applications.*
>
> *In Photoshop, file size is based on the number of pixels in the document. A common misconception is that if a document has 10 layers, it is 10 times the size of the original, 1-layer document. Instead, the size only increases by the number of pixels that are actually used on a layer. Areas of flat color in a layer use less room than if each pixel were a different color. Type layers (nonrendered) take up even less space. The status bar at the bottom of the document window shows the base size of the document (if the image were flattened), and the expanded size of the document including additional space taken up by additional layers.*
>
> *In Illustrator, file size is based on the number of paths and text objects added to the size of any embedded files in the Illustrator document. In addition, the complexity (number of points and points with control handles) and fill types of paths and amount of text per text object also relate to file size and speed. For example, 10 gradient mesh objects with hundreds of nodes each produce a much larger Illustrator document than 10 rectangles with a black fill.*
>
> *Both applications start to slow down at a certain threshold file size. This threshold depends on the speed of your system, the amount of RAM available to the applications, and a few other variables. A good rule of thumb for Photoshop is that an image that fits on your screen at 100% is within the threshold. For Illustrator, any document with fewer than 500 solid color paths is within the threshold. Adding layers to Photoshop documents and adding more or complex objects to Illustrator is likely to start slowing you down.*
>
> *Physical size in Photoshop is determined by the number of pixels divided by the image resolution. You can view the physical size of a Photoshop document at any time by clicking the status bar's File Size at the bottom left of the document window. To view the size in numbers (instead of the default picture), Alt/Option-click the status bar's File Size. In Illustrator, physical size is determined by the area taken up by all objects in the document (excluding guides and hidden-by-mask objects). Illustrator calls this the document "bounding box." Saving a document with a large physical size that has a preview (such as an EPS) takes longer than saving a smaller document, because the preview that is being created is larger.*
>
> —Ted Alspach

Completing your poster in Illustrator

To complete the poster, you'll make a shadow for type using type on a path in Illustrator, and paste the type into the Photoshop file. As a final step, you will reimport the Photoshop file into Illustrator to print your work.

Combining the spot-color and duotone images

First you will combine the spot-color saxophone image and duotone DCS file in Illustrator, in an Illustrator file that I have prepared for you. The Illustrator file already contains type on a path.

1 In Adobe Illustrator, open the 09Start.ai file, located in the Lessons/Lesson09 folder on your hard drive.

2 Save the file as **Poster.ai**. For Compatibility, choose Illustrator 8.0, and click OK.

3 In the Layers palette, notice that the type on a path is on a layer called Curved Type, and the type on the black bar is on a layer called Bottom Bar. Select the Working layer.

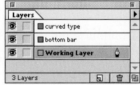

09Start.ai file and its layers

4 Choose View > Hide Page Tiling.

5 With the Working layer selected, choose File > Place, and select and place the Duo.eps file, located in the Lessons/Lesson09 folder on your hard drive.

6 Position the photo so that the left and right sides align with the black bar containing the Paris Metro text. The black bar should overlap the bottom edge of the photograph.

Positioning the Duo.eps file

7 Repeat step 3, choosing the Sax.asc.eps (Windows) or Sax.eps (Mac OS) file you created earlier. You need to line up the saxophone in the two images.

8 Select both saxophones, and use the Align palette (Window > Show Align) to first align them vertically, and then horizontally.

Aligning vertically   *Aligning horizontally*

9 Lock them in this arrangement by choosing Object > Group to group the two images.

10 Arrange the images and the curvy type so that the type aligns with the saxophone, as shown in the following illustration.

Curvy type aligned with saxophone

11 Save your work so far.

To make the curvy type more readable against the photo, you'll copy the Illustrator type into the Photoshop file to create a white shadow (or halo).

12 Select the three lines of curvy type, and copy them to the Clipboard.

💡 *To select the curvy type easily, click the blank square next to the Bottom Bar and Working Layer names in the Layers palette to lock them and make them unselectable. A pencil icon with a red line through it indicates that the layer is locked.*

13 Keep Illustrator open.

Creating shadow text in Photoshop

Now you will copy and paste into your Photoshop file to make a shadow.

1 In Photoshop, open the Duo2.eps file, located in the Lessons/Lesson09 folder. Paste the type you copied from Illustrator into the Photoshop image, selecting the Paste as Pixels option.

2 Double-click the new layer on which the type was pasted, and name it **Saxophone text**.

3 Select the new layer, and use the move tool to align the text with the saxophone.

To create the white type halo, you first need to make the type white.

4 Press D on the keyboard to set the foreground color to white. In the Layers palette, select the Preserve Transparency option, and then press Alt+Backspace (Windows) or Option+Delete (Mac OS) to fill the Saxophone text layer with white.

Saxophone text filled with white

5 With the Saxophone Text layer selected in the Layers palette, deselect the Preserve Transparency option.

6 Choose > Filter > Blur > Gaussian Blur. Set the radius to 2.0 pixels. Click OK.

7 In the Layers palette, choose the Hard Light mode. This helps to mix the halo with the image.

8 To make the halo brighter, duplicate the Saxophone Text layer by selecting it and choosing Duplicate Layer from the Layers palette menu. Click OK.

9 Flatten your image by choosing Flatten Image from the Layers palette menu.

Brightened halo, flattened layers

10 Select File > Save As, and name your file **Duo2.eps** to replace the file you saved earlier.

Preparing final files for printing

Now that you have created your final duotone artwork, you can finalize your Illustrator file. You'll update and align your duotone, draw crop marks, and prepare your image for final printing.

1 In Illustrator, open the Links palette if it is not already open by choosing Window > Show Links. In the Links palette, check that all layers are unlocked.

2 Select your duotone's thumbnail, and choose Update Link from the Links palette menu. (If you closed and reopened the file, the links will already be updated.)

3 Position the image so that white shadow is just below and to the right of black and red text.

💡 *To create the drop shadow easily, position the image so that the shadow type is directly behind the black-and-red type. Then press the arrow keys to offset the image down and to the right.*

Offset white shadow text

4 Select the rectangle tool, and Alt/Option-click the center of the page. Enter 11.75 inches for Width and 9 inches for Height in the dialog box. Don't worry about the fill and stroke.

5 With the selection tool, center the box on your poster. With the box selected, choose Object > Crop Marks > Make. Crop marks appear that define the area inside the rectangle you just made.

Making sure that two-color files print properly

When designing two-color projects, it is important to make sure that your final art separates into only two plates (in this case, black and PMS 485).

Some of the options in the Separation Setup dialog box can vary depending on your output device. Use these settings as a guide, but always consult your print shop technician on the best settings for the output device on which your artwork will be printed.

1 Choose File > Separation Setup or File > Print, and click the Separation Setup button to display the Separation Setup dialog box.

2 If the options are dimmed, select a PPD file by clicking Open PPD and choosing the PPD file for your output device. If necessary, get the correct PPD from your print technician.

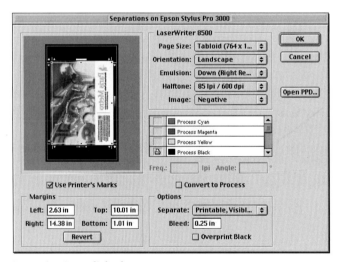

Separation Setup dialog box

The layout is best printed on tabloid-sized paper or film.

3 For Orientation, choose Landscape. For Page Size, choose 11x17.

4 Choose Emulsion and Image options:

• If you're outputting to a filmsetter, set the Emulsion option to Down and the Image option to Negative. (Verify the setting with your print shop technician.)

• If you're sending to an imagesetter, set Emulsion to Up and Image to Positive.

5 In the scrolling list of separations, check that only the Black and PANTONE 485 separations have a printer icon next to them (indicating that the separation contains information that needs to be printed).

If the other process colors show printer icons, one of your images may be CMYK or RGB. In Photoshop, open the Sax.eps and Duo2.eps files, and make sure they are in grayscale mode and duotone mode, respectively.

6 Set these remaining separation options:

• Select Use Printer's Marks.

• Deselect Convert to Process. If this option is selected, your PANTONE 485 CVC color will be converted to print in magenta and yellow inks.

• Leave the margins set to their default.

• For Separate, choose Printable, Visible.

• Set the Bleed to 0.25 inches.

• Deselect Overprint Black.

7 Click OK.

8 Save the file.

You've completed the lesson. You are now ready to output your two-color files as the finished poster.

9 Close the file, and quit Illustrator and Photoshop.

Lesson 10

10 | Creating an Animated Web Ad Banner

By Mordy Golding

Turn on the **light...**
...to a new **lôôk** at home
custom lampshades
CLICK HERE

Using Adobe Illustrator as a starting point when creating Web graphics means that you can always go backward without losing data—a capability you don't always have in a pixel-based program— and that's especially important when creating an ad banner campaign for fussy clients. Adobe Illustrator and Adobe ImageReady work seamlessly with each other to make preparing your art for the Web as easy as can be.

In this lesson, you will create a standard 468-pixel by 60-pixel animated ad banner for a custom lampshade company, and prepare it to conform with required specifications for placement on a Web site. You'll learn how to do the following:

• Use blends and layers to lay the groundwork for an animation.

• Import Illustrator art into ImageReady, without losing layer information.

• Understand how animation and color affect file size.

• Optimize an image to fit file size requirements.

This lesson will take about 1 hour to complete.

If needed, remove the previous lesson folder from your hard drive, and copy the Lesson10 folder onto it.

Getting started

Before beginning this lesson, restore the default application settings for Adobe Photoshop and Adobe Illustrator. For instructions, see "Restoring default preferences" on page 3.

You'll start the lesson by viewing the final Lesson file to see the Web banner image that you will create.

1 Start Adobe ImageReady 2.0.

2 Choose File > Open, and open the 10End.psd file, located in the Lessons/Lesson10 folder on your hard drive.

3 Click the Play button in the Animation palette to see the completed file you will create.

4 When you have finished viewing the file, either leave the End file open on your desktop for reference, or close it without saving changes.

For an illustration of the finished artwork for this lesson, see the color section.

To start the lesson, you'll open an existing art file in Illustrator.

5 Start Adobe Illustrator 8.0.

6 Choose File > Open, and open the 10Start.ai file, located in the Lessons/Lesson10 folder on your hard drive.

7 Choose File > Save As, name the file **Banner.ai,** and click Save. In the Illustrator Format dialog box, select version 8.0 of Illustrator and click OK.

Setting up your document

On the Web, everything is measured in pixels. You will use the points measurement system in Illustrator, because monitors typically display 72 pixels per inch, and there are also 72 points in an inch.

1 Choose File > Preferences > Units & Undo.

2 Set General Units to Points. Click OK.

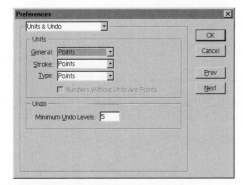

The Units & Undo Preferences dialog box

> #### Using the Adobe Illustrator Startup file
>
> *The Adobe Illustrator Startup file contains information that Illustrator uses each time a new document is created. By modifying this file, you can change the behavior of Illustrator in a much more dramatic way than you can using Preferences options.*
>
> *The Adobe Illustrator Startup file is located in your Plug-ins folder, inside the Adobe Illustrator application folder. You can open the file by double-clicking it, or through the Open dialog box. Once it's open, changes made to this document will be reflected in new documents (not existing ones) that you create. You can modify the following options in the Startup file to alter how documents behave:*
>
> *• Window size and placement. This lets you create each new document with a specific-sized window. For instance, you could set up a window that doesn't extend behind the column of palettes on the right edge of your monitor.*
>
> *• Zoom level. I like to start with the zoom level set to 100%. Many like the Fit in Window zoom option.*
>
> *• Document Setup options. The most important of these is Page Size, but all document setup options that are modified in the Startup file affect new documents.*
>
> *• Swatches. These include the colors, gradients, and patterns that appear with new documents you create.*
>
> *• Brushes. While the set of brushes that ships with Illustrator is great for getting started, you'll probably want to set this up with the brushes that you use all the time.*
>
> *• Actions. Instead of loading a set of actions each time you run Illustrator, just load them in the Startup file and save. They'll be available for each new document.*
>
> ——Ted Alspach

Designing your banner

A client's job is to make changes, or so it seems. The strength of designing your banners in Illustrator lies in the ability to make changes easily, without worrying about resolution issues.

One of the hardest things about designing Web banners is working within the required parameters specified by the Web sites on which the banners appear. Obviously, no one wants a site that takes years to download, so site designers do not let Web banners exceed 10K or 11K. The art of designing Web banners lies in the designer's ability to create eye-catching and effective banners that fit within the required file size.

When designing ad banners, the two most important factors to keep in mind are number of colors and animation. The fewer colors you have, the more you can do with animation. Of course, the less you have in the way of animation, the more room you have to design with more color.

Adding text to the banner

To begin, you will add the words *click here* to the banner.

1 Select the Custom Lampshades layer.

2 Using the type tool, type the words **CLICK HERE**. Set the font to Myriad Bold and the type size to 10 point. (Press Ctrl/Command+T to display the Paragraph palette.)

3 Rotate the text 90°, and position the text along the right side of the banner.

Positioning the words click here

4 To make the words stand out, draw a rectangle around the text, and give a fill of black and a stroke of None. (You won't be able to see the text.)

5 With the black rectangle selected, press Shift+Ctrl/Command+Left Bracket ([) to send it to the back.

6 Select the text (you'll be able to see the selected path), and apply a fill of white and a stroke of None.

Click here *in its finished state*

Using the Web-safe color palette

You are now ready to add color to your banner. To ensure that these colors will appear as specified on the Web, you will select colors from Illustrator's Web-safe color palette.

💡 *When you use Web-safe colors, you avoid the problem of using colors that may not be available on others' computer screens. If colors are unavailable, the computer screen tries to simulate them by dithering or mixing colors. Often, dithered colors produce nasty-looking moiré patterns.*

1 Choose Window > Swatch Libraries > Web.

2 In the Layers palette, select the Custom Lampshades logo layer.

3 Using the rectangle tool, click once at the upper left corner of the banner to open the Rectangle dialog box. For Width, enter **468**; for Height, enter **60**, and click OK. This will be the background of the banner.

Background rectangle created, filled and sent to back

4 Using the Web Swatch palette, select the first bright yellow color (R=255, G=255, B=0) for the rectangle's fill.

5 Press Shift+Ctrl/Command+Left Bracket ([) to send the rectangle to the back.

6 If necessary, position the rectangle so that it overlaps the banner.

The design calls for the banner to appear as though someone turned on a light. To achieve this, the banner will have a black background that will turn yellow when the chain is pulled. To keep the banner visually appealing and the logo visible at all times, the background behind the logo will always be yellow. For that effect, you will create a small gradation from yellow.

7 Draw a rectangle that covers the left two-thirds of the banner (285 points by 60 points), as shown in the following illustration. Fill it with 100% black.

Adding the black rectangle

8 Now draw a rectangle 6 points wide by 60 points tall. Align it next to the yellow rectangle, where the large black rectangle ends. Fill it with 100% black and no stroke.

9 Using the direct-selection tool, hold down Shift+Alt/Option, and drag a copy of the small black rectangle to the yellow rectangle, aligning it next to the logo. (See the following illustration for the placement.)

10 With the new rectangle still selected, press the I key to switch to the eyedropper tool, and click anywhere on the yellow background rectangle to make the new rectangle the same color.

11 With the selection tool, Shift-click to select both the small black rectangle and the small yellow rectangle.

Selecting the two rectangles to make the blend

12 Choose Object > Blends > Make. With the blend still selected, choose Object > Blends > Blend Options. For Spacing, choose Specified Steps, enter **10**, and click OK.

Using blends when creating elements for the Web is better than using gradients, because you can specify the number of steps a blend uses. A gradient uses as many color steps as it can to assure smooth color. On-screen, however, you may need only a small amount of steps to achieve what looks like a smooth color transition. Using blends, you can specify steps, see how smooth the blend appears, and then go back and make adjustments to the number of steps as needed—thus reducing the number of colors used in the art.

Adding a memorable element

You'll design one more thing to complete the artwork. To add that special touch, you will make the lamp in the logo appear to turn on when the animation has finished.

1 Choose View > Smart Guides. Using the rectangle tool, draw a box that begins directly under the lampshade and extends down to the bottom of the banner (it will snap to the border). Fill it with white and a stroke of None.

Drawing a rectangle for the light glow

2 Press the E key to switch to the free transform tool.

3 Click the lower left handle, and hold down the mouse button without releasing it.

4 Press Shift+Alt+Ctrl (Windows) or Shift+Option+Command (Mac OS), and drag toward the left. Notice that both bottom corners of the box extend in opposite directions. Release the mouse button.

Shaped light glow positioned behind letters

5 Press Ctrl/Command+Left Bracket ([ ) as needed to position the light beam behind the letters.

Specifying layers and exporting the artwork

You have now created all the art you need for your banner in Illustrator. Before exporting the artwork to ImageReady, you will place each art element on its own layer, so that you can keep control over the artwork and work with it easily.

1 In the Layers palette, create a new layer by clicking the New Layer button in the Layers palette and dragging it to the bottom of the list.

2 Double-click the new layer to open the Layer Options dialog box. Rename the layer **Yellow Background**, and click OK.

💡 *Alt/Option-click the New Layer button at the bottom of the Layers palette to create a new layer and display the Layer Options dialog box in one step.*

3 Using the selection tool, select the yellow rectangle that makes up the background of the banner.

4 In the Layers palette, to the far right of the Custom Lampshades Logo layer, notice the small square next to the pen icon. Drag the small square to the Yellow Background layer, to move the selected artwork to that layer.

Dragging square in Layers palette to move yellow rectangle in artwork

5 Create a new layer, and name it **Lamp Light for Logo**.

6 In the image, select the shape you created for the logo's light.

7 In the Layers palette, drag the small square, indicating the selection, to its new layer.

8 Create a new layer and name it **Black Background**.

9 In the image, select the black rectangle and the blend you created; in the Layers palette, drag the small square, indicating the selection, to the Black background layer.

10 Adjust the layer order, if necessary, according to the following illustration.

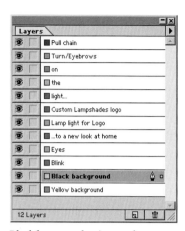

Black box moved to its own layer

Now you'll export the file for use in ImageReady.

11 Save your changes.

12 Choose File > Export. Name the file **Banner.psd**, and for Format, choose Photoshop 5. Click OK. In the Photoshop Options dialog box, choose RGB for the Color Model to RGB and Screen for Resolution. Select both Anti-Alias and Write Layers. Click OK.

Photoshop Option dialog box

13 Quit Adobe Illustrator.

Creating the animation and adding effects

You are now ready to begin animating your banner in ImageReady.

Adding color effects

You will start by opening the layered Photoshop file that you exported from Illustrator and adding some color effects.

1 Start Adobe ImageReady.

2 Choose File > Open. Select the **Banner.psd** file you just exported from Illustrator.

3 In the Layers palette, Alt/Option-click the eye icon next to the Yellow Background layer to hide all but that layer. (Expand the palette to view all layers.)

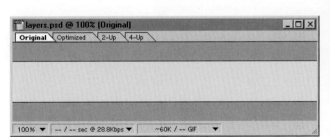
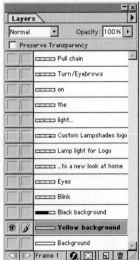

All layers but Yellow Background hidden

4 Now click the eye icon column next to these layers to turn them on: Pull Chain, Turn/Eyebrows, Custom Lampshades Logo, Eyes, and Black Background.

5 In the Layers palette, select the Pull Chain layer. Click the Layer Effect button at the bottom of the palette to add a Color Fill effect to the layer. In the Color Fill palette, select the color white.

6 Repeat step 5 for the Turn/Eyebrows and the Eyes layers.

Adding some action

Next, you will position the pull chain, to make it look as if it is turning on the light. The chain will start in the up position when the banner is dark, and then look as if it were pulled down when the banner lights up.

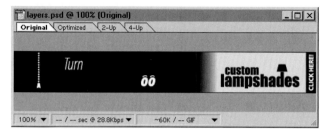

Pull chain in down position

1 In the Layers palette, select the Pull Chain layer. In the image, use the move tool and Shift-drag the chain up so that it comes only about halfway down the height of the banner.

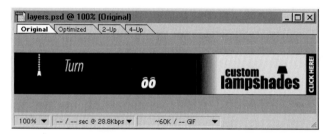

Pull chain in up position

Now you will create a series of duplicate frames, turning on layers and painting their artwork white.

2 In the Animation palette, click the Duplicate Current Frame button. In the Layers palette, select the On layer. Click the Layer Effect button to add a Color Fill effect to the layer. In the Color Fill palette, select the color white.

3 Repeat step 8 for the layers The and Light.

For visual interest, you will make the *O*'s that look like eyes in the word *look*, blink.

Frame 4 artwork, Animation palette, and Layers palette

4 In the Animation palette, click the Duplicate Current Frame button. In the Layers palette, turn off the Eyes layer. Turn on the Blink layer, click the Layer Effect button to add a Color Fill effect to the layer, and in the Color Fill palette, select the color white.

5 In the Animation palette, click the Duplicate Current Frame button. In the Layers palette, turn off the Blink layer. Turn on the Eyes layer, click the Layer Effect button to add a Color Fill effect to the layer, and in the Color Fill palette, select the color white.

6 Repeat steps 4 and 5. This will make the eyes blink twice.

Blinking O's

Now you'll gradually show text as the pull chain is lowered.

7 In the Animation palette, click the Duplicate Current Frame button. In the Layers palette, turn off the Black Background layer. Turn on the To a New Look at Home layer, click the Layer Effect button to add a Color Fill effect to the layer, and in the Color Fill palette, select the color white.

8 In the Layers palette, turn off the Color Fill effects for all of the visible layers by clicking the eye icon next to each layer's Effects icon.

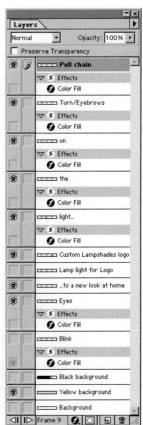

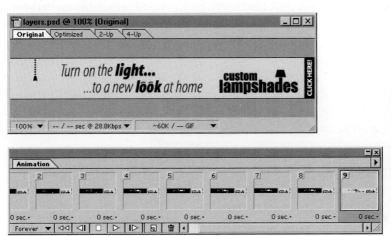

Banner in frame 9

You will move the pull chain to its down position, so that when the banner is animated, it will look as if someone pulled the chain.

9 In the Layers palette, select the Pull Chain layer. In the image, use the move tool and Shift-drag the chain down to position it near the bottom of the banner.

Positioning the pull chain

Now you will move the pull chain back up, to make it appear to pop up after being pulled.

10 In the Animation palette, click the Duplicate Current Frame button. In the image, use the move tool and Shift-drag the chain halfway up the height of the banner.

Pull chain moved to Up position

For added effect, you will make the O's blink again.

11 In the Animation palette, click the Duplicate Current Frame button. In the Layers palette, turn off the Eyes layer. Turn on the Blink layer. (If the Color Fill effect is visible for the Blink layer, turn it off.)

12 In the Animation palette, click the Duplicate Current Frame button. In the Layers palette, turn off the Blink layer. Turn on the Eyes layer.

Blinking O's

13 To make the eyes appear to blink twice, repeat steps 11 and 12.

Turning on the lights

As a final touch, you will now make the light in the logo turn on.

1 In the Animation palette, click the Duplicate Current Frame button. In the Layers palette, turn on the Lamp Light for Logo layer.

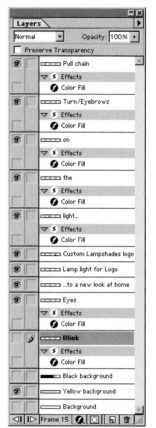

Logo with lamp glowing with light

As an added effect, you will now make the word *Light* fade in as it appears just before the light goes on in the banner.

2 In the Animation palette, select frame 3. Choose Tween from the Animation palette menu. Select All Layers, and for Tween with, choose Next Frame. For Frames to Add, enter **5,** and click OK.

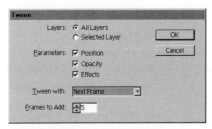

Tween dialog box

3 To view your animation, click the Play button at the bottom of the Animation palette.

4 Save your changes.

Setting the animation's timing

The animation moves much too fast and does not seem right. Timing, as they say, is everything.

For your animation to appear smooth and realistic, you must adjust the time or duration for each frame.

1 In the Animation palette, select the first frame. Click directly beneath the frame where 0 sec appears to display the Duration pop-up menu. Choose 0.1 Seconds from the pop-up menu.

Setting the timing duration for frame 1

2 Repeat step 1 for frames 2 and 3.

3 Now select frame 9. Repeat step 1, changing the duration to 0.5 seconds.

4 Continue to select frames and change their duration using the pop-up menu, as follows:

• Change the duration of frames 10, 11, and 12 to 0.1 seconds. This makes the eyes blink twice in rapid succession.

Shift-click frames in the Animation palette to select multiple frames.

• Change the duration of frame 13 to 0.5 seconds. This is the delay just before the light goes on.

• Change the duration of frame 1 to 0.2 seconds.

• Change the duration of frame 15 to 0.5 seconds.

• Change the duration of frame 16, 17, and 18 to 0.1 seconds. Again, these are the eyes blinking.

• Set the duration of frame 19 to 0.2 seconds.

5 As a final step, set the duration of frame 20 to 2 seconds. This lets the animation pause a bit before it starts again.

Animation palette showing the time duration of each frame

6 Now press the Play button and watch the animation.

Notice how it moves logically, and pauses when it has finished before looping again.

Optimizing and exporting the banner

As a final step before exporting your banner, you will optimize your file. To see how the file will look when optimized, you will preview several settings to see how each affects the banner's look. You can then decide to adjust your banner accordingly to which looks the best at the required file size. Remember that most sites limit banners to a file size no larger than 10K.

1 In the document window, click the 4-Up tab at the top of the window. This window lets you compare different settings, so that you can choose the best-looking banner at the smallest file size.

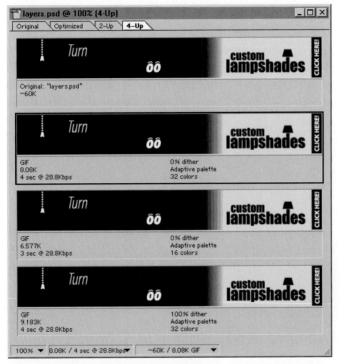

Previewing the artwork in the 4-Up window

2 With the second frame from the top selected in the Optimize palette, select these settings:

- Choose GIF with a Lossy setting of 0.

- Choose Adaptive from the pop-up menu, and set the number of colors to 64.

- Set the Dither to 0%.

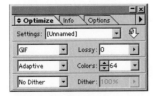

Optimize palette

3 Choose File > Save Optimized, name your banner **Banner_final.psd,** and click Save.

Experiment with the color setting to get the best-looking banner within the 10K file size limit. If you can't get the banner to look the way you want, you may have to remove some frames (for example, the blinking eyes) to allow for more colors and a more attractive result.

As an alternative, ImageReady also lets you set the file size. ImageReady then removes color and specifies the dither and loss amount needed to achieve the specified file size. Remember that this does not necessarily mean the banner will look great when it's done. Again, you must experiment and compromise with animation and colors to get the best-looking banner at the file size you need.

Now preview how ImageReady would optimize the file.

4 From the Optimize palette menu, choose Optimize to File Size.

5 Select Start with Current Settings. Enter the desired file size, and click OK.

Optimize to File Size dialog box

6 If desired, repeat step 3 to save your changes, either renaming the file or replacing the file you already saved.

7 Close the file, and quit ImageReady.

You've completed the lesson.

Exploring on your own

Now that you've gone through the steps of creating a Web banner, try exploring other techniques that will enhance the look and feel of the banner.

• Try using more colors in your banners. Keep in mind that the more colors you use, the less animation you can have.

• Explore how you can make subtle changes in an animation without sacrificing file size. The number of frames in an animated banner does not necessarily translate into larger file size. For example, a 30-frame banner could have only a small area that animates, and a 3-frame could have the entire artwork change.

• Work with the time duration of each frame to better control your animations. Remember that people viewing your ad may not read text at the same speed you do. Experiment with the timing to get a smooth feel across the board.

Lesson 11

11 | Animating With Photoshop, Illustrator, and After Effects

By dåv rauch

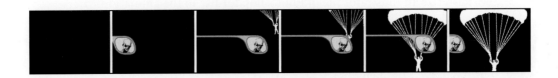

In this project you'll re-create graphics and animation used in the video intro-duction to the Masters of Visual Effects tape series. The Masters tape series has a decidedly retro "Secret Agent" aesthetic. It was created using Adobe Photoshop to integrate and prepare vector and raster graphics, which were then animated and rendered in Adobe After Effects®.

In this lesson, you'll use Adobe Illustrator, Adobe Photoshop, and Adobe After Effects to create an animation using elements from the Masters of Visual Effects clip. In a series of four projects, you will learn how to do the following in Illustrator and Photoshop:

• Create an Illustrator vector graphic using a still image as a reference.

• Integrate an Illustrator vector-graphic file into a Photoshop raster graphic, using a series of Photoshop layers.

• Use Photoshop's adjustment layers to prepare the file for video.

• Rasterize an Illustrator file in Photoshop for use in the animation.

• Compensate for flickering in NTSC video.

• Output color channels to NTSC-safe levels using Photoshop adjustment layers.

In After Effects, you'll learn how to the following:

• Create a composition.

• Animate elements, and edit and fine-tune the animation.

• Use the Easy-Ease feature to add more natural movement to animation.

• Compensate for flickering in NTSC video and intense colors.

• Set compression and output options for QuickTime videos in a broadcast format and a Webcasting format.

This lesson will take about 2 hours to complete.

If needed, remove the previous lesson folder from your hard drive, and copy the Lesson11 folder onto it.

Important: For this lesson, the CIB includes a tryout version of Adobe After Effects. Files can't be rendered or saved in the tryout version.

Getting started

Before beginning this lesson, restore the default application settings for Adobe Photoshop and Adobe Illustrator. For instructions, see "Restoring default preferences" on page 3.

Before you begin, you'll view the Masters of Visual Effects clip to see the animation you'll create.

1 From the Windows desktop or the Mac OS Finder, locate the file 11End.mv in the Lessons/Lesson11/11MV folder.

2 Double-click the file to open it and launch QuickTime. (If you have not already installed QuickTime, you will be prompted to do so. If your system is not equipped, log on to the Apple site at www.apple.com/quicktime/ and download the current version.)

3 Press the play button (large right arrow) located at the bottom of the frame to play the movie.

4 When you have finished viewing the file, either leave the End file open on your desktop for reference, or close it without saving changes.

Project 1: Adding vector graphics to a raster image

In the final animation, the silhouette of a parachutist floats down from a plane.

You will start the first project by creating a silhouette of a parachutist from a previously grabbed video frame. You'll edit the raster image in Adobe Illustrator, adding vector graphics.

For information on acquiring digital video, see "Acquiring frames from video" on page 100.

Cropped video frame

1 Restart Adobe Illustrator.

2 Choose File > Open, and open the parachute.eps file, located in the Lessons/Lesson11 folder on your hard drive.

3 Choose File > Save As, rename the file **parachute.ai,** and click Save. In the Illustrator Format dialog box, for Compatibility, select version 8.0 of Illustrator, and click OK.

Editing the image

First, you will create the silhouette that you will later animate.

1 In the Layers palette, create a new layer for tracing, and name it **Tracing**.

2 In the image, use the pencil tool to trace the outline of the parachute and the parachutist. Don't worry about tracing it perfectly—you can adjust the lines later.

3 Now fill the parachute with white to complete its silhouette.

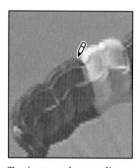

Tracing parachute outline   *Filling outline with white.*

Next, you'll draw the strings and stroke them. The strings between a parachute and jumper are always stretched tightly, but tracing the strings probably wouldn't result in perfectly straight strings. Using the pen tool, you can create straight lines and simple shapes easily.

4 Select the pen tool.

5 Click the start point of the line you wish to draw. Click the end point to draw the line. Deselect.

You must deselect the path before starting the next one, or you'll create zigzag lines. For more information on drawing with the pen tool, see Lesson 8, "Mastering the Pen Tool."

6 Repeat step 3 until you have enough lines for the parachute.

Parachute lines added

7 Using the selection tool, drag the marquee to select all of the parachute lines.

8 In the toolbox, set the fill to None. Stroke the lines with your choice of colors (white in this project). Set a stroke weight of at least 2 or 3 points.

💡 *When working with video with stroked lines, always use a stroke of 2 pixels or greater. Thin lines—especially horizontal ones—flicker noticeably on NTSC video displays (for an explanation, see "Correcting flickering in NTSC video" on page 345). Stroking graphics with a line at least 2-pixels thick avoids the high-frequency flicker.*

Adding crop marks

It's important when creating files in Illustrator for use in After Effects that you always set crop marks. Crop marks let you specify the location of the file edges, so that importing the file into After Effects brings in only exactly what you want.

Illustrator will create crop marks automatically by default, but setting them yourself gives you more control over their placement. When Illustrator sets the marks automatically, it creates a bounding box just large enough to fit the object. However, you may want to apply filters to the object that would expand it beyond its original size.

1 With the rectangle tool, draw a rectangle where you want the crop marks to be set, making the rectangle larger than the artwork. Be sure to allow at least 10 pixels to 20 pixels of elbow room for your artwork.

2 Convert the rectangle to crop marks (Object > Crop Marks > Make).

Crop marks added

Note: *If you make a mistake, just create a new rectangle and convert it to crop marks. Illustrator deletes the old ones automatically.*

Completing the vector graphic

Now you'll finish your work in Illustrator, and save the file.

1 In the Layers palette, select the original layer containing the video image.

2 Delete the layer by dragging it to the Trash button at the bottom of the Layers palette.

3 Save your changes.

4 Close the file, and quit Illustrator.

Project 2: Preparing Photoshop layers for animation

The animation masters are black-and-white caricatures peering out from mysterious bubbles (created in Illustrator). In this project, you'll integrate an Illustrator file into a Photoshop graphic, and use Photoshop's adjustment layers to prepare the file for video.

1 Restart Adobe Photoshop. Click Cancel to dismiss the color management dialog box that appears.

2 Choose File > Open, and open the toon.psd file, located in the Lessons/Lesson11 folder on your hard drive. In the Profile Mismatch dialog box, click Don't Convert. (For information on setting up a color profile, see "Setting up a color profile" on page 182.)

3 Save the file as **Scott.psd.**

Rasterizing artwork

Next, you'll open a vector-graphic, Illustrator image in Photoshop, and rasterize the vector graphic.

1 Choose File > Open, and open the Bubble.ai file, located in the Lessons/Lesson11 folder on your hard drive.

2 Choose File > Save As, rename the file **Bubble.psd**, and click Save.

Note: To have Photoshop automatically append a file's extension, choose Always for Append File Extension in the Preferences dialog box. To display the option, choose File > Preferences > Saving Files.

3 In the Rasterize dialog box, set display options for how Photoshop will interpret the file:

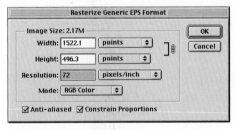

Rasterize EPS options

4 For Resolution, choose 72 pixels/inch. The only resolution you should use for video is 72 ppi.

Images made for video only appear on-screen, and screens are limited to a display resolution of 72 ppi. At best, a resolution higher than 72 ppi will end up being disregarded, and at worst, will cause problems for the video application that you are using.

Note: It's best to prepare graphics oversized in Photoshop and shrink them later in After Effects. If you scale a graphic any larger than 100%, the image will start to degrade—it will become very soft and eventually pixelated (and très unattractive). Shrinking a file doesn't degrade quality, because After Effects does a great job of resizing it. Play it safe, and save yourself time; make your files 50% to 100% larger than you think you'll need them.

5 For Mode, choose RGB Color.

Video images exist as light on-screen. RGB is the native color space for screens. (Plus, it offers you a much larger spectrum of colors, luminance, and saturation levels than does CMYK, for example.)

6 Click OK to rasterize the file and open it in Photoshop.

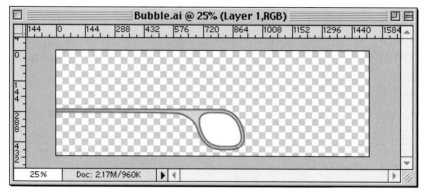

Bubble.ai file rasterized in Photoshop

Preparing the animation graphics

Now you'll place Scott inside the paddle-like bubble graphic. You'll place him so that he is behind the paddle, but in front of the white space in the center of the paddle. Just think of it as a Scott sandwich. Here's the recipe.

1 In the Layers palette, double-click Layer 1, and rename it **Paddle**.

2 In the image, use the magic wand tool to click inside the bubble to select it.

3 In the Layers palette, create a new layer, and name it **White Background**. Drag the White Background layer beneath the Paddle layer.

4 Expand the selection so that it extends beyond the current selection by choosing Select > Modify > Expand. Enter **6** pixels, and click OK

5 Fill the selection with white.

6 Deselect the image.

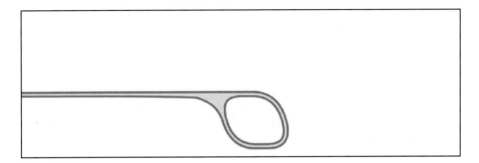

Combining the elements

Now you'll paste Scott's image into the paddle graphic.

1 Make the Scott.psd file active. Make sure that the Layers palette is visible.

2 Select the entire image (Ctrl/Command+A).

3 Choose Edit > Copy Merged to copy all of the layers as one.

4 Make the Bubble.psd file active, and choose Edit > Paste. Photoshop will merge the original layers into single new layer.

5 In the Layers palette, rename the layer **Scott**, and move it to the top of the palette.

6 With the Scott layer selected, select Edit > Free Transform (Ctrl/Command+T). You may need to enlarge the window to see the corners of the resizing box.

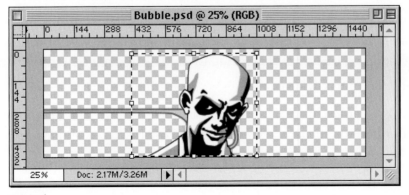

Original

7 Shift-drag any corner to shrink the Scott graphic. You want almost the entire graphic to fit inside the bubble, with Scott's forehead leaning almost directly against the right side of orange inner outline.

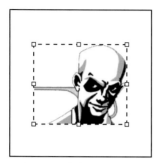 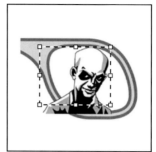

Resizing Scott's head   *Result*

8 When you've finished, press Enter to apply the transformation.

9 In the Layers palette, drag the Scott layer beneath the Paddle layer.

Now you'll remove the part of Scott's shoulder that extends outside the bubble.

Instead of erasing elements on a layer, you will hide them with a layer mask. A layer mask is an alpha channel attached to a single layer. If you decide to reposition Scott and need his shoulder back, you can simply change the layer mask; if you erase his shoulder with the eraser tool, you'd have to start over.

10 In the Layers palette, with the Scott layer selected, Ctrl/Command-click the White Background layer to create the layer mask. This action loads a selection based on any pixels on this layer.

11 Now select the layer with Scott on it, and click the Add Layer Mask button at the bottom of the Layers palette (or choose Add Layer Mask from the Layers palette menu).

Voilà! Scott's shoulder is hidden!

This looks like a finished image, ready to bring into After Effects. But since it's ultimately destined for video, you still have a few contrast and color adjustments to make.

Reproducing contrast and color in NTSC video

NTSC video reproduces well only a subset of the color models used for graphics, and tends to intensify the colors (particularly reds) that it displays. Colors outside this range look terrible, and in some cases, even cause playback problems—even on the video's sound track! If you are preparing graphics for video output, it's crucial to keep colors within the NTSC display range (called NTSC-Legal), limit RGB channel levels, and reduce the contrast and brightness of your image.

Photoshop's NTSC Colors filter does a pretty good job of fixing most of these display problems. Even better, adjustment layers let you control color and levels without altering the pixels in your image. With adjustment layers, you can come back and make further changes if the image still doesn't display well.

To reduce the output of the color channels to NTSC-safe levels, now you'll add an adjustment layer and use it to decrease the white output.

1 In the Layers palette, select the topmost layer, Paddle. An adjustment layer sits on top of the layer it affects.

2 Choose New Adjustment Layer from the Layers palette menu. In the dialog box that appears, keep Levels for the name and type. Click OK.

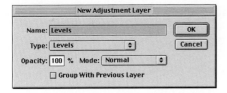

3 In the Levels dialog box, for white Output Levels, enter **234** in the second (lower right) box. Click OK.

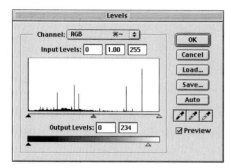

Reducing white output to NTSC-Legal levels

Theoretically, you have just placed everything safely within NTSC color space—without altering your original pixels! Don't worry if your image seems rather dull and blurry—after all, you've just dulled and blurred it!

Before you decide that your graphic looks terrible and you don't want to use it in the video, continue to work with it. You'll be amazed at how an image that looks so dull and blurry on a computer monitor can look bright and sharp on a television screen. And thanks to the flexibility of adjustment layers, you can come back and experiment with the level settings if the don't like the results when you see them on video.

Now you'll add another adjustment layer to reduce contrast.

4 Choose New Adjustment Layer from the Layers palette menu.

5 For Type, choose Brightness/Contrast, and click OK.

6 Reduce both the brightness and the contrast sliders to about –2. Select Preview to see the effect on the image.

Eventually you'll develop an eye for how much you need to change these settings. Every image needs slightly different corrections.

♀ *If your system can display NTSC video on a second monitor, you can place the image window on the NTSC display to judge your adjustments in real time.*

7 If you can preview your image on a television monitor, look for these warning signs of an illegally bright or sharp image:

- Bleeding colors (especially reds and yellows).

- Shadows and smears from high-contrast areas.

- Flicker around the edges of lines (especially around type and other hard-edged graphics).

- Flickering and strobing white areas.

If you see any of these signs of an illegal image, in Photoshop try reducing the white levels (as you did in steps 1 through 3) or adding blur to the image. You'll add a blur in the next section.

Correcting flickering in NTSC video

You can use several techniques to avoid flickering in full-screen NTSC video, including stroking all graphics by at least 2 pixels (or an even number), applying anti-aliasing, and blurring images.

Flickering is caused by the interlacing of NTSC video. The 480 horizontal lines that make up a full-screen NTSC are displayed as alternating fields: every 0.6 second, half of the lines are displayed—first the odd-numbered lines, and then the even. If a graphic has a 1-pixel line, the television will first display it on the odd line, and then 0.6 second later display it on the even line, creating a high-frequency flicker. To avoid this, you should make all graphics at least 2 pixels thick—or better yet, keep their width to an even number of pixels, which further reduces flickering.

Using anti-aliasing at every stage is also a good idea. Aliasing creates single-pixel borders that not only flicker, but also accentuate the "jaggies," and generally amplify a sense of low-resolution. Resizing Scott's image resulted in some pretty thin black lines—and they'll get smaller if he's scaled down further in After Effects.

Another technique for improving the appearance of thin graphics on NTSC is blurring. Blurring is absolutely essential for effectively translating digital graphics to NTSC. Although blurring may seem to blur and defocus images on your monitor, the technique will result in much sharper images for video playback. In fact, it's a good idea to apply a light blur to your entire image as a finishing touch.

Now, you'll apply a slight Gaussian blur to the Scott and Paddle layers.

1 In the Layers palette, make the Paddle layer active. Choose Filter > Blur > Gaussian Blur. Leave the Preview box selected, and use the hand icon to locate a good spot for checking the filter's effect.

2 Using the slider, reduce the Radius value until the lines are just barely blurred—a 0.3 radius should be about right. Click OK.

Original   *Gaussian blur of –0.3*

3 Select the remaining layers in turn, and apply the Gaussian Blur filter with the same Radius value. (Select a layer and press Ctrl/Command+F to reapply the filter.).

Remember that even though the image will look a little soft on your display, the image will actually look sharper on an NTSC screen.

4 Save your changes.

5 Close the file, and quit Photoshop.

You've finished the process of preparing a graphic for use in an NTSC-destined animation. Now you're ready to animate.

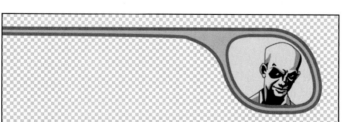   

Completed Photoshop image, ready to import into After Effects for animation

Project 3: Making it move

Now for the fun part: animating all the elements you've created. The first step is importing all of the elements into After Effects.

Importing a file

You can select a layer or an entire image to import into After Effects.

1 Start After Effects.

2 Choose File > New Project. Save the project as **MVFX.aep.**

Note: If you are using the tryout version, you cannot save.

3 Choose File > Import > Footage File, and select and import the parachute.ai file, located in the Lessons/Lessons11 folder.

4 In the dialog box that appears, for Choose a Layer, select tracing and click OK. You want to import the tracing layer and not the entire image.

Importing a single Illustrator or Photoshop layer

Creating a composition

Next, you need to create a composition before you can animate any elements.

1 Choose Composition > New Composition to create a composition.

2 In the Composition Settings dialog box, set the options as follows:

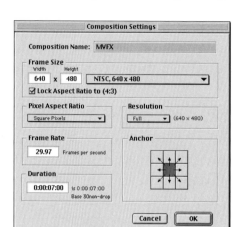

Composition Settings dialog box

• For Composition Name, name your composition **MVFX** (short for Masters of Visual Effects), an intuitive, descriptive name. You can change the name later. The movie will default to this name when you finally make a a movie from the composition.

• For Frame Size, choose the standard NTSC frame size of 640 pixels by 480 pixels, entering the values or choosing the option from the pop-up menu. This option is suitable for output to videotape. (You can make a smaller version for Web use.)

• For Pixel Aspect Ratio, choose Square Pixels.

• For Resolution, choose Full.

• For Frame Rate, enter 29.97 frames per second. Use this value if you'll output to full NTSC video or the Web; for output for computer use, use a value of 30.

• For Duration, enter 7 seconds. (You can simply type 700 in the Duration field; it will be interpreted as 7 seconds.) If you don't know exactly how long an animation will be, guess and add a few more seconds to give yourself the benefit of the doubt. You can always change this value.

• Leave the Anchor setting as is.

3 Click OK.

4 Drag the tracing/parachute.ai file from the Project window to the Time Layout window.

5 Save your changes if you're working in the full After Effects version.

The parachutist may look a bit pixelated. Until you instruct After Effects otherwise, it displays all elements at a lower resolution to speed up processing. This display has no effect on the movie you eventually render.

About setting keyframes and tweening

To animate any attribute over time, you must set keyframes. Instead of changing the parachutist for each and every frame in the animation (a process that would take far too much time and energy), you can set just a few keyframes, and the computer will inter-polate the layer between each keyframe—a process called *tweening*. By default, each attribute stays constant over time.

To make a keyframe change over time, you click the stopwatch icon next to an attribute name to have After Effects automatically set a new keyframe.

Before animating the parachutist, think about which attributes are changing as she floats down from the heavens. By breaking down her movement, you'll know which attributes to animate. In this case, you need to animate her position, rotation, and scale.

In After Effects, anything you do, including transformations (changes to size, scale, and opacity) and filters can be changed at any time without consequence. You don't have to get the animation perfect the first time. You can always refine it or completely change it whenever you like.

Scaling the graphic

The parachutist is much bigger than you want. You'll scale the graphic.

1 In the Time Layout window, select the Parachutist layer.

2 Press the S key to display the Scale attribute.

3 Change the view to 50% so that you can see the entire bounding box.

4 Shrink the image to the size you want it to appear when it first enters the frame. Either enter a new scale value in the Time Layout window or simply drag the corner of the bounding box in the composition window (Shift-dragging will preserve the aspect ratio).

5 Drag the parachutist to her position when the animation starts, just outside of the upper right corner of the frame.

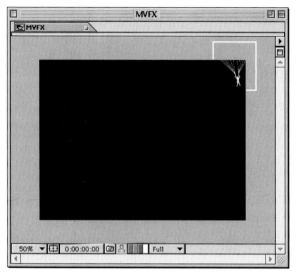

First frame of the animation with parachutist properly positioned

Note: *The intrepid parachutist is none other than the editor of this book, Luanne Cohen.*

Congratulations! You've just set the first keyframes for the parachutist.

Moving in time

You must instruct After Effects to change attributes (such as motion) over time to have After Effects create new keyframes, rather than simply resetting the attribute value.

1 If the attributes aren't visible, press the S key to display the Scale attribute, the R key for rotation, and the P key for position.

2 Click the stopwatch icon (the round icon) to the left of the Scale, Rotation, and Position attributes.

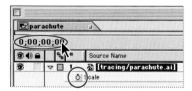

Clicking the stopwatch next to the Scale attribute

Clicking the stopwatch interpolates the attribute over time; when you jump to a new point in time and change the attribute (say, by rotating or scaling) After Effects automatically sets a new keyframe.

Important: *Once you click the stopwatch, don't click it again—unless you want to change the attribute back to a constant keyframe. Clicking the stopwatch each time you want a new keyframe is a common mistake that erases all the keyframes you've worked so hard to create!*

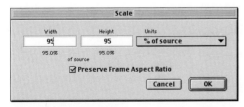

Setting keyframing by clicking the stopwatches for Scale, Rotation, and Position

The parachutist will float for the duration of this animation. Now that the you've set up for the first frame, you'll set up the last frame.

3 Move to the last frame of the composition: Drag the time marker where you want the next keyframe, click the Current Time counter in the upper left corner of the Time Layout window, or press Ctrl/Command+G.

4 Press the End key on the keyboard. Now you'll set the scale attribute.

5 Increase the size of the parachutist to 95% of the source file:

• Drag the bounding box (press the Shift key to maintain the aspect ratio).

• Click the Scale attribute value (the underlined value expressed as a percentage next to the word *Scale* in the Time Layout window). Enter a new value, expressed as a percentage of the source file, a percentage of the composition, or as pixels. (To change aspect ratio, deselect Preserve Aspect Ratio.) Click OK.

Changing the Scale value

6 Drag the parachutist near the bottom of the frame as seen in the video. Now you have the basic path established.

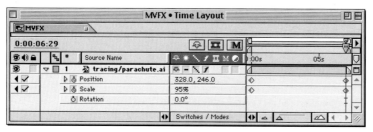

Time Layout window with beginning and end keyframes

7 If you are using a full version of After Effects, save your changes. (You cannot save in the tryout version.)

You've established the basic path of animation.

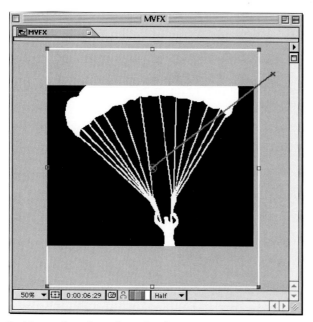

Position, scale, and rotation at last frame in Composition window

Now you'll preview your work and make any necessary changes to the middle.

Previewing

You can preview your work in After Effects in several ways. Which method you use depends on how much time you have, how much RAM you have, how complicated your composition is, and how much detail you need to preview.

1 To preview your work so far, choose an option:

• Press 0 (zero) on the number pad. The preview should render fairly quickly. This is the quick way of getting the RAM preview. After Effects will step through and render each frame of the composition and put it back in RAM for accelerated real-time playback. This gives you the most thorough preview, leaving little to the imagination.

• If you're short on RAM or time, then press Alt/Option+zero (0) to get a wireframe preview of the selected layers (or all the layers if none are selected). This option is by far the fastest and will be able to preview much longer sections of the composition.

You now have a very basic animation path blocked out. It needs a lot of finesse, but the timing, scaling and general position are all correct.

2 If you don't like the size or exact position of your parachutist, feel free to adjust the scale and position keyframes so that they work for you. (See the preceding section, "Scaling the graphic" on page 349.) Remember, After Effects is procedural: you can always finesse and change things later.

Adding detail to the motion

As you know, parachutists in the real world just don't float down from the sky in a perfectly straight line at a perfectly even velocity. To make the motion feel more natural and organic, you can jump to several points in the middle of the composition and offset their position so that the resulting path isn't so straight and perfect.

1 In the Time Layout window, drag the time marker to 3:00.

2 In the Composition window, drag the parachutist to a new position; or press Shift+Left arrow key four times, and press the Down arrow twice. (Pressing Shift nudges the layer in 10 pixel increments.)

Notice that repositioning the parachutist adds a new keyframe to the timeline. Remember that once you've clicked the stopwatch to interpolate attributes, After Effects automatically sets a new keyframe whenever you go to a new point in time and make a change.

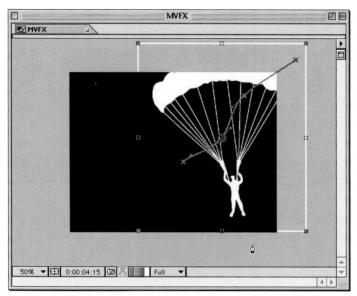

Parachute with slightly offset path made up of Bézier splines

A you repositioned the path of the parachutist, After Effects also automatically created a smooth, Bézier path with handles. You know from working with Photoshop or Illustrator paths, how flexible, powerful and easy to use they are. For this animation, Bézier paths will let you create the smooth, flowing curved paths typical of descending parachutists.

3 To edit the path with the pen tool, select it in the toolbox (press G), and edit the path by adjusting the handles.

4 Preview the new path to see if you like it (press 0 on the number pad).

5 Continue to offset the path every 1 second to 3 seconds, and preview it until you are satisfied with it.

6 If you are using a full version of After Effects, save your changes. (You cannot save in the tryout version.)

Adding rotation

You'll finish the animation of the parachutist by adding some rotation.

1 In the Composition window, start at time 0:00. Add just a little bit of rotation by selecting the rotation tool (press the W key) and dragging the bounding box; or simply type a new value (7 degrees) in the Time Layout window.

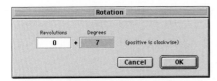

Rotation dialog box

2 Adjust the rotation as desired, about 5° to 10°, using positive values for clockwise rotation, and negative values for counterclockwise rotation. Add new rotation values every so often. You don't need as many rotation keyframes as position keyframes—two or three will work just fine.

To add new rotation keyframes at the same points in time as the position keyframes, Shift-drag the time marker to jump quickly to the points in the timeline where the position keyframes are located. (The Shift key makes the new keyframe snap to any other visible keyframes.)

As long as you have already clicked the stopwatch for rotation, After Effects will set a new keyframe every time you change the value.

3 Preview the parachutist to see the movement. Continue to adjust the movement until you're satisfied.

4 Save your changes if you're working in the full After Effects version.

Adding a new element to the composition

Now you'll add Scott to the animation.

1 Choose File > Import > Footage File, and select and import the Bubble.psd file, located in the Lessons/Lesson11 folder.

2 In the dialog box that appears, for Choose a Layer, select Merged Layers, to merge the layers of the file into one for use in your composition.

3 Go to time 0:00 by pressing the Home key or dragging the time marker to the beginning of the composition.

4 Drag the Bubble.psd file from the Project window into the composition.

When you drag a new element into a composition, After Effects adds that element at the current time marker (so if the time marker is at 2:08, the new file you add will start at 2:08). Although you can change the In point of a layer, it's easier and more efficient to move the time marker to the desired location before dragging in an element.

As you can see, this image is much bigger than you want it to be.

Image at 75% scale with fine resolution   *Image scaled to 400% with pixelation*

It's good to have an image larger than you want. It's never a problem to shrink layers in After Effects—but it's always a problem to scale them to more than 100% of their original size. Shrinking a graphic increases the number of pixels per inch increase, resulting in denser and higher resolution. Scaling an image larger than 100% decreases the number of pixels per inch, resulting in thinner, lower resolution. The application tries to fill in the missing information, but it usually ends up softening or pixelating the image.

5 Select the Bubble.psd layer in the Time Layout window.

6 Press the S key to view the Scale attribute. Scale the image to 75%.

Important: *Be sure to not click the stopwatch. Remember that you've already selected the stopwatch to interpolate the attribute; clicking the stopwatch again will erase the keyframes you've already created.*

7 Save your changes if you're working in the full After Effects version.

Positioning elements in the composition

Now that Scott is properly sized, you'll position him.

1 Click the small button in the lower left corner of the Composition window to turn on the Title-Action Safe grid.

Title-Action Safe button

2 Position the image in the lower left corner of the frame, so that Scott is just 1 or 2 pixels above the Action-Safe zone, and the arm of the Paddle graphic that frames him extends beyond the visible frame.

3 Adjust the scale and the position so that it's just right. This is the position that Scott will be in after he is animated into the frame.

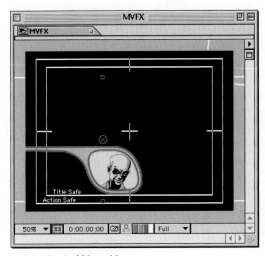

Positioning Bubble.psd layer

This part of the animation should take about 10 frames to execute.

4 Go to frame 10 of the composition (drag the time marker, or press Ctrl/Command+G and type in 10). Click the stopwatch for the position, to mark this as a keyframe.

5 Go to time 0:00 (or press the Home key).

6 Reposition Scott slightly out of the left frame by pressing the Shift + Left arrow key (press Shift to move in increments of 10), until he is completely out of frame. You should now have two keyframes: one at time 0:00, and one at time 0:10.

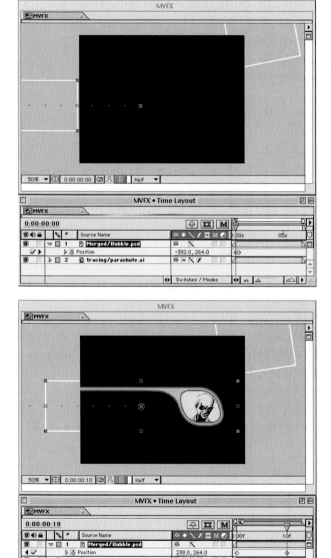

Bounding box for Bubble.psd extending out of frame;
two keyframes in the Time Layout window

7 Go to the last frame of the animation (press the End key).

At this point you want Scott to be all the way off-screen, as he was at time 0:00.

8 Select the keyframe at time 0:00 by clicking it, and then copy and paste the keyframe (choose Edit > Copy and Edit > Paste). After Effects always pastes keyframes at the current time on the selected layer. So your new keyframe should be just where you want it—on Scott's layer on the last frame of the animation.

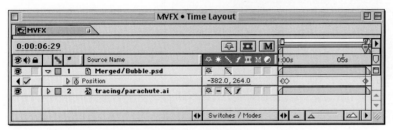

*First keyframe selected, with the current time marker in position
where keyframe will be pasted.*

Previewing the animation so far shows Scott moving into 10 frames, and then starting to slowly move back out of frame. After Effects has simply interpolated between the three keyframes that you just created. To have Scott remain on-screen until the end of the animation, you must add another keyframe for After Effects to interpolate.

You'll copy the second keyframe and paste it 10 frames before the end of the animation. This will freeze Scott's motion, and then zip him out of frame at the end.

9 To move 10 frames back in time, press Shift+Page Up.

10 Select and copy the second keyframe (at time 0:10) and paste it. You now have four keyframes to create a simple slide on, hold, and slide off.

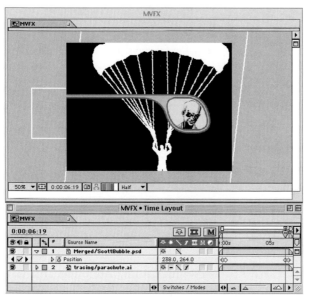

Four keyframes making a simple slide on, hold, and slide off

11 Preview to check your work.

Preview of slide on, hold, and slide off

12 Save your changes if you're working in the full After Effects version.

Applying Easy-Ease

Next, you'll add a few finishing touches that will apply some finesse and grace to the movement.

The animation's movement is rather linear. The keyframes used linear interpolation by default, giving a uniform velocity to the element as it moves. The element moves at one velocity; it doesn't slow down, it just stops. Linear interpolation can feel a bit robotic. In the real world, things tend to speed up over time, and then slow down before stopping. Creating this movement is more complicated because it involves constantly changing the velocity by adding acceleration and deceleration.

However, After Effects includes a super-easy, built-in way to apply acceleration and deceleration to your animations—Easy-Ease. You'll apply it now.

1 Right-click (Windows) or Control-click (Mac OS) the second keyframe, or choose Layer > Keyframe Assistant > Easy-Ease In.

Applying Easy-Ease to keyframe

2 Choose Easy-Ease In, so that the second frame comes smoothly to a stop. Easy-Ease In applies ease from the previous keyframe as it interpolates to the selected keyframe.

3 Repeat step 1, selecting the third keyframe. Apply Easy-Ease Out, so that the third frame gently accelerates as it leaves. Easy-East Out applies ease from the selected keyframe to the next one.

The third option, Easy-Ease, applies ease both coming in from the previous keyframe and out to the next keyframes.

4 Preview the animation to see the difference Easy-Ease makes.

5 Save your changes if you're working in the full After Effects version.

Adding motion blur

The final finesse you'll add to all of the elements that move, scale, or rotate is true, automatic motion blur.

If objects are moving faster than the shutter of a camera, they will blur with the direction and velocity of the movement. You can manually apply motion blur to layers and create keyframes to match movement. You can also apply motion blur automatically.

1 Locate all layers that have motion, rotation, scaling applied to it (both layers in this case).

2 To the right of the layer name, select the Motion Blur (M) box at the top of the column. When this box is checked, After Effects will calculate a realistic camera blur velocity (amount) and vector (direction), based on the movement of the layer and the Shutter Angle preference (set in File > Preferences > General Preferences).

3 To view the motion blur, turn on motion blur for the entire composition. (By default, motion blur is turned off to make previews faster.)

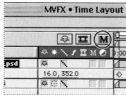

Turning on motion   Turning on motion blur
blur for layer   for composition

Compensating for NTSC flicker

On page 346, you blurred the elements of the Bubble.psd to compensate for NTSC flicker. You'll apply a blur to the Illustrator file, parachute.ai. Illustrator doesn't support blur. The file was imported directly into After Effects without first being rasterized in Photoshop.

1 In the Time Layout window, select the tracing/parachute.ai layer.

2 Choose Effect > Blur&Sharpen > Gaussian Blur to add a Gaussian blur.

3 For blur, enter **0.3**. Click OK.

4 Save your changes if you're working in the full After Effects version.

Now that you've animated the elements, you've almost completed the lesson. The next project will show you how to set up your animation for rendering.

Project 4: Compressing the composition for video and the Web

In this exercise, you'll learn how to use the After Effects Render Queue, Render Settings, and Output Modules to create final versions of your work in two formats: one for broadcast, and one for streaming over the Web.

The Render Queue lets you line up one or a series of compositions for output. The Render Settings determine which elements of the composition will be rendered, and in what manner. The Output Module determines how the final file will be compressed.

Lining up compositions for output

You'll start by adding a composition to the Render Queue.

1 Open the Render Queue window from the Window pop-up menu.

2 Drag your MVFX composition from the Project window to the Render Queue window.

After Effects immediately adds two items under your composition in the queue: Render Settings, and an Output Module.

♀ *When you have two output formats with the same frame rate, you can set up a composition in the queue to render with two output modules using a single render setting. This saves rendering time, because After Effects will render common information for both files at the same time. You can't use this technique if you need files with different frame rates, because the frame rate in the render settings overrides the frame rate in the output module's video settings.*

Although a frame rate box appears under an output module's video settings, it is overridden by the rate specified in the render settings. You will need to set up two different renders. You will duplicate the composition in the Render Queue:

3 Click the Composition Name in the Render Queue.

4 Press Ctrl/Command+D to duplicate the composition in the queue.

Setting broadcast render options

You'll modify the first render in the queue for its intended output to NTSC video.

1 Click the arrow next to the Render Settings name.

2 Choose Custom from the pop-up menu.

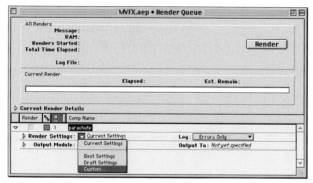

Selecting Render Settings Custom option

The Render Settings dialog box appears.

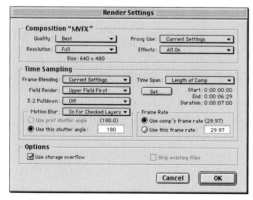

Render Settings

3 In the Render Settings dialog box, set the following general options for the MVFX composition:

• For Quality, choose Best for any final output. The Draft and Wireframe modes are only useful for low-quality drafts used to check your work.

- For Resolution, choose Full. The other resolution settings speed up render time when you need a quick preview file.

- Leave Proxy Use as is. This option doesn't apply to your composition.

- For Effects, choose All On. This setting determines whether effects used in your composition are rendered.

4 Select the following Time Sampling options:

- Leave Frame Blending at the default. Frame blending smooths the choppy effect seen in video clips that have been slowed down. Your composition doesn't have such material in your composition.

- For Field Render, choose Upper field dominance, the setting used by most hardware. This setting determines the order in which QuickTime renders the two fields of each video frame. To set this correctly, you must consult the documentation for the hardware you will use to send your file out to videotape. Video boards have specific codecs associated with them, with different settings for field rendering. If you don't have access to this information, try rendering a short clip and playing it back through your video hardware; if the playback looks strange, you'll know you had this set incorrectly.

- Leave 3:2 Pulldown off. This special formula removes extra fields and frames in material that has been transferred from film to video.

- For Motion Blur, choose On for Checked Layers, because you applied motion blur in this composition. Enter a Shutter Angle of 180; this option lets you simulate a specific camera shutter angle.

- For Time Span, choose Length of Comp, to output the entire composition. This setting determines which portion of the composition will be rendered to a file. You can set this to render only the work area (determined by the sliders above the time ruler in the Time Layout window), the entire composition, or set custom in and out points.

- For Frame Rate, enter 29.97, unless you know that your video board uses a different rate. Although NTSC video is often described as running at 30 fps, it actually runs at 29.97 fps. Again, consult the documentation for your video board to determine which setting to use. A few boards automatically interpret 30 fps as 29.97, but most want a file rendered at 29.97. If you don't know which setting your hardware requires, 29.97 is the safest guess.

5 Select Use Storage Overflow as a precaution if the files to be rendered are large but you don't have enough space on one hard drive to accommodate them. If you have set up After Effects' preferences for overflow storage volumes, you can select this as a precaution.

6 Click OK when you've finished setting the render options.

7 For Log File, choose Errors Only.

8 Save your changes if you're working in the full After Effects version.

Setting Web render options

A few of the render settings that you just set in the previous section are inappropriate for the file you'll render for viewing on the Web. Now you will make new custom settings for this render.

1 In the Render Settings dialog box, click the arrow next to the Render Settings name for the second item in the queue.

2 Choose Custom from the pop-up menu.

3 Set the pop-up menus and input boxes as you did for the first render, choosing Off for Field render; because the file isn't destined for NTSC video, its fields won't be rendered.

4 In addition, for Frame Rate, choose the slowest connection speed at which you want the file to be viewable.

There are several considerations to keep in mind, and no one setting is perfect for every file. The frame rate you set works in combination with the data rate you'll set later in the output module to determine the quality of the rendered file. Within a given data rate, slower frame rates will result in higher quality individual frames, at the expense of choppy playback. Also keep in mind that material with a great deal of complex motion is more difficult to compress than simple graphics with very little motion.

Here are a few guidelines for frame rates intended for different connection speeds:

• For 28.8K to 56K modems, use a frame rate of between 2.5 and 7.5 fps. At slower frame rates, the codec will render each frame at a higher quality, at the expense of temporal resolution.

• ISDN connections can handle a higher frame rate of between 7.5 and 12 fps.

- If your viewers will be connected via DSL or cable modems, try a setting of between 12 and 15 fps.

Note: It is not advisable to use frame rates higher than 15 fps for Web streaming.

5 When you've finished making the settings, click OK.

6 Save your changes if you're working in the full After Effects version.

Setting compression for broadcast

Next, you will customize the Output Module for your broadcast file. The Output Module determines how the final file will be compressed.

1 Click the arrow next to Output Module name for the first file in the queue.

2 Choose Custom from the pop-up menu.

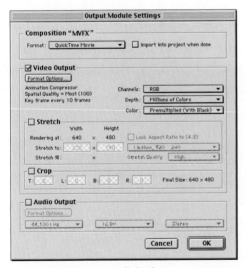

Output Module Settings dialog box

3 For Format, choose QuickTime Movie. Select Import into Project When Done to have the file imported into the Project window when the file has been rendered.

4 Choose Format Options to display a standard QuickTime compression settings dialog box:

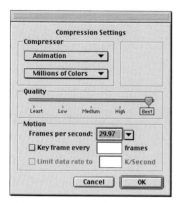

QuickTime Compression Settings dialog box

5 In the Compression Settings dialog box, select the following Compressor options:

• For broadcast video, choose the compressor used by your hardware (for example, Media 100, Targa, and so on); to archive the file for later use on various systems, choose the Animation codec, which uses a lossless compression scheme, thus letting you recompress the file for use on another system with minimum data loss.

• For color depth, choose Millions of Colors if your codec lets you choose a color depth. Do not select Millions of Colors+; this option adds an alpha channel to the file.

6 Deselect the Keyframe Every Frame option for broadcast video. Some codecs use keyframes as reference points for calculating compression. This type of keyframe is different than the keyframes you set in an animation. The codec stores a complete frame at the interval you specify, then tracks the changes from that frame to the next keyframe to compress motion efficiently.

7 Select Limit Data Rate if your codec lets you specify data rate, and enter the highest rate at which your hardware can play a video stream. (This rate is determined by the speed of the bus connecting your system to your storage media, the speed at which your storage media can perform a sustained read, the speed of your CPU, and the particular limitations of your video hardware.) Consult the manual for your video hardware before setting this option.

8 Click OK to close the Compression Settings dialog box and return to the Output Modules Settings dialog box.

9 In the Output Modules Settings dialog box, set these options:

• For Channels, choose RGB.

• For Depth, choose Millions of Colors.

• Leave the default Color setting. This option won't apply because you are not rendering an alpha channel (Millions of Colors +).

• Leave deselected the Stretch, Crop, and Audio options. You would use these options if you needed to change the size and/or aspect ratio of a composition, apply a matte (such as a letterbox), or export audio from your composition.

10 When you've finished the settings, click OK.

11 Save your changes if you're working in the full After Effects version.

Setting compression for the Web

Because your second file is intended for use on the Web, as with the Render Queue, you must set some of its Output Module settings differently.

1 Click the arrow next to Output Module name for the first file in the queue.

2 Choose QuickTime Movie from the pop-up menu.

3 Click Format Options. The Compression Settings dialog box for Sorensen Video appears. This compression scheme does not change frames per second.

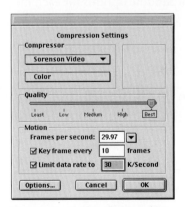

Compression Settings for Sorenson

4 For Compression, choose Sorenson Video. This codec is designed to produce low-data rate files at the best possible quality—exactly what you need for the Web.

5 For Frames Per Second, leave the frame rate as is. Your render settings have already specified the frame rate.

6 For Key Frame Every, enter **10** frames. Compressing an animation with a lot of fast motion—meaning each frame would be very different from the one immediately before and after it—might require a lower value for more frequent key frames to improve quality.

7 Set Limit Data Rate to the slowest connection speed you expect your viewers to have, as follows:

- For 28.8K and 33.3K modems, enter 2K/second to 2.5K/second.

- For 56K modems, enter 4K/second to 5K/second.

- For ISDN, enter 7K/second to 12K/second.

- For DSL or cable modems: 15K/second to 40K/second.

8 Keep the remaining other Output Module settings the same as those you set for the first file in the queue. (See "Setting compression for broadcast" on page 367.)

9 When you've finished making the settings, click OK.

10 Save your changes if you're working in the full After Effects version.

Rendering final broadcast and Web versions

Once you've completed setting Render and Output Module options for each file you will create, you're ready to render.

1 In the Render Queue next to the Output Module for your first file, click Output To: Not Yet Specified. Name the file **MVFX_broadcst.mv**.

2 Repeat step 1 for your second file. Name the file **MVFX_Web.mv**.

3 Save the project.

4 Click Render.

After Effects will render the files in the queue, in order of appearance, with the settings you've specified. If you like, you can untwirl the Current Render Details to watch After Effects work and get an idea of how large the resulting files will be and how long they will take to render. In general, expect 7 seconds of full-screen video to require about 125 MB of disk space, and the Sorenson Compressed version to require about 1 MB of disk space.

That's all folks!

Index

Project Designers

Lessons 1 and 2

Laura Dower

Laura Dower is an illustrator, painter, and writer, who works in both digital and traditional media. Laura is a former art director at Adobe Systems, where she continues to consult as a designer and writer while pursuing a painting degree at the California College of Arts and Crafts in San Francisco, CA.

Lesson 3

Glen Janssens

As a founding partner at eMotion studios, Glen has directed and produced several projects, ranging from rich interactive experiences to commercial visual effects. When not leading eMotion's clients in broadband and rich-media communications, Glen can often be spotted pushing a running stroller off-trail, much to the amusement of his silly daughter.

Lesson 4

Jen Alspach

Jennifer Alspach is a nationally known artist and author. Her other books include: *Teach Yourself Photoshop* (IDG Books Worldwide), *Photoshop and Illustrator Synergy Studio Secrets* (IDG Books Worldwide), *PhotoDeluxe for Windows Visual Quickstart Guide* (Peachpit Press), and *Illustrator Complete* (Hayden Books). When not feverishly drawing or writing, she keeps busy with her two kids, five cats, dog, horse, and husband.

Lesson 5

Karen Tenenbaum

A photographer and designer, Karen Tenenbaum has been working with digital imaging since 1988. Over the years, she has used these skills in several different industries—as a T-shirt designer, photographer, picture editor at the San Francisco Examiner, and senior graphic designer at Adobe Systems. Karen has been a part of the team creating learning materials for Adobe's software since 1994. She now freelances as a photo illustrator, and sometime Photoshop teacher.

Lesson 6

Rita Amladi

Rita Amladi is a nationally regarded independent trainer and industry consultant. Hired to work for Adobe Systems 10 years ago when Photoshop first became an Adobe product, she has been involved with it ever since! She worked as the Product Support Engineer for Photoshop at Adobe before leaving to start her own training company. Her company, Orion Arts & Communications, is a certified Adobe Training provider providing digital imaging solutions.

Lessons 7 and 10

Mordy Golding

Mordy Golding (mordy@mordy.com) is a trainer, consultant, writer, graphic designer, production artist, network manager, husband, and a father—not particularly in that order. Residing in New York, he has been a panelist at Macworld and the author of several books including *Teach Yourself Illustrator 8 in 24 Hours*.

Lessons 8 and 9

Andrew Faulkner

Andrew is a principal in the Bay Area-based design studio, TonBo Designs. He and partner Lori Barra provide design and illustration with a focus on editorial and corporate design. Their work includes books, magazines, Web sites, and brochures. Andrew has earned his reputation as the "Photoshop & Illustrator rebel" by breaking all the rules and even inventing some new ones. Clients include Apple Computer Inc., Adobe Systems Inc., Chronicle Books, *Newsweek*, and Sunset Publishing Corporation.

Lesson 11

dåv rauch

As art director and motion graphics designer at eMotion studios, dåv enjoys working on experimental video, Internet, and theatrical projects which incorporate technology and art. A Taurus on the cusp of Aries, dåv enjoys sunset jaunts along the beach, cooking, and eating anything that is in the refrigerator.

Efficient production sidebars

Ted Alspach

Ted Alspach is the author of more than two dozen books, including the best-selling *Illustrator Bible* series, *PDF with Acrobat Visual QuickStart Guide*, and *PageMaker 6.5 Visual QuickStart Guide*. Ted is the Illustrator Product Manager at Adobe Systems, Inc.

Editor

Luanne Seymour Cohen, Mountain View, CA

Production

Jan & Eric Martí, Command Z, Palo Alto, CA

Copyeditor

Judy Walthers von Alten, San Francisco, CA

Proofreading

Lasselle Ramsey, Palo Alto, CA

Production Notes

This book was created electronically using Adobe FrameMaker®. Art was produced using Adobe Illustrator, Adobe ImageReady, and Adobe Photoshop. The Minion® and Myriad® families of typefaces are used throughout the book.

Photography and illustration

Photographic images are intended for use with lessons only.

Adobe Image Club: Lesson 3 (sunset, woman in hard hat) Lesson 7 (construction worker images) ©Adobe Systems Inc.

Laura Dower: Lesson 1 (Portrait painting) painting and photograph

Lesson 2: (BBQ Betty); (Bee) ©1999 Laura Dower

eMotion studios / Glen Janssens: Lesson 3-photo CD sample (girders, sailboats) © eMotion studios / Glen Janssens 1996

eMotion studios / Bill Dierssen: Lesson 3-photo CD sample (lighted tank, pencils) © eMotion studios / Bill Dierssen 1996

eMotion studios: Lesson 3 (parachutist) Lesson 11 (parachutist footage) © eMotion studios/1996

eMotion studios: Lesson 11 (Masters of Visual Effects video) © eMotion studios/1999

Andrew Faulkner: Lesson 6 (Lotus image) Lesson 9 (Paris metro) ©1999 Andrew Faulkner

Amy Faulkner: Lesson 6 (Background image) ©1999 Amy Faulkner

Mordy Golding : Lesson 10 (animated banner) ©1999 Mordy Golding

Josepha Haveman: Lesson 4 (flowers) ©1993 Wayzata Technology

Glen Janssens: Lesson 3 (little girl, girl in glasses, girl with stroller) ©1998 Glen Janssens

PhotoDisc, Inc.: Lesson 2 (Old West Photo); (Country Store, New Mexico)

© 1997 PhotoDisc, Inc., 2013 Fourth Ave., Seattle, WA 98121, 1-800-528-3472, www.photodisc.com.

Rial Solutions (Joe Jones of Artworks Studios): Lesson 4 (Illustrator masking art) ©1999 Rial Solutions

Karen Tenenbaum: Lesson 5 (woman) ©1999 Karen Tenenbaum